CREATING A
REAL WEALTH ECONOMY

With every passing day it is apparent that the really existing capitalist economy offers a dreary present and a dismal future for humanity. Perhaps the greatest task before us is to begin the important work of rethinking how to structure an efficient, fair, humane and sustainable economy, one that nurtures freedom and democracy. Finley Eversole's new book, *Creating a Real Wealth Economy*, is a giant step in that direction. He brings together some of our most visionary thinkers to produce a book that is both thoughtful and bold.

—Robert W. McChesney, PhD, Gutgsell Endowned Professor in the Department of Communication, University of Illinois, and Author, Digital Disconnect: How Capitalism Is Turning the Internet Against Democracy

CREATING A
REAL WEALTH
ECONOMY

From Phantom Wealth to
a Wiser Future for All Humanity

Edited by

FINLEY EVERSOLE, PhD

THE CREATIVE AGE
Aiming for a Wiser World

The Creative Age
1300 Beacon Parkway E., Suite 305
Birmingham, AL 35209
www.creativeagepublishing.com

Library of Congress Control Number: 2013923510

Keywords: new economics, Occupy Wall Street, public banking, bioregional currencies, public assets, social spending, worker-ownership, democratization of wealth, capitalism, neoliberal economics, debt, recessions, tax-payer bailouts, private banks, predatory loans, Federal Reserve, world financial crisis, austerity measures, privatization of wealth, income inequality, international trade currency, green economy, Lincoln greenbacks.

Summary: Workable alternatives to the troubled US and global financial system exist which could reduce reliance on private banks, halt rising national debt, and free society from a debt-based economy. Several leading world economists here present a number of proven alternative solutions which could replace the current system with a real wealth economy. This is the book Occupy Wall Street activists should have had in 2011.

ISBN: 978-0-9913079-0-6 (paperback)—ISBN: 978-0-9913079-1-3 (e-book)

CHOOSING A WORLD BASED ON SHARING

Certain facts are obvious. The old order has failed. The resources of the world have fallen into the hands of the selfish, and there has been no just distribution. Some nations have had too much, and have exploited their surplus; other nations have had too little, and their national life and their financial situation have been crippled thereby.

Three things will end this condition of great luxury and extreme poverty, of gross over-feeding of the few and the starvation of the many, plus the centralization of the world's produce under the control of a handful of people in each country. These are: first, the recognition that there is enough food, fuel, oil and minerals in the world to meet the need of the entire population. The problem, therefore, is basically one of distribution. Second, this premise of adequate supply handled through right distribution must be accepted, and the supplies which are essential to the health, security and happiness of mankind must be made available. Third, that the entire economic problem and the institution of the needed rules and distributing agencies should be handled by an economic league of nations. In this league, all the nations will have their place; they will know their national requirements (based on populations and internal resources, etc.) and will know also what they can contribute to the family of nations; all will be animated by the will to the general good—a will-to-good that will probably at first be based on expediency and national need but which will be constructive in its working out.

This period of adjustment offers the opportunity to effect dramatic and deeply needed changes and the establishing of a new economic order, based on the contribution of each nation to the whole, the sharing of the fundamental necessities of life and the wise pooling of all resources for the benefit of everyone, plus a wise system of distribution. Such a plan is feasible.

?!   The solution here offered is so simple that, for that very reason, it may fail to make an appeal. The quality required by those engineering this change of economic focus is so simple also—the will-to-good—that again it may be overlooked, but without simplicity and goodwill
! little can be effected…. The great need will be for men of vision, of wide sympathy, technical knowledge and cosmopolitan interest. They must possess also the confidence of the people. They must meet together and lay down the rules whereby the world can be adequately fed; they must determine the nature and extent of the contribution which any one nation must make; they must settle the nature and extent of the supplies which should be given to any nation, and so bring about those conditions which will keep the resources of the
!! world circulating justly and engineering those preventive measures which will offset human selfishness and greed.

Can such a group of men be found? I believe it can.

The world is one and its sufferings are one…. The sins of humanity are also one. Its goal is one and it is as one great human family that we must emerge into the future. I would emphasize this point: *it is as one humanity, chastened, disciplined but illumined and fused, that we must emerge into the future.*

Djwhal Khul

Take courage. The human race is divine.

Pythagoras

Money is not yet used divinely, but it will be.

Djwhal Khul

Also from Finley Eversole

Author, Art and Spiritual Transformation:
The Seven Stages of Death and Rebirth

Editor, Infinite Energy Technologies: Tesla, Cold Fusion,
Antigravity, and the Future of Sustainability

Editor, Energy Medicine Technologies: Ozone Healing,
Microcrystals, Frequency Therapy, and the Future of Health

Editor and Contributor,
Christian Faith and the Contemporary Arts

Dedicated to Abraham Lincoln

"No scheme of amelioration (of our ills) has the least chance of success unless and until the money ceases to be the master and becomes the servant of mankind, thus that no financial barrier is ever again interposed between man and his ability to create wealth."

"We gave the people of this Republic the greatest blessing they have ever had—their own paper money to pay their own debts."

This time, like all times, is a very good one, if we but know what to do with it.

Ralph Waldo Emerson

The people of Earth are a superpower themselves, if united.

Jeane Manning

We have it in our power to begin the world over again.

Thomas Paine

World conditions today—precipitated as they are by human greed and ignorance—are nevertheless basically conditioned by the will-to-good which is the primary quality of the energies and forces coming forth from the great Lives in which all that exists live and move and have their being. The Law of the Universe…is to all eternity the good of the whole and naught can arrest this happening; for who can arrest the impact of those energies which play upon and through our planet.

We stand at the gateway of the new world, of the new age and its new civilizations, ideals and culture. What is coming is a civilization of a different yet still material nature, but animated by a growing registration by the masses everywhere of an emerging spiritual objective which will transform all life and give new value and purpose to that which is material.

The best is yet to be.

Djwhal Khul

I know of no more encouraging fact than the unquestionable ability of man to elevate his life by a conscious endeavor.

Henry David Thoreau

Another world is not only possible, she is on her way. On a quiet day, I can hear her breathing.

Arundhati Roy

The real gift isn't freedom. It's what we get to do with it.

Nikita, final TV episode

ACKNOWLEDGMENTS

My first thanks go to all the authors who have contributed so gener-ously of their time and wisdom to write the chapters contained in this volume, and for their quick responses to my many communications and requests.

I would like to say thanks to John Perkins for taking time from his busy schedule to writing the Forward. I wish also to express my gratitude to David Korten, Ellen Brown, and Hazel Henderson who gave generously of their time to serve as advisors and consultants at many points along the way as this book was being planned and edited.

A special word of appreciation goes to my friends Halina Bak-Hughes and Sheldon Hughes who were the first to introduce me to the writings of David Korten and Bernard Lietaer.

And I owe a huge debt of gratitude to Olivia Hansen and John Toomey for their generous support which is helping to made possible the comple-tion of the final three volumes in this 5-volume series on solutions to global problems. (Other available volumes are reviewed at the back of this book.)

I wish to acknowledge the graphic artists who have assisted with graphic designs: Adina Cucicov in Spain, Rita Toews in Canada, Stanley Parrish, Jr. in Alabama, and Steven James Catizone in Pennsylvania.

The world's economy has never before been as massive, so fraught with *!!!* problems, or so unevenly distributed among the world's population as it is today. When 400 Americans control as much of the nation's wealth as the bottom 150 million citizens—half of the US population—clearly justice, democracy, human rights, and the virtues of compassion suffer. In the words of Jeffrey Sachs, "America became a place where money buys everything." Everything except those values which show *respect* for life, human dignity, the untapped potential of billions of people deprived of opportunities, and the earth's resources and ecosystems. All this must change, and calls for massive global demonstrations to protest current economic corruption and political favoritism.

The authors in this volume present us with a deeper understanding of the global economy, its exploitation, problems and failures, and a number of lines along which creative and lasting solutions may be found. It is time we end the massive human suffering due to economic scarcity and create a real wealth economy based on wisdom, compassion and sharing which is beneficial to every member of our global family.

I feel therefore a debt of gratitude to and wish to acknowledge *every person on earth* who is working to help make this a better world for all. It is in your hands that the destiny of the planet and humanity truly lies.

TABLE OF CONTENTS

FOREWORD

John Perkins

Author of *Confessions of an Economic Hit Man*

We have entered a time of the greatest revolution in human history: a Consciousness Revolution.

People across the globe are waking up to the need for change. We know we've been hoodwinked, conned into believing that this system is the best one possible. On every continent, we are understanding that it simply isn't so and it is time for us to act.

We've lost faith in the ability of government and business leaders to resolve the problems facing humanity. The global economic depression has shattered the lives of Andean peasants, African fishermen, corporate executives, and the average household alike. Despite claims that the current economic malaise is ending, the general public remains unconvinced, suspicious, and shaken. The promised *recovery* is uneven and uncertain; monumental issues still remain to be resolved.

In our cash-strapped economy, privatization is proffered as a solution for many of our financial woes. The fire sale is so intense that we cannot be faulted for thinking there is a *going out of business* sign over the doors of government on every continent.

Officials at all levels are hocking whatever they can—roads, bridges, national monuments, prisons, and even water—to stave off what seems like an inevitable bankruptcy. Furthermore, and perhaps most disconcertingly, the very foundations of our social contract, the institutions we once believed would always be honored such as education and social services, are gutted and sold to private companies. Today, the US taxpayer supports more privately owned soldiers in Afghanistan then members of our national military.

Although the public is told that these solutions are more efficient, the fact is that they are usually more costly in the long run. Government ownership of these services served us extremely well in the past. Against this emerging social and economic backdrop, the agenda of the *Economic Hit Man* that unfortunately worked so well in other parts of the world, taking advantage of developing countries to enslave them with indebtedness to international financial institutions, has come home to roost in what is referred to as the *developed world*, including the United States.

Circumstances like these generate revolutions. The Agricultural Revolution. The Industrial Revolution. The American Revolution. We have entered such a time. Future historians, I believe, will define this as a Consciousness Revolution. People around the world are waking up to the fact that a very few extremely wealthy individuals are enslaving the rest of us. The shackles take the form of the currencies and debt that are interwoven into global monetary systems.

When Asian, African, and Latin American countries experienced economic problems and found themselves unable to make their loan payments, they were forced to accept *structural adjustment programs* (SAPs) which mandated that they dramatically reduce government spending, raise interest rates (often to 30% or higher), privatize sectors of their economies, and sell national assets to multinational corporations.

SAPs have been severely condemned by political and social scientists around the world because they:

- threaten national sovereignty and undermine the democratic process by transferring control to foreigners;
- benefit the largest donors (especially the United States, European Union, Canada, and Japan) whose corporations end up owning the privatized sectors and whose financial institutions receive high interest rate payments;
- privatize resources that have been in the public domain;
- encourage foreign corporations to exploit workers and corrupt local officials as they lobby for lax environmental and labor regulations and tax loopholes;
- discourage agriculture and land reform, thereby protecting aristocracies and facilitating the growth of slums and poverty;
- increase the use of fertilizers and pesticides that damage the environment and make farmers dependent on foreign chemical companies;
- force cutbacks on health, education, and other social services by diverting money to interest payments;
- disenfranchise women who dominate workforces in the education, health, and other social services; and
- cause the abandonment of women and children as rural men migrate to cities and other countries.

However, the most important criticism is that they DO NOT WORK. *!!* Or, restated, structural adjustment programs do not help the countries they are touted as helping. In fact, they drive them deeper into crisis, while making the multinational corporations and big banks richer.

Clearly, our current economic system must undergo a profound trans- *!!!* formation which places people, freedom, human rights, and the environment above profits.

It is decision time. Time to answer some basic questions. Do we want *!!* a world ruled by a few billionaires, intent on controlling the planet's resources with the goal of serving their increasingly voracious appetites?

Do we want more debt, privatization, and markets where robber barons elevate themselves above the rules and regulations that apply to the rest of us? Accounting systems that fail to record the most egregious costs? Magazine-cover *heroes* who exploit their workers, pay fortunes to lawyers and lobbyists to defend the status quo, and ship their money to overseas tax havens? Do we want to buy from or invest in corporations that finance the overthrow of democratically elected governments? And undermine our own presidents and elected officials? Do we want to raise our children on a planet where less than 5% of the population consumes more than 25% of the resources, less than 10% of that 5% control the assets, and roughly half the world lives in poverty? Where violence continues to rise and our militaristic tactics against *terrorism* force us into a constant state of siege?

Or do we want a world envisioned by the organizations that are striving to create a socially and environmentally responsible economy—the type of organizations we find at Green Festivals and local markets, and in cooperatives, employee-owned businesses, and stores, and on websites that are committed to the triple bottom line? Don't we want a world where the models for our children are the founders and managers of institutions that restore rainforests and polluted lakes, promote sustainable energy, and help starving people feed themselves? Where no one is denied medical care and the right to live out the last days of life in dignity? In short, don't we want to break the old pattern, rid ourselves of the viral form of predatory capitalism that is failing us so badly, and bequeath a world to future generations that reflects the ideals of true democracy, a world headed toward sustainable, just, and peaceful societies for us all? The choice is ours.

Recently I traveled to Vietnam—a country that in many respects was the door-opener for what I've come to think of as a Death Economy—one that is based on military conquest, killing and enslaving people, and on raping and pillaging the earth's resources while at the same time polluting the air, water, and soil. When we in the US sent our young men off to die and kill in Vietnam we entered an era that redefined global economics.

After Vietnam, I journeyed to Myanmar (formerly Burma)—a country whose brutal dictators threw it into the economic turmoil of isolationism and trade sanctions for decades.

These two countries tell stories that should be lessons for us all. Today Vietnam is thriving. It has come to represent the innate ability of human beings to overcome great odds, to not only survive but to excel. Myanmar was changed by a series of events that culminated in the terrible destruction caused by Cyclone Nargis in 2008 that killed more than 140,000 people. When the government blocked international relief efforts, it generated worldwide condemnation and the probability of internal revolts supported by outside financial aid. In the end, the cyclone turned the country's leaders around.

We all need to rally, as the Vietnamese did, to the call to overcome the odds, to not only survive but to excel. Nature is now speaking to people everywhere, not just to Myanmar. Disastrous events like Cyclone Nargis happen frequently. It seems as though every week we read about a new catastrophe caused by massive storms, floods, tsunamis, tornadoes, or earthquakes. Science leaves no doubt that many of these events are caused by the activities of the Death Economy.

The time has come for us to stand up to those who insist on perpetuating a Death Economy and to create a better life that is based on a Life Economy, a Real Wealth Economy. The status quo depends on us to support it. By understanding that we have the power to change the system through the ways we shop, invest, and live our lives, and by taking the appropriate actions, we will create a Real Wealth Economy.

It is time for us to pull ourselves back from the edge of the precipice, to insist that our corporations and the growing numbers of entrepreneurs focus on cleaning up our polluted planet and developing technologies for helping the starving billions grow food and store and distribute it more efficiently; and to create better systems for banking, transportation, energy, marketing, education, healthcare, and so many other areas. Moving into a Real Wealth Economy is not about giving up jobs or sacrificing living standards. It is about creating more jobs—in areas that count—and improving living standards for all.

I feel blessed to be born into this time of transformation—to be able to play a role in the greatest revolution in human history, the Consciousness Revolution. You, dear reader, were born into this time also. How fortunate you and I are! Read on in this fine collection of essays by some of the world's most insightful economic thinkers and commit to feeling the great joy of participating, to taking actions that will make a better world for ourselves and generations to come...

INTRODUCTION

The Perils of a Debt-Based Economy and Its Alternatives

Finley Eversole, PhD

Adolescents know where babies come from but only about one adult in every hundred knows what money is and where it comes from.
   Paul Hellyer

It is well enough that the people of the nation do not understand our banking and money system, for if they did, I believe there would be a revolution before tomorrow morning.
   Henry Ford

Bankers literally own and control our medium of exchange, and before we can obtain it we must obligate ourselves to pay interest upon it. Interest is nothing more than a tax, which a privileged class is permitted to impose upon trade.
   Mary E. Hobart

I am afraid the ordinary citizen will not like to be told that the banks can and do create money. And they who control the credit of the nation direct the policy of Governments and hold in the hollow of their hand the destiny of the people.

Reginald McKenna, Chairman of Midland Bank, 1924

There are two ways to conquer and enslave a nation. One is by the sword. The other is by debt.

John Adams

The money power preys on the nation in times of peace, and conspires against it in times of adversity. It is more despotic than monarchy, more insolent than autocracy, more selfish than bureaucracy. It denounces, as public enemies, all who question its methods or throw light upon its crimes.

Abraham Lincoln

Our period is simply one in which human selfishness has come to its climax and must either destroy humanity or be brought intelligently to an end.

Djwhal Khul

In the early twentieth century a well-known African-American author, poet, educator, and civil rights activist by the name of the Weldon Johnson once began a talk at a dinner for Congressmen by saying, "I intend to explain the unexplainable...and to unscrew the inscrutable." If America, Europe and the world at large are to understand how the economy actually works or, rather, why it works to the advantage of a small minority and against the well-being of most of humanity, and brutally so for the poor and exploited Third World countries, we need honest, enlightened economic thinkers willing to explain the unexplainable and unscrew the inscrutable.

Bankers and economists go to great lengths to make what they do seem arcane and impenetrable, including hiding from the public the very process by which money is created, along with the strategies employed by bankers to create periods of prosperity with easy loans, only to follow them with periods of tight money, causing recessions and depressions created for the sole purpose of foreclosing on businesses, farms, homes and other assets and thereby acquiring for themselves the *real wealth* of nations and the masses. As John Kenneth Galbraith said, "The study of money, above all other fields in economics, is one in which complexity is used to disguise truth or to evade truth, not to reveal it."

Once it is understood that bank loans are created out of thin air with a few leger entries or computer keystrokes and are backed up by nothing more the bank's name and your pledged collateral as security, the seizure of tangible assets and properties during hard times will be seen, in all honesty, as nothing more than a confiscation of working people's real wealth in exchange for the phantom wealth (money conjured out of an empty hat) of the bankers' loans.

This brilliantly conceived master game—call it *The Greed of the Exploiters*—has been going on ever since the founding of the Bank of England in 1694.[1] Even before that, in many societies a crafty, unscrupulous few had found ways to gather the wealth of the people to themselves. History shows that in every case, once the bulk of the wealth is held by less than 4% of the population, that nation or society has collapsed. Today we are facing the possibility of a global economic meltdown, thanks to greed and exploitation having become the guiding principles of our economic system.

This system serves the self-interests of private bankers brilliantly, but it clearly does not contribute to the welfare and wellbeing of nations, the masses who have been granted no such privilege as creating their own money with slight-of-hand trickery, or the world at large which is held captive to the greed and self-interest of a small group of international bankers and money manipulators. Profit, the bankers' god, renders them blind to all other human values.

The Downside of Debt-Money

The creation of money through loans makes *debt* the basis of our economic system. In a real wealth economy, *productivity*—the creation of value by contributing something useful to society—ought to be the basis of all money-creation. All bank-created money, which in the United States includes everything except coins minted by the US Mint, is created as *debt*-money. In other words, it is created as debt owed to the banks, along with interest which must be paid to the banks on money they never had, but which magically appears—shazam!—from thin air each time a loan is created or a credit card is swiped. The money needed to pay the interest is not created along with the loan, so borrowers must make up the difference from their salaries or profits from the sale of their products or services, or, as is all too frequently the case, by the forfeiture of their collateral!

Because nearly all money placed into circulation is debt-money, the amount of money due the banks always exceeds the total amount of money in existence. And because banks are owed more money than actually exists, someone—in truth, many someones—must lose their homes, land, businesses, or other assets if the bankers are to balance their books. You can readily see that recurring recessions and financial failures are built into the very fabric of our existing economic system. What you need to understand is that this is by design and intent and has nothing to do with naturally occurring economic cycles, which might be caused by drought, wars, or other disasters. For more than 300 years bankers have deliberately designed their banking systems to serve as a giant sucking machine to suck up the real wealth of the masses and Third World nations and concentrate more and more of it in the hands of a small super-rich minority, a mere fraction of 1% of the world's population. At least 40% and as much as 50% of the cost of everything we manufacture, build, purchase or consume is interest paid to private bankers. They have created this system through secrecy, treachery, deception, trickery, bribery, control of governments, even murder. More on this to come.

The burden of making up the difference between the amount of money in circulation and the amount owed banks invariably falls on those least able to absorb the losses—farmers, small-business owners, homeowners, salaried workers, small investors, the elderly and the poor. Not being wealthy, they lack the resources to ride out hard times when banks decide to tighten the money supply. Homes are foreclosed on. Lands are seized. Businesses downsize or go out of business, and millions lose their jobs. The latest growing threat to the public interest is the *bail-in* template originated by the G20's Financial Stability Board in 2011, and first implemented in Cyprus, which allows private banks to re-capitalize their losses by dipping into the pensions and savings of their depositors. Even city and state governments are not immune to this grab for wealth by the bankers—bail-ins having been designed to override their constitutional protections of their people. Thus does the war of the wealthy against the masses rage on, generation after generation. As a child of the Great Depression, I remember all too vividly the broken lives and destroyed families such exploitation produces.

Moreover, the credit reporting system in the US is designed to force us into debt. Anyone who is truly responsible, always paying his/her bills on time and never incurring debt—but choosing to live within, not beyond, that which his/her labors can create—will be denied a high credit score and shut out of the system. The bankers want to us—individually, as nations and as a world—in perpetual bondage to them. Adam Smith had warned of what he called the "vile maxim"—"All for ourselves, nothing for other people."

Meanwhile, the world's 225 richest individuals have a combined wealth in excess of 1 trillion US dollars, equal to the annual income of the poorest 50% of the earth's population. The seven richest men could single-handedly wipe out world hunger. Today, 90% of international capital goes into financial speculation and only 10% into long-term productivity. In the words of Heidi Moore, "Wall Street is a poor indicator of the real wealth of the nation." The world's economy has become the casino of the super-rich, who pocket their wins while demanding that taxpayers pick up their loses.

Our Banking System is Unconstitutional

Our present banking system is designed to exploit the weakest and poorest in order to enhance the wealth of the privileged few to whom Congress granted the privilege of creating the nation's money. This is a clear violation of the provision of the US Constitution which, in Article 1, Section 8, places responsibility for creating the nation's money squarely in the hands of Congress. Article 1, Section 1 of the Constitution also states, "*All legislative powers herein granted shall be vested in a Congress of the United States, which shall consist of a Senate and House of Representatives*"—making it abundantly clear that transferring any constitutional power vested in Congress to any private entity or group of individuals is a deliberate violation of the Constitution. In transferring the right or power to create the nation's money from Congress to private bankers, Congress itself has abrogated its Constitutional powers. If the American people were willing to defend and uphold the above constitutional provisions with the same passion they bring to upholding the Second Amendment, guaranteeing the right to keep and bear arms, or the right of free speech, or the rights of women and minorities, who knows what might happen? Maybe, in time, we might get the economic system we deserve—the one the Founding Fathers intended us to have.

Recessions, depressions, unemployment, and foreclosures on homes, lands and business will continue unless and until we radically alter the way money is created and spent into circulation. The American revolutionaries, in 1776, created their own paper money—$350 million which they distributed among the people—and used it to win the War of Independence from England. Once the war was over, British bankers quickly destroyed the value of the new Continental currency, plunging the

new nation into poverty. So, from its earliest days, the United States has
struggled to create a currency not controlled and manipulated by bankers.

Any sovereign government can be granted, *by the will of its people,*
the right to create that nation's money supply in whatever form is most
conducive to sound business practices, maintenance of all the nation's
financial responsibilities, the providing of all essential public services, and
the creation of a stable economy free of inflation, recessions and depressions. The awarding of the right to create the nation's money supply to a
privileged class, which is then left free to charge whatever rate of interest
it can extort by controlling the issue and circulation of money, is clearly
subversive of the self-interest of a sovereign nation and its people. More
importantly, to deny the people of any nation the right to create their
own debt-free money for all financial transactions is to deny them FULL
constitutional self-government. It opens the doors to economic tyranny. It
was to escape such tyranny that the American colonialists fought the War
of Independence from England.

Even the money created by bankers is good only to the extent that it is
backed up by the full faith and credit of the government and its willingness to bail out failing banks with taxpayer money. It is the sovereign
power of a government, supported by its publicly-owned assets, which
stand behind and guarantee that any monetary system can be trusted by
its citizens. A *debt-free* dollar issued by a government is of *more real value*
that an interest-bearing dollar created out of thin air by a private for-
profit bank and having only the promise of borrowers and their pledged
collateral to back it up.

Today, the nations of the world are caught in a powerful struggle between
the citizens of the earth, with all their hopes, aspirations and dreams for
a better world in which all human beings are recognized as having value,
and a small group of greedy exploiters of humanity seeking world domination regardless of the cost in human lives and suffering, depletion of
the world's resources, or long-term damage to the earth's environmental.

Debt-money, issued by private bankers, is the linchpin holding together their nefarious schemes. As Thomas Paine said at the time of the American Revolution, "We have it in our power to begin the world over again." Has this time not come?

The American Revolution will remain unfinished until such time as we the people take full control of our own economic destiny.

Lincoln, Civil War, the Bankers, and Assassination

There was a moment, immediately following the American Civil War, when the United States and the world could have charted a new monetary course. That moment was lost with the death of Abraham Lincoln. Is it any wonder the true story behind Lincoln's assassination has been buried for 149 years, once the role played in Lincoln's death by British bankers is revealed? Lincoln thoroughly understood the nature of the banking problem and knew what it was doing to his beloved nation. As a writer in the 1930s said, "No government, up to Lincoln's time, had ever been able to figure out any way for the government itself to gain and keep control of its own money and finances." Lincoln did, and for that he paid the supreme sacrifice. As long as the Civil War raged on, he said he could not fight wars on two fronts at once. "I have two great enemies," Lincoln said, "the Southern army in front of me and the bankers in the rear. And of the two, the bankers are my greatest foe."

Our present monetary system came into existence with the establishing of the Bank of England in 1694. This bank was chartered by a consortium of people who loaned the British government £1,200,000 and received in exchange a perpetual annuity. In other words, it created a permanent debt for the people of England on which they continue even today to pay interest. Thus was born the modern monetary system which spread throughout Europe and eventually to the United States. England, France, Germany and Switzerland would become the great centers of money and credit manipulation with the same small group of families controlling virtually all national and international banking. They had but one goal: economic control of the entire world.

To the best of my knowledge, the true story behind Lincoln's assassination has never appeared in any of our history books or Lincoln biographies. The recently aired National Geographic film, *Killing Lincoln,* failed to offer a single hint of the *real* conspiracy behind Lincoln's death. The people of the United States are yet to realize that their greatest president, Abraham Lincoln, was targeted for assassination by British bankers because they feared his monetary policies.

Because the truth behind Lincoln's assassination bears directly on the question—Who should create our nation's money?—it is a story that deserves to be better known. Had Lincoln lived, in addition to preserving the Union and freeing the slaves, he might very well have given the American people their own national bank and their own debt-free money in perpetuity. Lincoln was fully aware of the machinations of the private bankers and ran for reelection in 1864 on a platform which included a proposal for a national bank. While we cannot say with certainty, based on available evidence, whether Lincoln intended to establish his greenbacks as a permanent national currency, whatever his intentions may have been, he did not live to carry them out. But there were many—and this definitely included England's bankers—who believed that once the war was over Lincoln would put up legislation at the first opportunity to repeal the National Bank Law which had restored to bankers the money-creating power. Lincoln had opposed the law because he had seen that the government could finance itself. So there were those who feared he might decide to create a financial system that would free his countrymen permanently from the bankers' economic slavery.[2]

What follows is an abbreviated account of the relatively unknown story of the conspiracy behind Lincoln's assassination, based on known facts.[3]

On April 12, 1861, a month after Lincoln's inauguration as President, the Civil War broke out. Needing money to finance the war, Lincoln, together with his Secretary of the Treasury, Salmon Chase, went to New York to secure funding for the war. But the bankers, wishing the Union to fail, offered Lincoln loans at the exorbitant interest rates of 24% to 36%.

Knowing such terms would create an impossible debt for the nation, Lincoln declined their offer. Germany's Chancellor, Otto von Bismarck, said in 1865 that slavery was not the only cause of the American Civil War: "I know of absolute certainty that the division of the United States into two federations of equal power was decided long before the Civil War by the high financial powers of Europe. These bankers were afraid that the United States, if they remained as one block and were to develop as one nation, would attain economic and financial independence, which would upset their financial domination over the world."

Col. Edmund Dick Taylor, father of the Lincoln Greenbacks

Lincoln then turned to an old Chicago acquaintance, Col. Dick Taylor, for advice on funding the war. Taylor replied, "Why Lincoln, that is easy, just get Congress to pass a bill authorizing the printing of full legal tender treasury notes or greenbacks, and pay your soldiers with them and go ahead and win your war with them also." When Lincoln asked if Taylor thought the people would accept them, Taylor replied, "The people or anyone else will not have any other choice in the matter, if you make them full legal tender. They will have the full sanction of the government and be just as good as any other money, as Congress is given the express right by the Constitution, and the stamp of full legal tender by the Government is the thing that makes money good anytime."

The question whether the Constitution granted Congress the right to issue paper money was hotly debated, but the decision was made that it was a wartime necessity in order to save the Union. The Legal Tender Act was passed into law on February 25, 1862, and on February 27, Lincoln authorized the issue of the full legal tender paper currency known as greenbacks—the nations' first paper money, printing $450 million to help finance the war. They were printed on the finest paper with no interest due the government and issued directly into circulation by the US Treasury to fund the war.

Lincoln would be the last president to issue debt-free US notes, but an important lesson had been learned. He would later say: "The Government should create, issue and circulate all the currency and credit needed to satisfy the spending power of the Government and the buying power of consumers. The privilege of creating and issuing money is not only the supreme prerogative of Government, but it is in the Government's greatest creative opportunity. By the adoption of these principles...the taxpayers will be saved immense sums of interest. Money will cease to be master and become the servant of humanity."

1862 Lincoln Greenback

¡¡ The issue of the Lincoln greenbacks by the US Treasury as interest-free money was immediately seen as a threat to the existence of private bankers who realized how effective it could be in addressing a nation's economic needs. What if Lincoln, after the war, were to establish a permanent national currency? Lord Goschen, speaking for the bankers, wrote in the *London Times:* "If this mischievous financial policy [Lincoln's greenbacks], which has its origin in North America, shall become indurated down to a fixture, then that Government will furnish its own money without cost. It will pay off debts and be without debt. It will have all the money necessary to carry on its commerce. It will become prosperous without precedent in the history of the world. That Government must be destroyed, or it will destroy every monarchy on the globe." The "monarchy" referenced here is, of course, that of the bankers.

In fact, Lincoln's Treasury notes, bearing no interest, worked so well that when the National Bank Law came up for renewal in 1863, British bankers persuaded certain Congressmen and Senators to include an exception clause in the bill for the next issue of greenbacks. This exception clause, forced on Lincoln during the crisis of war, would allow bankers to devalue the greenbacks and eventually force them out of circulation, restoring to bankers the exclusive right of creating money.

¡¡ The London bankers saw Lincoln as a man so foolish as to believe ordinary citizens should have a voice at all matters that concerned them. In this respect he was a true Jeffersonian. This made him a danger to the banking aristocracy. They believed he could neither be controlled nor reasoned with. Should he wish to do anything about the money issue, given Lincoln's popularity, it would have been virtually impossible for Congress to stand in the way. Lincoln needed to be removed from power as quickly as possible. It mattered little that it might cost England's bankers a few hundred thousand pounds to get Lincoln out of office. They would recover their investment many millionfold in years to come. In the past 150 years, that goal has been realized many times over.

In the early fall of 1864, a British banker by the name of Rothberg, *!!*
a relative and close associate of one of Britain's leading banker families,
possibly the Rothschilds, was sent to North America with one mission
and unlimited access to gold to carry it out. His one and only objective
was the removal of Abraham Lincoln from power.

He quickly settled in Montréal. Canada was the perfect place from
which to carry out his mission as many Confederate conspiracies were
being hatched there, and it was easy to get information from both the
Northern and Southern states. Rothberg soon discovered people in the
Northern States who were sympathetic to his plans. But by now Lincoln
had been reelected to the presidency by a large majority and was quickly
becoming a national hero in the North. He was also letting it be known
that he was a friend of the South and that, in the event of surrender,
there would be no mistreatment of Southerners. All of this was making
Rothberg's mission more difficult, and his British counterparts were
making frantic and urgent demands for Lincoln's removal, with promises
of additional gold and a free hand in using it.

Rothberg had informants in both the Northern and Southern States
gathering newspaper reports and other information for him. An ad
appeared in a newspaper in Selma, Alabama on December 1, 1864, with
an offer to assassinate President Lincoln, Vice President Andrew Johnson,
and Secretary of State William H. Seward for the sum of $1 million. A
copy of this ad reached Rothberg. He decided this was exactly what he
had been looking for but offered the scheme to his accomplices initially
as a kidnapping plan.

Soon thereafter, Rothberg got word of an actor by the name of John
Wilkes Booth who was quite hostile toward Lincoln and had been heard to
say, while performing at McVickers' Theatre in Chicago two years earlier,
"What a glorious opportunity there is for a man to immortalize himself
by killing Lincoln."[4] Booth was promptly brought to Canada, and he and
Rothberg began planning Lincoln's removal from the White House.

When Booth returned from Canada[5] he was in possession of a substantial amount of gold which he claimed to have acquired speculating in real estate and petroleum. He returned to Washington with the intention of kidnapping Lincoln on the day of the Inauguration. Gold and silver were scarce during the war, so Booth's possession of gold made it easy for him to hire accomplices. There is no evidence however that he ever consulted with Confederate leaders about his kidnapping plans to ascertain how they might feel about them.

Initially, Lincoln's kidnapping was all the British bankers thought they could accomplish and were willing to chance that Lincoln might be killed once inside Confederate lines. Then a letter Lincoln would write to his friend, Col. William F. Elkins, on November 21, 1864, all but assured his death:

"We may congratulate ourselves that this cruel war is nearing its end. It has caused a vast amount of treasure and blood.... It has indeed been a trying hour for the Republic; *but I see in the near future a crisis approaching that unnerves me and causes me to tremble for the safety of my country. As a result of the war, corporations have been enthroned and an era of corruption in high places will follow, and the money power of the country will endeavor to prolong its reign by working upon the prejudices of the people until all wealth is aggregated in a few hands and the Republic is destroyed.* I feel at this moment more anxiety for the safety of my country than ever before, even in the midst of war. God grant that my suspicions may prove groundless."[6]

This was the Lincoln the British bankers had feared. Rothberg now realized that Lincoln was fully aware of the gravity of the money situation. In spite of the turbulent final days of the war, solving the nation's financial problems was never far from Lincoln's mind.[7] Given his knowledge and experience, it now seemed likely he would put through legislation, once the war ended, to repeal the 1863 National Bank Law which had revoked the Greenback Law and restored to privately-owned banks the power of issuing interest-bearing money. Would Lincoln endeavor to put into place a monetary system to free his country economically, and for all time, from the debt-money of the international bankers? Could he do for all citizens on the economic front what he had done for the slaves with the passage of the Thirteenth Amendment—free them from slavery? These are the questions Lincoln's death would leave unanswered.

Having already missed two opportunities to abduct Lincoln, Rothberg now became quite passionate in urging Booth to complete his mission. Conditions were rapidly changing, and Rothberg realized kidnapping Lincoln could prove increasingly difficult.

Around this time, Lincoln made a trip down the Potomac on the boat *River Queen* to meet with Generals Sherman and Grant. He gave them his last secret instructions regarding the surrender of the Confederacy which, when carried out a short time later, would prove the true character of the Great Emancipator. After their surrender, every Confederate officer and soldier was to be fully pardoned and each soldier permitted to take a horse or mule of his choosing for his journey home. In the eyes of the people of both North and South, this was proof of Lincoln's intention to heal the nation after its brutal war. His popularity now was such that he could have gotten through the Congress any legislation he might have wanted.

By now Rothberg was frantic over Booth's delays and slipped across the US border in the dead of night during the jubilation over the ending of the war, making his way to Washington, DC. On April 11, Booth and David Herold, one of Booth's accomplices, were in the crowd at the White House when Lincoln gave the most famous speech of his last days, pleading with his people for mercy and forgiveness for their fellow citizens in the South. He was concerned to protect Southerners from the radical revenge-seekers of the North and promised not to turn former slaveholders over to their former slaves. Lincoln's words were proof that he was the South's best friend. But for Booth it seemed his last chance to kidnap Lincoln and deliver him to the South was disappearing. He urged Herold to shoot Lincoln on the spot. Herold refused, saying they would surely be caught.

Rothberg was waiting for Booth when he returned to his hotel that night. With Rothberg's urging and more of Rothberg's gold in his pocket,

Booth was finally ready to finish the job. It was decided the plan published a few months earlier in a Selma, Alabama paper would be followed. Lincoln, Johnson, and Seward were to be killed. When in Canada, Booth had demonstrated to Rothberg that he was an excellent shot with a pistol. So he was given the principal role of assassinating Lincoln.

After Booth shot Lincoln around 10:15 PM on April 14, 1865, in Ford's Theater, then managed to escape, Rothberg was quick to spread rumors and gold around the Capital. It was essential that Booth be found and killed to keep the British bankers' murderous conspiracy silent. The remainder of the story is well known.

Twenty years after Lincoln's death, Jefferson Davis, former President of the Confederacy, would say that second only to the Civil War itself Lincoln's assassination was the greatest tragedy ever to befall the nation.

Several decades later, a Canadian attorney, Gerald McGeer, addressing the Canadian House of Commons, made statements based on evidence he had obtained from Secret Service Agents present at the trial of John Wilkes Booth. The evidence showed that Booth was a mercenary working for the international bankers. McGeer's speech, reported in the *Vancouver Sun*, May 2, 1934, stated: "Abraham Lincoln, the murdered emancipator of the slaves, was assassinated through the machinations of a group representative of the International Bankers, who feared the United States President's National Credit ambitions. There was only one group in the world at that time who had any reason to desire the death of Lincoln. They were the men opposed to his national currency program and who had fought him throughout the whole Civil War on his policy of Greenback currency." McGeer's speech went on to say, "They were the men interested in the establishment of the Gold Standard and the right of the bankers to manage the currency and credit of every nation in the world. With Lincoln out of the way they were able to proceed with that plan and did proceed with it in the United States. Within eight years after Lincoln's assassination, silver was demonetized and the Gold Standard system set up in the United States."

Because silver was plentiful in the United States (and Lincoln had plans to mine it after the war), and because much of the world's gold was already concentrated in the hands of bankers, demonetizing silver would give them greater control over the amount of money circulating in the US economy. The bankers' schemes have always been about keeping control over the money supply. Mayer Rothschild, founder of the House of Rothschild, had said, "Let me issue and control a nation's money and I care not who writes the laws." Lawmakers can always be bought.

The United States went off the Gold Standard in 1933. The global economy was already becoming too large to be tied to precious metals as a standard of worth. What was true in 1933 is even truer today. The time has come for humanity to realize the *real wealth* of the planet resides in the resources of the earth—being so ruthlessly exploited today by private interests—plus humanity's rich cultures, amazing inventions, wealth of knowledge, love of family and neighbors, and the labor, skills and creative imagination of its peoples. We are the world's True Wealth—all of us, working together. "The people of Earth are a superpower themselves, if united," says my friend, Jeane Manning. Once we have realized this, there is nothing we, the people, cannot accomplish. The united will of humanity can transform the world, and we shall see this will manifesting more and more as time goes on.

1913: The Birth of the Federal Reserve

When plunder becomes a way of life for a group of men living together in society, they create for themselves in the course of time, a legal system that authorizes it and a moral code that glorifies it.
Frédéric Bastiat, *Economic Sophisms*, 1845

The aims of the international bankers to establish the US currency as a bank-created debt-currency were fully realized in 1913 with the establishing of the Federal Reserve Board—the word *Federal* being inserted into the name for the sole purpose of misleading the American people into believing the Fed is a governmental agency, not a private banker-owned enterprise. The scheme to establish the Fed was hatched in 1910 by the six wealthiest men in the world meeting in secret at the home of J.P. Morgan on Jekyll Island off the coast of Georgia.[8] Even though the bill to establish the Fed passed the House of Representatives, it was fiercely opposed by a number of US Senators. Nevertheless, late in the evening of December 23, 1913, after nearly all members of Congress had gone home for the holidays, three Senators remained in Washington and passed the bill to establish the Federal Reserve by unanimous consent. Just three men, voting in the dead of night during a Congressional Christmas recess, would decide the financial fate of the United States up to the present day. We can assume they were well compensated for bowing to the bidding of the bankers. But the wrongness of that vote would be powerfully demonstrated by the Great Depression and every financial recession since—all of them artificially created by bankers for their own benefit.

Secrecy, deception, manipulation, subterfuge, bribery and, yes, even murder have long been the tools employed by private bankers and international banking cartels to control most of the world's money and credit and increasingly concentrate the people's real wealth in the hands of a small super-rich aristocracy.

As John Perkins so superbly shows in his books and alludes to in his Foreword to this volume, the US-controlled World Bank and International Monetary Fund, along with the central banks of the European Union, have employed similar strategies to financially enslave Third World countries—and recently also the cash-strapped countries of the European Union—in order to exploit their rich resources, confiscate public assets, eliminate social programs, and enslave the peoples. If we are to have any hope of creating an economically just world, we must create new regional, national and global economic systems, created and controlled by the people themselves—a Real Wealth Economy which reflects our democratic rights and values, our creative genius as a people, our compassion for each other, and our respect for the Earth and its ecosystems.

This brief bit of history provides a backdrop against which to view both new economic ideas and the revival of old ones as we search for lasting solutions to our national and global economic problems. Alexis de Tocqueville wrote in *Democracy in America*, "They will put up with poverty, servitude, and barbarism, but they will never endure aristocracy." The tide of opposition to an economic system which increasingly concentrates the nation's and world's wealth in the hands of a tiny minority triggered the 2011 Occupy Wall Street protests as well as demonstrations against austerity measures in Spain, Greece, Ireland, Italy and Portugal. It remains to be seen what will follow, but the old economic order has now been challenged. Once out of the chrysalis, the butterfly cannot be put back in. The entrenched financial system which largely dominates today's world will no doubt fight to the death to preserve itself, but the tide of evolution is on the side of *liberation* from all forms of oppression and a new global economic vision is now called for.

The machinations and manipulations of the international bankers must come to an end if humanity as a whole is ever to prosper. Christ spoke truly when saying, "Men love darkness because their deeds are evil." He also said, "There is nothing hidden that shall not be revealed, nor any secret that will not be brought into the light." The day of revelation for the world's greed-driven economies is now upon us. May the spotlight of truth, justice and compassion expose the greed from which all humanity suffers!

A Bird's Eye Overview of This Volume

This book is about *the democratizing of wealth*—locally, regionally, and globally. Many new economic ideas are being put forth, old ideas re-examined, new regional currencies floated, new community and regional economic experiments conducted, and the long-range benefits to humanity of stable, noninflationary, environmentally sensitive economic systems studied. If I may be permitted to say so, this is the book I wish could have been in the hands of Occupy Wall Street activists in the fall of 2011.

Every citizen needs to be educated about what money is, how it works, who controls it, who benefits from it, who suffers from its exploitation, how that exploitation can be ended, and what other options humanity has at its disposal should we decide we care enough about the health and well-being of our global fellow citizens and the Earth to want to insure their survival. Money is merely a tool for transformation—a way of influencing change, not a value unto itself. The authors you will read in this book bring a wealth of wisdom, experience and insight to the rethinking of money and the economy. They, and others like them, are the boundary-riders of evolution scouting the way ahead for the rest of humanity. They are the voices of a new economic age.

James Gustave Speth, in "Building the New Economy: Ten Steps We Can Take Now," calls for progressives to unite around a common agenda—a new progressive operating system—of pro-democratic reforms committed to social justice, job creation, new economic models, environmental sustainability, cooperation and peace. Noting that nothing changes until demands are made, Speth urges direct action through a rebirth of marches, protests, demonstrations, and nonviolent civil disobedience.

David Korten, in "The Naked Emperor," exposes the fraudulent claim that global capitalism champions a market economy. He describes global capitalism as a financial pyramid scheme devoted to circumventing democracy and market discipline; extracting subsidies; monopolizing control of resources, money, markets, and technology; and misleading consumers to gain unearned profits—all violations of basic market principles.

Ellen Brown, in "How We the People Lost the Money Power and How We Can Get it Back," shows how the private banking system, IMF and World Bank are responsible for massive world debt with all its adverse consequences, and how we can restore fiscal sanity to the states, nation and world by exercising sovereign power to create state- and federally-owned banks able to issue their own debt-free money.

Michael Hudson, in "Europe's Transition from Social Democracy to Oligarchy," describes a new form of financial warfare in which European governments—through austerity programs, the selloff of public assets, and the strangling of social programs—are being compelled to serve as enforcers against their own citizens for the gain of foreign bankers and domestic financial elites. He says this goes against the long history of Progressive Era principles and threatens to subvert Europe's social democracies by replacing them with an oligarchy of unelected, international financiers.

Paul Hellyer, in "Ending the World Financial Crisis," examines the economic problems the world has suffered in light of 300+ years of bank-created debt-money, the mistake made in creating the Federal Reserve in 1913, and the economic miscalculations of the Friedman-Chicago school of economics. To create a real world economy that works for everyone, Hellyer urges citizens to take back the power to create their own money and calls for a publicly-owned Bank of the United States as a first step in that direction.

Riane Eisler, in "Roadmap to a New Economics: Beyond Socialism and Capitalism," documents the failure of old thinking and details a new economics that recognizes the enormous social and economic value of caring for nature and for people, starting with children. She shows trends in this direction, as in the *caring societies* of Nordic nations, which focus on human development, gender equality, environmental protection, and partnership.

Bernard Lietaer, in "The Role of Bioregional Currencies in Regional Regeneration," illustrates, by negative example, the adverse effects on regional economies of a centralized national debt-currency and contrasts that with the positive example of Curitiba, Brazil, which flourished after creating its own regional currency. There is a clear lesson here: regional currencies can significantly enhance regional economic stability and growth.

Gar Alperovitz and **Steve Dubb**, in "The Possibility of a Pluralist Commonwealth and a Community-Sustaining Economy," address what they call *evolutionary reconstruction*. Recent financial and economic crises have contributed to the emergence of a vast array of new democratized ownership models at national, state, municipal and neighborhood levels—which they discuss in some detail, leading to a slow transformation of institutional structures and power. They observe that for today's young, "A non-statist, community-building, institution-changing, democratizing strategy could well capture their imagination and channel their desire to heal the world."

Hazel Henderson, in "The Growing Green Economy," says current economic models are too narrow to deal with today's ecologically-aware, information-rich societies and that we must seize the opportunities created by recent blowups in financial markets to shift toward a Main Street economy based on real people creating real products and services. "Real wealth," she says, "is generated by productive people using the Earth's resources wisely."

Bernard Lietaer, in "Terra: A Currency to Stabilize the World Economy," explores the many ramifications of a new global trade currency called the Terra, the Latin word for Earth. Designed specifically to counter the fluctuations of conventional economic cycles, the Terra provides a stable complementary currency for world trade, plus protection against currency speculation. As a hedge against inflation, it can also foster long-term economic and environmental planning; promote greater investment in less developed countries, add stability to the global economy, and lead to reductions in unemployment.

The Times They Are a-Changin'

The tests and difficulties and pains of this era are symptoms or indications of the "entering into manifestation" of the new civilization and culture. They portend the birth of a new era for which the entire world waits.

Djwhal Khul

The times in which we live are chaotic and demanding. This is due to the very profusion of all that is struggling to come to birth in a rapidly changing world. Civilizations come and go and in the going overlap. The old order, the passing civilization which once marked a new high point of advancement for humanity, once its purpose has been served, becomes increasingly a confining prison for the expanding consciousness, soul and creative powers of humanity. When this happens, there is growing unrest on the part of millions to break free of the past, to give birth to new ideas, new strategies, and a new vision of what is possible. At such times new creative powers struggle for expression the way a seed struggles to break through the dark earth in order to reach into the light and unfold all its hidden beauty. This is the case with humanity today. Nothing remains static. Everything advances. Were it otherwise, life would truly be death, not life. Today, a higher vision of humanity's possibilities is emerging in the consciousness of many and the vital imagination of the race is being drawn toward wiser and more universal principles.

When civilizations are undergoing transformation, carried forward by the dying of the old order and the gradual emergence of a new civilization and culture (a process which is necessarily slow, for only what is slowly and carefully built endures), cross-currents of conflicting energies can create the appearance of societal breakdown. But this is only an illusion, akin to that of a wheel which appears to be rotating backward in the early stages of its acceleration. True, from one point of view a reasonable case could be made that, for all our advances, these are the true Dark Ages: greed, corruption, violence, exploitation, secrecy, deception, old animosities, loss of dignity on the part of millions, indifference to the suffering of others, and contempt for mother Earth seem to rule the day. Life is seriously out of balance. Such things have always been with us, but never on the massive scale seen today. What is new is that all around the world humanity is *awakening* to these evils and injustices, and with such knowledge comes power—the power to re-imagine the future. What we are now experiencing are the growing pains of humanity's successful evolution which has prepared us for the birth of a new global civilization, new freedoms, and a new recognition that, in spite of all apparent differences, humanity is One. The brotherhood of suffering unites us all. The healing of the wounds of humanity is the next great task calling to all.

Everywhere today we are witnessing conflicting ideas and values in politics, in religion, in economics, and in society generally. Many feel deeply threatening by these events. But as Winston Churchill put it, "This is not the end. It is not even the beginning of the end. But it is, perhaps, the end of the beginning." Humanity is on the verge of taking its greatest evolutionary leap forward since our kind appeared on earth. And the next twenty years will play a deciding role in the transformations that are coming. Never before in our long history has humanity had more reason for hope. Closer beyond the horizon than we might imagine a new world awaits an awakened humanity.

The sheer numbers of new discoveries, scientific breakthroughs, creative ideas, and social experiments undertaken in all fields of human endeavor, together with clashes between conflicting and unifying values and interests driving human debate and actions—all this is *forcing* a quickening of humanity's mental evolution. In other words, humanity is undergoing an accelerated awakening of consciousness without which we would not be adequately equipped to function wisely in the increasingly complex and highly integrated world that is emerging. (Evolution always proceeds from the simple and amorphous toward the complex and more highly integrated—toward unity. Evolution is also an accelerating process.) Pain produces awareness and calls attention to what needs changing. All of this is good and necessary. In past ages, people typically handed control of their lives over to some external authority, usually religious or political. Now, the Age of Adolescence for our species is ending, and the Age of Responsibility is dawning. Our survival depends on achieving maturity and recognizing our new global interdependence as One Humanity, One World.

Times like these are the great periods in world history because they represent an evolutionary advance and a further unfolding of the unknown Purpose (unknown as yet *to us*) which guides the evolutionary process. Such times bring about a liberation of the human spirit for higher and nobler achievements ahead. The forces guiding evolution are divine and purposeful and therefore cannot be thwarted by humanity. However, endowed as we are with free will, we have the choice of delaying progress or of hastening it. But in the end, resistance is futile.

It is not the international nature of today's global economy that presents a problem. Even quantum physics is showing us how interconnected all things are. The achievement of unity and universal brotherhood between all living beings is perhaps the principal driving force of the coming age. The problem is that the wrong people are in control of the world's economy, and money is being wrongly used, with violent results. The belief that everything is fair in war and economics is an idea whose time is passing. The battle for humanity's future is being fought out by two opposing forces: conservatives and reactionaries on one side, who are committed to upholding the status quo and the entrenched values of a privileged few—which include greed and a callous indifference to the needs and suffering of others, and on the other, progressives and evolutionary—and at times visionary—forces working toward a new world rooted in compassion, sharing, inclusiveness, freedom, democracy, understanding, equality, respect for human rights and individual worth, concern for the Earth's environment, and an ardent desire to heal humanity's suffering. Someone once said, "Truth is eternal, but a lie ends when no one any longer believes it." Belief in the economic status quo is dying, at least among those who are *aware* of its greedy and deceptive practices and also realize that real wealth alternatives truly exist which can bring healing, justice and opportunity to all people everywhere. This book is intended to increase their numbers.

Humanity has entered the time of the Great Awakening, and we each need to choose which side of the battle for humanity's future will command our loyalties, dedication, and service. All that is veiled by secrecy, propaganda, and subterfuge must be brought to light. There is but one creative power that never leaves us as it finds us—the Truth. We must be informed of all decisions and action which impact our lives and affect the wellbeing of the planet. With truth comes revelation, and in its light the Way Ahead for humanity will stand revealed. The dark ages of materialism and greed will in time begin to dissipate, and we shall start to realize the long-veiled truth stated by Pythagoras at the front of this volume: "The human race is divine." This revelation also is rapidly on its way, and the light it brings will reveal and nurture all the dreams of humanity. For that end all humanity should work.

Creating a Real Wealth Economy is the third volume in a series addressing solutions to global problems. To see other available volumes, go to page 332.

BUILDING THE NEW ECONOMY

Ten Steps We Can Take Now

James Gustave Speth, JD

NOTE: Address at the New Economics Institute conference,
Strategies for a New Economy, June 2012

Power concedes nothing without a demand. It never has and it never
will.

Frederick Douglass

Are we ready for a new economy? And a new politics? First, some
definitions. I think we can define the new economy as one where
the overriding purpose of economic life is to sustain and to strengthen
People, Place, and Planet, and is no longer to grow Profit, Product (as in
gross domestic), and Power.

And a new politics? No surprises here. A new politics in America is
one that replaces today's creeping corporatocracy and plutocracy with true
popular sovereignty.

Well, then, let's explore how we can begin the process of transformation to a new economy and a new politics. This afternoon, I want to offer ten steps we can take now that would start us on our journey. Time is short, so here they are.

Step 1. The journey to a new political economy begins when enough Americans have come to two important conclusions. The first is that something is profoundly wrong with our current political economy—the operating system on which our country now runs. That system is now routinely generating terrible results—failing us socially, economically, environmentally, and politically. When big problems emerge across the entire spectrum of national life, as they surely have in our country, it cannot be for small reasons. We have encompassing problems because of fundamental flaws in our economic and political system. The second conclusion follows from the first. It is the imperative of system change, of building a new political economy that routinely delivers good results for people, place and planet.

A growing number of Americans are already finding it impossible to accept the deteriorating conditions of life and living. They see frightening gaps between the world that is and the one that could be. So, our first step is to become teachers—to help bring these Americans, and many more, to see the basic relationships: that the huge challenges we face are the result of system failure, that our current system of political economy no longer deserves legitimacy because it doesn't deliver on the values it proclaims, and that, therefore, the path forward is to change the system. As the slogan goes, "System change, not climate change." This is the core, foundational message, and we must pursue many ways to reach ever-larger numbers of Americans with it.

Step 2 is what I call progressive fusion. If the various US progressive communities remain as fragmented and as in-their-silos as today, we won't be able to take advantage of positive opportunities opened up by rising popular disenchantment and by the inevitable crises ahead. What's needed, for starters, is a unified progressive identity, a concerted effort to institutionalize coordination, a common infrastructure capable of formulating clear policy objectives and strategic messages, and a commitment to creating a powerful, unified movement beyond isolated campaigns.

Critical here is a common progressive platform. It should embrace a profound commitment to social justice, job creation, and environmental protection; a sustained challenge to consumerism and commercialism and the lifestyles they offer; a healthy skepticism of growth mania and a democratic redefinition of what society should be striving to grow; a challenge to corporate dominance and a redefinition of the corporation, its goals and its management and ownership; a commitment to an array of prodemocracy reforms in campaign finance, elections, the regulation of lobbying; and much more. A common agenda would also include an ambitious set of new national indicators beyond GDP to inform us of the true quality of life in America.

Coming together is imperative because all progressive causes face the same reality. We live and work in a system of political economy that cares profoundly about profit and growth and about international power and prestige. It cares about society and the natural world in which it operates primarily to the extent the law requires. So the progressive mandate is to inject values of justice, democracy, sustainability, and peace into this system. And our best hope for doing this is a fusion of those concerned about environment, social justice, true democracy, and peace into one powerful progressive force. We have to recognize that we are all communities of a shared fate. We will rise or fall together, so we'd better get together.

Step 3. A powerful part of the drive for transformation must be a compelling envisioning of the world we would like to leave for our children and grandchildren—a new American Dream, if you will. When systemic change does come, it does so because the people agitating for change have painted a compelling vision of a better future. And this new dream should be accompanied by a new narrative or story that explains America's path from yesterday to tomorrow. Harvard's Howard Gardner stresses that "leaders...can change the course of history...by creating a compelling story, embodying that story in one's own life, and presenting the story in many different formats so that it can eventually topple the counterstories in one's culture…. The story must be simple, easy to identify with, emotionally resonant, and evocative of positive experiences."

Bill Moyers has written that "America needs a different story…. So let me say what I think up front: The leaders and thinkers and activists who honestly tell that story and speak passionately of the moral and religious values it puts in play will be the first political generation since the New Deal to win power back for the people."

We can realize a new American Dream, America the Possible, if enough of us join together in the fight for it. This new dream envisions an America where the pursuit of happiness is sought not in more getting and spending but in the growth of human solidarity, real democracy, and devotion to the public good; where the average American is empowered to achieve his or her human potential; where the benefits of economic activity are widely and equitably shared; where the environment is sustained for current and future generations; and where the virtues of simple living, community self-reliance, good fellowship, and respect for nature predominate.

Step 4. One key task for progressives of all stripes is not merely to have a compelling vision but also to pioneer the development of a powerful set of new ideas and policy proposals which confirm that the path to this better world does indeed exist. We must show that when it comes to defining the way forward, we know what we're talking about. We are dreamers, perhaps, but dreamers with tools. The good news here is that system-changing proposals already exist in many of the key areas of transformation—ideas for dethroning GDP, transcending consumerism, transforming corporations, revitalizing communities, building a different system for money and finance, and more. The goal here is to design and test a new operating system. Carrying forward this work is something to which I know many of the groups represented here today will contribute.

Which brings me to **Step 5**. It's vital that we continuously strengthen the intellectual capital of the new economy movement, as well as regularly link ideas to action and prepare for the crises that will surely come. This means that we need to dramatically strengthen the institutional capacity to do these things. That is why we have created the New Economics Institute, for example. And here, let's face it, the desperate need for most institutions working these issues is funding. Given the stakes involved, financial support for new economy work from foundations and individuals has thus far been much too limited. Together, we can help to change this situation.

Step 6. This is the step I suspect many of you have been waiting to have recognized. It is certainly the step that many of you are already taking!

I have reference, of course, to the extraordinary work being done today in America's communities and regions to bring the future into the present, without waiting on the rest of the world to catch on and catch up. Many of you are already building a new world from the ground up with a proliferation of real-world, predominantly local initiatives—new forms of community revitalization and innovative community action—new business models focused on local living economies, rootedness, and sustaining people and nature (for example, B-Corps, public-private and profit-nonprofit hybrids, mission-protected corporations) as well as new growth of older models (worker owned coops and other forms of employee ownership)—and new lifestyles and work-styles adopted at the individual, family and organizational levels. These initiatives are not only worthy in themselves, they provide inspirational models that can be replicated as the movement grows. They provide opportunities for people to get involved. And they also change peoples' minds. As they say, seeing is believing. This may be the most hopeful thing going on in America today. So more power to you.

Step 7. This step embraces another area where numerous of you are already active. Many of the ideas needed to transition to a new political economy must await better times, or they need further development. But many do not, and should be pursued now, even in today's political process. Of particular importance here are what we can call non-reformist reforms—they may look like mere reformist incrementalism, but they plant the seeds of deeper changes. The New Economy Working Group, the Institute for Policy Studies, *Yes!* Magazine and the New Economy Network, for example, have collaborated on path-breaking work on reforms in banking and finance and on jobs in the new economy. Demos is pushing new indicators of progress beyond GDP. The Democracy Collaborative is developing and promoting new models of community revitalization and business ownership. And on and on. Again, more power to you. We need to define a new economy policy agenda that has a fighting chance today, and we need to pursue it with all our strength.

Step 8 takes us into politics. Clearly, America faces a daunting agenda, one that requires far-sighted, strong, and effective government leadership and action. Inevitably, then, the drive to respond to these challenges leads to the political arena, where a vital, muscular democracy steered by an informed and engaged citizenry is needed. That's the democracy we need, but, unfortunately, it is not the democracy we have. Right now, Washington isn't even seriously trying to address most of the country's challenges. It is unimaginable that American politics as we know it will deliver the responses needed.

The deep transformations we need—and even most of the proposals for reform offered by progressives in Washington today—will not be possible without a new politics in America. As Michael Waldman, director of one of the key reform groups, the Brennan Center for Justice, has said, "Progressives have to grapple with this central truth—we can't solve the country's problems if we don't fix the systems of democracy." The antidote to creeping corporatocracy and plutocracy in America is a strong, muscular democracy in America.

We know what must be done here—and done with urgency before we decline into terminal corporatocracy and plutocracy. We need to guarantee the right to vote and ensure that all votes are counted equally, effectively challenge the two-party duopoly with fusion voting and otherwise, overturn Citizens United and enact meaningful public and citizen financing of elections, regulate lobbying and the revolving door, reform Senate rules on holds and filibusters, for starters.

Step 9. How do progressives begin to drive real change? The short answer is that we need to build a powerful citizens movement. In today's America, progressive ideas are unlikely to be turned into action unless they are pushed relentlessly by citizen demand. The more serious the change sought, the louder the demand must be.

This reality has been stressed by many of our most perceptive observers. Washington Post columnist Harold Meyerson wrote in 2010, "If there's a common feature to the political landscapes in which Carter, Clinton and now Obama were compelled to work, it's the absence of a vibrant left movement.... In America, major liberal reforms require not just liberal governments, but autonomous, vibrant mass movements, usually led by activists who stand at or beyond liberalism's left fringe." Successful movements for serious change are launched in protest against key features of the established order. They are nurtured on outrage at the severe injustice being perpetrated, the core values being threatened, and the future prospects that are unfolding. And they insist that power concede to their demands. As Frederick Douglass famously said, "Power concedes nothing without a demand. It never did and it never will." If progressives hope to succeed, then the movement must capture the spirit of Frederick Douglass.

Achieving meaningful changes will require reaching out to diverse communities, and it will require a rebirth of marches, protests, demonstrations, direct action, and nonviolent civil disobedience. No one who followed recent events in Egypt or at the Wisconsin State House, or who remembers the civil rights and antiwar protests of the 1960s and 1970s, or has seen the impact of Occupy and other protests, can doubt their importance. Author and social critic Chris Hedges reminds us that "Civil disobedience, which will entail hardship and suffering, which will be long and difficult, which at its core means self-sacrifice is the only mechanism left." Those words ring true to those who have worked for decades to elicit a meaningful response to the existential threat of climate change and who find, after all the effort, only ashes.

Step 10. The final step we need to pursue is a little different. An imperative we face is to preserve the possibility of a bright future by preventing any of today's looming disasters from spinning out of control or otherwise becoming calamitous or so overwhelming that they monopolize resources of time, energy, and money.

So, while the struggle to build a new system goes forward, we must do everything we can to make the old system perform to head off such calamity. For example, climate disruption is already well under way. Should we fail to act decisively on the climate front, the world will likely become so nasty and brutish that the possibility of rebirth, of achieving something new and beautiful, will simply vanish, and we will be left with nothing but the burden of climate chaos and societies' endless responses to it.

To sum up, I believe we can already see how the dynamics of fundamental change might emerge—how systemic change can come to America. As conditions in our country continue to decline across a wide front, or at best fester as they are, ever-larger numbers of Americans lose faith in the current system and its ability to deliver on the values it proclaims. The system steadily loses support, leading to a crisis of legitimacy. Meanwhile, traditional crises, both in the economy and in the environment, grow more numerous and fearsome. In response, progressives of all stripes coalesce, find their voice and their strength, and pioneer the development of a powerful set of new ideas and policy proposals confirming that the path to a better world does indeed exist. Demonstrations and protests multiply, and popular movements for prodemocracy reform and transformative change gain strength. At the local level, people and groups plant the seeds of change through a host of innovative initiatives that provide inspirational models of how things might work in a new political economy devoted to sustaining human and natural communities. Sensing the direction in which things are moving, our wiser and more responsible leaders, political and otherwise, rise to the occasion, support the growing movement for change, and frame a compelling story or narrative that makes sense of it all and provides a positive vision of a better America. The movement broadens to become a major national force.

Demands for immediate amelioration—for jobs, for tax justice, for climate action—will at best be met with proposals for modest accommodations and half measures, and the struggle for deep, systemic change will be met with fierce opposition and determined resistance. So all-important conclusions emerge—namely, that the prospects for systemic change will depend mightily on the health of our democracy and the power of the popular movement that is built. And those prospects will also depend mightily on our willingness to take real risks, to struggle together, to sacrifice, to put it all on the line.

In the end, it all comes down to the American people and the strong possibility that we still have it in us to use our freedom and our democracy in powerful ways to create something fine, a reborn America, for our children and grandchildren.

Bankers Seek Global Domination

Let me issue and control a nation's money and I care not who writes the laws

Mayer Amschel Rothschild, 1790

I believe that banking institutions are more dangerous to our liberties than standing armies. If the American people ever allow private banks to control the issue of their currency, first by inflation, then by deflation, the banks and corporations that will grow up around the banks will deprive the people of all property until their children wake-up homeless on the continent their fathers conquered....The issuing power should be taken from the banks and restored to the people, to whom it properly belongs.

Thomas Jefferson, letter to Treasury Secretary Albert Gallatin, 1802

The bold efforts the present bank has made to control the Government...are but premonitions of the fate that awaits the American people should they be deluded into a perpetuation of this institution, or the establishing of another like it.

Andrew Jackson

Whosoever controls the volume of money in any country is absolute master of all industry and commerce.... And when you realize that the entire system is very easily controlled, one way or another, by a few powerful men at the top, you will not have to be told how periods of inflation and depression originate.

President James Garfield, 1881. Garfield was assassinated four months after making this statement

The powers of financial capitalism had another far-reaching aim, nothing less than to create a world system of financial control in private hands able to dominate the political system of each country and the economy of the world as a whole. This system was to be controlled in a feudalist fashion by the central banks of the world acting in concert, by secret agreements arrived at in frequent private meetings and conferences. The apex of the systems was to be the Bank for International Settlements in Basel, Switzerland; a private bank owned and controlled by the world's central banks which were themselves private corporations. Each central bank...sought to dominate its government by its ability to control Treasury loans, to manipulate foreign exchanges, to influence the level of economic activity in the country, and to influence cooperative politicians by subsequent economic rewards in the business world

Prof. Carroll Quigley, *Tragedy & Hope*

Most of the money in the world—all but the three or four percent that we use in banknotes and coins in everyday commerce—is not issued by central banks and guaranteed by governments but is created by commercial banks in the form of credit.... Economic growth fuels economic confidence and leads to an increase in borrowing—which means an increase in the amount of the debt-money that drives the system. The system is self-fuelling: debt, if it is to be repaid with interest, requires economic growth; growth leads to more lending and thus to more debt-money, which in turn leads to more growth—and more debt-money. In this system, rich people and multinational corporations are the main beneficiaries: They can qualify for credit and obtain debt-money. Poor people and small business are left on the margins.

Ervin Laszlo

An aspect of a 'free' market is the freedom to steal, which is why economics must be tempered with the Constitution and the law.

Ellen Hodgson Brown

2

THE NAKED EMPEROR

David C. Korten, PhD

This chapter was originally written by Korten in 1998 for *The Post-Corporate World: Life After Capitalism,* which was published in 1999 shortly after the collapse of the high tech bubble of the 1990s. Wall Street had not yet begun playing into the housing bubble that led up to the financial crash of September 2008. This in many respects heightens the chapter's significance, because it so clearly identifies the underlying fallacies and distortions that went uncorrected at the time and subsequently led to the growth and collapse of the housing bubble.

The consequences of the housing bubble were more devastating than the consequences of the high tech bubble. The responsible Wall Street edifice was saved from its housing bubble foolishness only by a massive public bailout that in total ran to the trillions of dollars. The concentration of Wall Street power is now even greater than it was in 1998 and the financial games that Wall Street plays are even more esoteric, removed from reality, and at odds with foundational market principles.

Until the myths that capitalism is the champion of markets and that rule by Wall Street bankers is the only alternative to rule by socialist bureaucrats are finally put to rest, the dynamic identified so clearly in this chapter virtually guarantees ever more devastating financial boom and bust cycles.

For we are all capitalists now, are we not? These days the victory of the market over state is taken quite for granted.
The Economist, 1997

Although members of other species trick one another, humans are the expert self-deceivers: as the best symbol users, the most intelligent species, and the only talkers, we are the only being accomplished enough to fully fool ourselves.
Lynn Margulis & Dorion Sagan

We are subjected to a constant refrain: the victory of capitalism is the triumph of the market and democracy. Capitalism is an engine of wealth creation. Freed from the oppressive hand of public regulation, market forces will cause the world's great corporations to bring prosperity, democracy, a respect for human rights, and environmentally beneficial technologies to all the world. If some must suffer temporarily to make way for greater progress for all, it is only capitalism's creative destruction at work on the path to a better tomorrow.

The mantra continually propagated by our most powerful institutions brings to mind the human capacity for self-deception immortalized in the story of the emperor's new clothes. Many of us are like the emperor's subjects. We see the truth, but lack the courage to speak. The time has come to speak the truth that so many of us know in our hearts. Though the Siren known as capitalism wraps herself in the cloak of markets, democracy, and universal prosperity, she is the mortal enemy of all three. We tolerate her triumph to the peril of nearly all we truly value.

In this chapter we will examine the ways capitalism actively erodes the conditions necessary to the market's efficient social function. Understanding the extent to which markets and capitalism are mutually exclusive forms of economic organization is the key to answering those who maintain there is no alternative to global capitalism. The most obvious and promising of such alternatives is an economy that honors foundational market principles that capitalism systematically violates.

The Emperor's New Clothes

Once upon a time a vain emperor who fancied himself a stylish dresser sent forth word that he would give a great prize to the tailor who sewed him a cloak woven of the finest cloth. A clever rogue came forward with an offer to make him a cloak from a cloth so fine that it would be neither seen nor felt against his skin. The Emperor was elated. When the cloak arrived, his terrified aides could only express their admiration for the emperor's fine taste. As the emperor ventured forth on his great horse to display his new finery to his subjects, they dared only to applaud—until the voice of a small and innocent child was heard, "Why doesn't the Emperor have any clothes?"

Capitalism Against the Market

The theory of the market economy traces back to the Scottish economist Adam Smith (1723-1790) and the publication of *Inquiry into the Nature and Causes of the Wealth of Nations* in 1776. Considered by many to be the most influential economics book ever written, it articulates the powerful and wonderfully democratic ideal of a self-organizing economy that creates an equitable and socially optimal allocation of a society's productive resources through the interaction of small buyers and sellers making decisions based on their individual needs and interests.

Market theory, as articulated by Smith and those who subsequently elaborated on his ideas, developed into an elegant and coherent intellectual construction grounded in carefully articulated assumptions regarding the conditions under which such self-organizing processes would indeed lead to socially optimal outcomes. For example:

- Buyers and sellers must be too small to influence the market price.
- Complete information must be available to all participants and there are no trade secrets.
- Sellers must bear the full cost of the products they sell and pass them on in the sale price.
- Investment capital must remain within national borders and trade between countries must be balanced.
- Savings must be invested in the creation of productive capital.

There is, however, a critical problem, as international financier George Soros has observed: "Economic theory is an axiomatic system: as long as the basic assumptions hold, the conclusions follow. But when we examine the assumptions closely, we find that they do not apply to the real world." Herein lies the catch: the conditions of what we currently call a capitalist economy directly contradict the assumptions of market theory in most every instance.

Bear in mind that the optimally efficient market exists only as a theoretical construction. No economy has ever fully satisfied its assumptions and probably none ever will. The challenge facing those of us who would create an economy that approximates the markets promised outcomes of fair but modest returns to capital, full employment at a living wage, and socially optimal allocation of society's productive resources is to establish a framework of rules that create as closely as possible the conditions that market theory assumes.

It is in contemplating this task that we encounter the reality of capitalism's true relationship to the market economy. Historians have traced the first use of the term capitalism to the mid-1800s, long after Adam Smith's death, when it was used to refer to an economic and social regime in which the ownership and benefits of capital are appropriated by the few to the exclusion of the many who through their labor make capital productive. This, of course, describes with considerable precision the characteristics of the current global capitalist regime—which bears no discernible resemblance to the concept of a market economy articulated by Adam Smith and those who followed in his tradition. Those who rejoice at the triumph of capitalism are rejoicing at the triumph of the few over the many.

Indeed, capitalism's claim to the mantle of the market has no more substance than the rogue's claim that he has cloaked the emperor in a fine gown. In selectively culling out bits and pieces of market theory to argue that the public interest is best served by giving globe-spanning mega-corporations a license to maximize their profits without public restraint, capitalism has distorted market theory beyond recognition to legitimate an ideology without logical foundation in the service of a narrow class interest.

Wearing the mantle of the market, capitalism's agents vigorously advance public policies that create conditions diametrically opposed to those required for markets to function in a socially optimal way. Table 2.1 provides an overview of some of the major differences that are examined in greater detailed below.

Table 1. Capitalism Against the Market

	Capitalism	Healthy Markets
Dominant attractor	Money	Life
Defining purpose	Use money to make money for those who have money	Employ available resources to meet the basic needs of everyone
Firm size	Very large	Small and medium-size
Costs	Externalized to the public	Internalized by the user
Ownership	Impersonal, absentee	Personal, rooted
Financial capital	Global with no borders	Local/national with clear borders
Purpose of investment	Maximized private profit	Increase beneficial output
The role of profit	An end to be maximized	Incentive to invest productivity
Coordinating mechanisims	Centrally planned by megacorporations	Self-organizing markets and networks
Cooperation	Among competitors to escape the discipline of competition	Among people and communities to advance the common good
Purpose of competition	Eliminate the unfit	Stimulate efficiency and innovation
Government role	Protect the interests of property	Advance the human interest
Trade	Free	Fair and balanced
Political orientation	Elitist, democracy of dollars	Populist, democracy of persons

As with the cancer cells that attempt to hide from the body's immune system by masking themselves as healthy cells, capitalism's agents attempt to conceal themselves from society's immune system by masquerading as agents of a healthy market economy. Capitalism has become so skilled in this deception that we now find our economic and political leaders committed to policies that serve the pathology at the expense of the healthy body. To restore health we must recognize the diseased cells for what they are and repair their damaged DNA, destroy them directly, or deprive them of the body's nutrients.

The nature of capitalism as a market pathology can be readily demonstrated by examining how it vigorously and systematically eliminates the five conditions mentioned above as basic to market theory. What follows is a grim picture of our collective affliction. We must, however, be willing to look our affliction squarely in the face if we are to exorcize it.

Competition: Small Firms vs. Mega-Corporations

Beginning with Adam Smith, market theory has been quite explicit that the efficiency of the market's self-organizing dynamic is a consequence of small, locally owned enterprises competing in local markets on the basis of price, quality, and service in response to customer-defined needs and values. No buyer or seller may be large enough to individually influence the market price.

By contrast, what we know as the global capitalist economy is dominated by a few financial speculators and a handful of globe-spanning mega-corporations able to use their massive financial clout and media outreach to manipulate prices, determine what products will be available to consumers, and reshape the values of popular culture to create demand for what corporations choose to offer. The alleged anti-competitive practices of the Microsoft Corporation in its systematic domination of the software industry and the Internet make it only one of the better known examples. Furthermore, the mega-corporations and financial houses continue to concentrate and consolidate their power over markets, technology, and capital through mergers, acquisitions, and strategic alliances—even as they shed their responsibility for people by downsizing and contracting out. The statistics are sobering.

In 1995, the combined sales of the world's top 200 corporations—which employed only 18.8 million people, less than 1/3 of one percent of the world's population—equaled 28 percent of total world GDP. The total sales of Mitsubishi Corporation were greater than the GDP of Indonesia, the world's fourth most populous country and a land of enormous natural wealth. The annual sales of Wal-Mart, the twelfth largest corporation, made its internal economy larger than the internal economies of 161 of the world's countries—including Israel, Poland, and Greece.

Meanwhile the consolidation of unaccountable corporate power is accelerating. In the United States the total value of corporate mergers and acquisitions increased at a rate of nearly 50 percent a year in every year save one from 1992 through 1998, with no end in sight. Most of these mergers and acquisitions are accompanied by large scale layoffs. The greatest concentration is taking place in the financial and telecommunications sectors—with deeply ominous implications for the future of democracy. In the United States alone, from the beginning of 1993 to the end of 1997, there were 2,492 commercial bank mergers worth more than $200 billion, 5,114 deals worth a total of $110 billion in the insurance industry, and 1,435 radio and television mergers worth $162 billion.

The increasingly arrogant defiance of law and the public interest embodied in these mergers was epitomized by the 1998 announcement by Citicorp banking corporation and Travelers Group insurance corporation of the largest merger in history to create the world's largest financial institution. It signaled that the titans of the money world no longer intended to be bound by the laws of the land—in this case the Glass-Steagall Act, a legal restriction passed by the US Congress during the Great Depression that prohibited banks from owning insurance corporations and brokerage houses to prevent a repeat of the disastrous financial collapse of 1929.

Other industries in which concentration has moved at a rapid clip include health services, investment brokers, utilities, oil and gas refining, and hotels and casinos. In the United States there are now only three large military contractors and one producer of large commercial airliners.

Though the United States led the world in merger mania during the 1990s, mergers world-wide totaled $1.63 trillion in 1997, up 48 percent over 1996. Merger activity is rapidly accelerating in Europe as Wall Street investment banks become more active there—aggressively promoting hostile take-overs that advance the concentration of European industry and the shift of wealth from workers to managers, investment houses, and shareholders. European mergers and acquisitions set a record of $400.6 billion in 1996—double the level of just two years earlier. American investment banks were involved as advisors in two-thirds of these deals. The move of eleven European countries to a single currency at the beginning of 1999 is expected to unleash a further wave of mergers and acquisitions

New agreements fashioned under the auspices of the World Trade Organization in Geneva plus terms imposed by the International Monetary Fund following Asia's 1997 financial meltdown opened Asia's financial markets to greater intervention by Wall Street investment houses to the same end. The US financial press referred to it as a great "fire sale" opportunity.

The accountancy industry may be the harbinger of things to come. In the 1980s, the world had eight large international accountancy firms. Four mergers in 1997 reduced the number of four. With these firms providing an increasingly diversified range of consulting and management services to large clients, interests become so intertwined that the concept of the independent audit is becoming nearly meaningless.

The global cartel is another favored mechanism by which the largest global corporations avoid competing with one another in the global economy by agreeing on mutually protective pricing formulas. In July 1998, the US Justice Department had 25 grand juries investigating international price-fixing cases in industries as diverse as vitamins, glass, and marine equipment. It is estimated that cartels are transferring billions of illegal dollars from consumers to corporate coffers.

Competition is a key to the self-organizing dynamics of a market economy. In contrast, capitalism loves monopoly with a passion equaled only by its abhorrence of the competition that limits its ability to extract monopoly profits.

Complete Information: Sharing vs. Monopolization

Market theory stipulates that information should be freely available. Adam Smith specifically condemned trade secrets as a form of monopoly power that prevents market entry by competing producers. Market efficiency requires that such artificial barriers be removed and relevant knowledge and expertise be freely shared. It also requires that buyers and sellers enter into each transaction fully informed regarding the nature and quality of the product and the current market price of comparable items. This is possible only to the extent that market participants freely share the information available to them.

Capitalism functions under quite different norms. Its corporations presume a right to withhold information about dangers posed by their products, deny consumers access to information that would allow them to make informed choices about the products they buy, and aggressively pursue the creation of government-enforced monopolies over critical technologies, including those essential to life.

In one of the more notorious examples of industry attempts to deny consumers their right to accurate product labeling, the United States Department of Agriculture (USDA) on December 16, 1997 released a 600 page technical document proposing changes in federal regulations regarding organic standards. Backers of the proposed changes included the National Food Processors Association, the Grocery Manufacturers of America, and the Biotechnology Industry Organization. The changes would have significantly lowered the organic standards maintained by an association of 40 non-governmental and state organic certifiers. In their place it would have introduced a mandatory standardized "USDA Organic" label that would permit the use of genetic engineering, nuclear irradiation, toxic sewage sludge, intensive confinement of farm animals, and other conventional factory farm practices in the production of organically certified products. Furthermore, the rule change would have given the USDA a monopoly over use of the word organic and prohibit any organic certifier or producer from setting any standard higher than those established by the USDA.

The response from consumers was strong and unanimous. The USDA received 220,000 citizen comments, 20 times greater than to any previous USDA proposal, and nearly all denounced the proposed rule change.

On a related front, corporations have also pushed through food liable laws in a number of states making it a crime to make a statement not backed by conclusive scientific evidence that might cause people to doubt the safety of their food. Thus the agents of capitalism not only seek the right to mislabel their own products, but also to deny others the right to accurately inform the public that they are holding themselves to higher standards or to raise critical issues of food safety for public discussion and debate.

With regard to trade secrets, corporations have been engaged in an increasingly intense campaign to strengthen and extend government protection of technology and information monopolies in the name of intellectual property rights. In response to the demands of global corporations, governments wrote strong safeguards for intellectual property rights into the North American Free Trade Agreement (NAFTA) and into the General Agreement on Tariffs and Trade (GATT) that created the World Trade Organization. The corporate goal is to establish an international intellectual property rights system that makes a patent granted in one country immediately enforceable in all countries to give the holder a strictly enforced global monopoly.

Currently, biotech corporations are engaged in a vigorous campaign to gain monopoly control over life itself through the patenting of genetic materials and processes. One favored strategy is to force farmers into dependency on patented genetically engineered seeds that give the holder of the patent virtual monopoly power over a commodity such as soya bean or cotton. Other biotech companies are in a race to patent every human gene they can identify. It is increasingly common for individuals to learn that without their knowledge or permission a corporation has acquired exclusive ownership rights to genetic material extracted from their bodies.

A brief segment in a television documentary I viewed some years ago on overpricing in the drug industry illustrates the extent to which some academic economists are revising economic theory to defend monopoly pricing. The documentary looked into a case in which a drug company was charging a price far above its costs for a patented drug a small number of desperate patients depended on for their lives. An economist who was invited to comment argued that since the patients who use the drug have no alternative, the drug company has a fiduciary responsibility to its shareholders to raise the price to the highest level the user is willing to pay to save her life. Since the drug's current high price was clearly below this amount, in this economist's opinion the company was in fact under-pricing the product. Adam Smith must have been turning in his grave.

Full access to information and an absence of artificial barriers to entry into the production of beneficial products are basic to the efficient function of the market and to meeting the needs of a troubled and resource scarce world. Capitalism is an ardent champion of the right to withhold relevant information from customers and the public and to establish government protected monopoly control of critical technologies.

Accurate Prices: Full Costs vs. Public Subsidies

Another major difference between a capitalist economy and an efficient market economy lies in the way they deal with subsidies and other exter-nalized costs. Market theory explicitly states that for the market to allo-cate resources efficiently, the costs of a product must be borne fully by its producer and passed forward in the price charged the consumer. Similarly, investors must bear the risks of their investments. Any subsidy, direct or indirect, distorts the incentives of the market's self-regulating pricing mechanisms and reduces the social efficiency of resource allocation.

By contrast, the institutions of capitalism are unabashed proponents of corporate subsidies. Using mechanisms that range from threatening to move jobs elsewhere to political contributions and fabricated grassroots lobbying campaigns, they convince those who control public expenditures to provide them subsidies for research, the extraction of resources, advertising products in foreign markets, insuring overseas investments against political risks, and an endless range of other activities. Banks and investment houses regularly run to government to save them from the costs of bad investment, as in the savings and loan bailout and the repeated IMF and US bailouts of bad loans to countries such as Mexico, Thailand, Indonesia, Malaysia, and Korea.

Corporations are constantly upping the ante on what they demand from state and local governments to bring jobs to their jurisdictions. For example, the incentive package given by the State of Virginia to Motorola to entice it to locate a research and manufacturing facility there included a $55.9 million grant, a $1.6 billion tax credit, and a reimbursement package worth $5 million for employee training. In New York City, investment banks threaten to leave the city for the suburbs, to which the cash-strapped city responds with ever greater tax breaks and other public subsidies. By 1998, $439 million had been granted to 18 financial institutions—including the New York Mercantile Exchange, New York's largest commodity market—during the administration of Mayor Giuliani. Big corporations now increasingly expect states to pick up a portion of their wage bill, commonly by returning to the company a portion of the state taxes withheld from qualified employees. In Tulsa, Oklahoma the county sales tax for one year was diverted from public purposes to pay for construction of a new Whirlpool factory. In addition, the state will reimburse Whirlpool 4.5 cents for every dollar paid in wages to 1,100 workers for ten years.

Corporations have been especially aggressive over the past 30 years in seeking to avoid paying a fair share of taxes to cover the public services and infrastructure they demand, including roads and port facilities, the protection of their assets by the US military, and the public education of their workers. In the 1950s, corporate income taxes accounted for 39 percent of all federal income tax revenue. From 1990 to 1995 it was only 19 percent. During that same period the share of federal income tax revenues coming from individuals rose from 61 percent to 81 percent. If in 1996 corporations had paid taxes at the same effective rate as during the 1950s, it would have produced an additional $250 billion in federal revenues and wiped out the federal deficit for that year.

It has been much the same story at local levels. In 1957, corporations provided 45 percent of local property tax revenues in the United States. By 1987, their share had dropped to about 16 percent.

The Cato Institute, a conservative Washington, DC based think tank, estimates that the US government each year provides corporations $75 billion in direct cash subsidies plus another $60 billion in industry-specific tax breaks. Worldwide, government subsidies for energy use—the vast majority for fossil fuel and nuclear sources—are estimated to be from $235 billion to $350 billion—a clear case of using public funds to encourage environmentally destructive practices. Business analyst Paul Hawken has compiled data suggesting that corporations in the US may now receive more in direct government financial subsidies than they pay in taxes.

Then there are the costs of straightforward corporate crime such as overbilling by defense contractors of some $25.9 billion, and by Medicaid contractors, primarily insurance companies, of an amount estimated by federal auditors at $23 billion in 1996.

Still another type of subsidy takes the form of unreimbursed costs imposed on society by the products corporations sell. These include health costs of $53.9 billion a year from smoking cigarettes, $135.8 billion for the consequences of unsafe vehicles, $141.6 billion for injuries and accidents from unsafe workplaces, and $274.7 billion for deaths from workplace cancer.

In *Tyranny of the Bottom Line,* CPA Ralph Estes compiles an inventory of those public costs of private corporations that have been documented by authoritative studies—not including direct subsidies and tax breaks—and comes up with a conservative total for the United States alone of $2.6 *trillion* a year in 1994 dollars. This is roughly five times the corporate profits reported in the United States for 1994 ($530 billion) and the equivalent of 37 percent of 1994 US GDP of $6.9 trillion. If we were to extrapolate this ratio to a global economy that had an estimated total output of $29 trillion in 1997, it suggests that the cost to humanity of maintaining the corporate infrastructure of capitalism may be upward of $10.73 trillion.

In short, while capitalism claims to be an engine of wealth creation, in fact, its primary vehicle, the corporation, is more accurately described as a powerful engine of wealth extraction—its profits dependent on imposing enormous costs on the rest of society so that a few top executives and large shareholders may enjoy unconscionably high financial rewards. If market rules were applied, most of the dominant corporations would have long ago found themselves unable to cover their own costs and gone bankrupt or been restructured into smaller, more efficient firms.

Balanced International Accounts: Rooted vs. Global Capital

Market theory's requirements that trade be balanced and capital national (that is, be nationally owned and remain within national borders) are fundamental to classical economist David Ricardo's *theory of comparative advantage*, a cornerstone of market theory. Much cited by capitalist interests pushing to remove barriers to the free flow of international trade and investment, Ricardo's theory makes the case that open trade between two nations is beneficial to the national interests of both—so long as a number of very specific conditions are met. Among these required conditions, trade must be a balance between the two countries, both countries must have full employment, and investors must not be able to transfer their production facilities from one country to another. In typical fashion, those of the capitalist persuasion take no note of these conditions. For them it is enough that the free movement of money and goods increases profit opportunities for global capitalists. National interests are not their concern.

Consequences of Foreign Debt

When a country spends more on imports then it earns from its exports, it incurs a foreign debt that must be covered by some form of foreign loan or other portfolio investment. In the end, whatever has been loaned or invested must be repaid with interest and profits in foreign exchange. Because there is rarely a reason to borrow or attract portfolio investments from abroad except to generate foreign exchange to pay for imports beyond what can be purchased with export earnings, the net amount of foreign exchange a country receives from foreign lenders and other portfolio investors generally equals the difference between its import expenditures and its export earnings.

It is much the same as for an individual. If you wish to spend more than you earn, you have to borrow money from someone to cover the difference. The person or bank making the loan is investing in you by acquiring a stake in your future earnings. You, of course, would be foolish to mortgage your future earnings simply for the pleasure of having the money sitting in your account. Normally people borrow only when they have in mind something they wish to buy beyond the means of their current savings and income. Of course, you will eventually have to increase your income or reduce your expenditures so you will have surplus income to repay the bank.

When a bank makes a foreign exchange loan to a government or business in another country, it is essentially providing the country with money that can be used to buy something from abroad it could not pay for from current export earnings. To repay its foreign obligations, the borrowing country must either earn the money for future repayment by making more on the sale of its exports than it spends on imports or by borrowing still more from abroad and thereby compounding its foreign debt. This makes it very difficult to pay off a major foreign debt once incurred because to do so, a country must shift its whole economy from an export deficit to an import surplus and find a trading partner willing to incur a corresponding export deficit. So long as trade between countries is balanced, there is no need for one country to borrow from another and thus no need to mortgage its assets and future production to foreigners.

Ricardo's reasoning is quite straightforward. If trade between countries is balanced, labor is fully employed, and investors are unable to transfer their assets abroad, the investor who finds she cannot compete against foreign imports in one industry will shift her investment and the related jobs to another industry in which her country has some natural comparative advantage. For example, if for reasons of climate Portugal has an advantage in growing grapes and producing wine, and if for reasons of climate, technology, cheap energy, and labor skills England has an advantage in growing wool and producing woolen cloth, both countries stand to benefit if Portuguese woolens producers shift to wine production and English wine producers shift to production of woolen cloth, and the products are then exchanged through trade. Workers and capital remain fully employed in both countries, the British are able to enjoy more wine, and the Portuguese are able to enjoy more woolen clothing.

It's an entirely different matter if both investments and goods are free to flow where they will—which is the goal the new global capitalists are advancing through international trade and investment agreements and organizations with names like NAFTA, GATT, WTO, OECD, APEC, and MAI. Negotiated without public discussion and ratified by legislative bodies with limited debate and no opportunity for amendment, these agreements are used to eliminate economic borders and regulatory restraints on the power of the institutions of capitalism to move goods and capital freely, without regard to national interests or trade balances, wherever they see prospects for quick profit.

Assume under a regime of completely open borders Portugal has both a more favorable climate and a substantial labor surplus that keeps wages deeply depressed, and that the retail prices of both cloth and wine tend to be higher in England. In this instance British investors will find it profitable to move their looms and wine presses to Portugal and ship both cloth and wine back to England.

Unable to compete with the lower-cost imports, the remaining British wine and textile producers will likely be driven out of business—depressing wages, increasing unemployment, and ultimately substantially reducing the British market for both Portuguese wine and cloth. In the meantime, the Portuguese may find their economy increasingly controlled by British investors intent on keeping Portuguese wages low and repatriating as much profit as possible back to England to finance purchases of Portuguese textiles and wine by the remaining elite. This may result in additional wage employment in Portugal, but with wages low and much of the output exported to a narrow market, Portuguese workers may find they are unable to afford to buy the products of their own labor. The only winners are the investor classes, who point out that the Portuguese workers should be happy to have any kind of job at all given the sad state of both the British and Portuguese economies. It is toward this latter world that capitalism has moved us.

Capital Accumulation: Productive vs. Extractive Investment

The fifth market condition discussed here addresses the question of whether savings are directed to productive investment or diverted to unproductive speculation. One of the most basic axioms of market economics is the simple equation: personal savings equals investment. In other words, market theory assumes that when people save, they defer current consumption in favor of investing in future productive output. As in the previous example, the wine maker might invest some of his earnings in a new wine press to increase future production.

The most advanced stage of capitalism's pathology is known as *finance capital* or *finance capitalism*. At this stage, the ownership of capital becomes increasingly separated from its application to production as power shifts from the entrepreneurs, inventors, and industrialists who are engaged in actual productive activity to financiers and rentiers who live solely from the income generated from the ownership of financial or other assets. The financial markets and the owners of capital become "increasingly purified in purpose—detached from social concerns and abstracted from the practical realities of commerce" and develop expectations regarding the returns invested saving ought to earn that increasingly "diverge from the underlying economic reality."

The focus at this point is on using money to make money by expanding bank lending, creating financial and real estate bubbles, and speculating on fluctuations in the prices of currencies and other financial instruments. Consumed by their own illusions, capitalism's foremost proponents and practitioners come to pride themselves on having accomplished the equivalent of the ancient alchemists' dream of turning baser metals into gold. The financial excesses we are now witnessing on a global scale are much like those that preceded the Great Depression of the 1930s. They are all a part of the *new global capitalism,* and virtually every country and person on the globe is to some extent subject to the resulting economic dysfunction and instability.

The mechanisms employed by finance capitalism to make money from money without the intervening necessity of engaging in productive activity allow those with money to increase their claims against society's stock of real wealth without contributing to its production. While the activities involved make a few people very wealthy, from a societal perspective they are extractive rather than productive. Finance capitalism's inability to tell the difference between productive and extractive investment seems almost to be one of its defining attributes.

The process of making money without creating wealth starts with banks creating money out of nothing each time they issue a loan. When I studied economics some years ago I was taught that banks are financial intermediaries. They take in money from those who have savings and make it available in the form of loans to those who invest it in productive activities. It is rather like one individual making a loan to another, except that as intermediary the bank translates the short-term savings of one group into long-term loans for another, does the paperwork, and takes the risk—or so I was led to believe.

In truth there is another and more basic difference. If I loan $1,000 to another person, call her Alice, I no longer have the use of that money until Alice repays me. If, however, I deposit my $1,000 in a bank and the bank loans the $1,000 to Alice, Alice has her money and I still have mine. Between Alice and me we now have access to $2,000 in ready cash rather than $1,000. The bank did not in fact loan Alice "my" money. Rather it created the second $1000 out of nothing simply by opening an account in Alice's name and typing in $1,000.

Clearly the bank has something more going on here than simply playing the role of intermediary between savers and borrowers. It is in the literal sense *making money*—creating it, putting it into circulation, and collecting interest on it—simply by posting a number to an account. Furthermore, the only thing of value that stands behind that money is the willingness of the rest of us to exchange our labor and other property for it. In a very real sense, the bank makes/creates the money and we guarantee its value with our labor and whatever other forms of real wealth we agree to exchange for it.

Another way to make money out of nothing without contributing to the creation of any real wealth is to create a financial bubble, which is a sophisticated version of the classic pyramid or Ponzi scheme. The fraudulent investment scheme that created a national crisis in Albania in the mid-1990s is an example. People were invited to participate in investment funds that promised returns as high as 25 percent a month. Impressed by the good fortune brought to them by the triumph of capitalism, some people handed over their savings. Though the investment scheme was not backed by any productive activity, with so much money pouring in it was easy for the promoters to use a portion of the money from new investors to pay the promised interest to the earlier investors. These payments established the credibility of the scheme and convinced still more people to invest. Soon the country was caught up in a speculative frenzy. Farmers sold their flocks and urban dwellers their apartments to share in the promised bonanza of effortless wealth. The inevitable collapse sparked widespread riots, arson, and looting when the Albanian government failed to make up the losses.

The speculative financial bubble, which involves bidding up the price of an asset far beyond its underlying value, is little more than a sophisticated and less obviously fraudulent variant of such pyramid scams. One of history's more famous financial bubbles occurred in 17th century Holland when it was found that certain tulip bulbs, when attacked by a particular virus, produced flowers of brilliantly variegated colors. These bulbs came to be highly valued by collectors. Then speculators began acquiring them, pushing prices higher. Others came in to profit from the bonanza of prices that seemed to rise without limit. Soon everyone, from nobles to chimney sweeps, was in on the action, bidding up the price of a single bulb of a particularly prized variety to the equivalent of $60,000 in current dollars. The inevitable bursting of the bubble came in 1637.

Those of us inclined to laugh at the innocence of the Albanians or the 17th century Dutch speculators should first consider our own participation in the world's stock markets. We operate on the mistaken belief that the money we use to buy stock or mutual fund shares goes into financing future productive output. However, in all but the rare instance in which we are buying shares sold in an initial public offering, not a penny of our money goes to the company whose shares we are buying.

According to 1993 Federal Reserve figures, equity financing raised through the sale of new shares contributed only 4 percent of the total financial capital of US public corporations. The rest came from borrowing (14 percent) and retained earnings (82 percent). Furthermore, from 1987 to 1994, corporations paid out more to buy back their own shares than they received from new stock issues. In early 1998, what is loosely called *investment capital* was flowing from corporations to the stock market at an annual rate of $110 billion.

We live in an era in which even as billions of dollars in new *investment* flow into the stock market and pump up prices at record rates, the net flow of funds from the stock market to the corporations in which we are in theory *investing* is actually negative. In truth, the stock market is a sophisticated gambling casino with the unique feature that through their interactions the players inflate the prices of the stocks in play to increase their collective financial assets and thereby their claims on the real wealth of the rest of the society.

So when I buy stock shares through my broker not a penny goes to the company I'm presumably buying. After the broker takes a commission what is left goes to the person who sold the shares. When I make my purchase I'm simply betting that in the future someone else will be willing to pay me more for that piece of paper than I've just paid for it. If I were a really sophisticated investor I would be betting on future price declines as well as future price increases and I would be borrowing money to leverage my bets. No matter how I go about it, however, it has no more to do with real investing than betting on a number on a Las Vegas roulette wheel.

The Asian financial crisis provides a fascinating window into how the game works and how the resulting gyrations in the world's stock markets have an impact on the lives of real people. In 1997 Asia's much touted financial miracle suddenly turned into the Asian financial meltdown. It began in Thailand and rapidly spread like falling dominoes through Malaysia, Indonesia, South Korea, and Hong Kong. Although specifics differed, we see in each instance a similar pattern. [See below: "Thailand's Encounter with Global Finance Capitalism."] During the miracle phase large inflows of foreign money fueled rapidly growing financial bubbles in stocks and real estate and a rapid increase in the importation and sale of luxury consumer goods—creating an illusion of economic prosperity unrelated to any increase in actual productive output. The growing bubbles attracted still more money, much of it created by international banks issuing loans secured by the inflated assets. Since returns on productive industrial and agricultural investments could not compete with the returns to stock and real estate speculation, the faster foreign investment flowed into a country, the faster money actually flowed out of its productive sectors to join the speculation. In the meltdown phase, investors rushed to pull their money out in anticipation of a crash, stock and real estate prices plummeted, banks and other lending institutions were left with large portfolios of uncollectible loans, and financial collapse threatened, as liquidity dried up.

Like the losers in the Albanian pyramid scheme, the Wall Street bankers and investment houses that created the crisis through reckless lending—inveterate champions of the free market when the profits were rolling in—responded in typical capitalist fashion. They ran to governments for public bailouts. The International Monetary Fund (IMF), with strong support from the Clinton administration, rushed to the aid of the bankers with emergency loans backed by public guarantees from its member governments. *The New York Times* reported, "One thing is clear: Whatever it takes, the Clinton administration will push to make sure that the size of the bailout is large enough to persuade investors to return." In translation, this means the US government intended to put up sufficient public money so that the private speculators would be attracted back into the market to restore the financial bubbles and get finance capitalism's party going again.

The IMF provided South Korea with a $57 billion bailout in December 1997. The Korean stock market rebounded smartly for a brief time. Then the speculators took the IMF money and ran. Korea's stock market suffered a 50 percent drop to an 11-year low. Korea's taxpayers were left with an IOU to the IMF for $57 billion plus interest to be paid in foreign currency.

We see in the Asian experience an all too common reality of capitalism's ability to create an illusion of prosperity by creating a speculative frenzy, while actually undermining real productive activity. The US financial collapse in 1929 and savings and loan crisis in the late 1980s, the gradual deflation of Japan's financial bubble that began in 1989, the Mexican collapse that followed the introduction of NAFTA, and the Brazilian crash that followed the Asian meltdown and the subsequent Russian crisis all shared the characteristic that they involved the crash of financial bubbles created by financial speculation and reckless bank lending.

Still, it seems, the members of capitalism's inner circle remain impervious to the difference between productive investment—using savings to increase the base of productive capital—and extractive investment—making money through speculation to establish claims on the existing real wealth of others. A 1996 *Foreign Policy* article titled "Securities: The New Wealth Machine" is unusually revealing of the mindset behind this blindness and the willingness of governments to align themselves behind finance capitalism's destructive power. The following are excerpts.

"Securitization—the issuance of high-quality bonds and stocks—has become the most powerful engine of wealth creation in today's world economy.... It has broadened the market for income-producing assets by separating ownership from management and is creating wealth rapidly. . . .

Historically, manufacturing, exporting, and direct investment produced prosperity through income creation. Wealth was created when a portion of income was diverted from consumption into investment in buildings, machinery, and technological change. Societies accumulated wealth slowly over generations. Now many societies, and indeed the entire world, have learned how to create wealth directly. The new approach requires that a state find ways to increase the *market value* of its stock of productive assets. [Emphasis in the original].... Wealth is also created when money, foreign or domestic, flows into the capital market of a country and raises the value of its quoted securities....

Nowadays, wealth is created when the managers of a business enterprise give high priority to rewarding the shareholders and bondholders. The greater the rewards, the more the shares and bonds are likely to be worth in the financial markets.... An economic policy that aims to achieve growth by wealth creation therefore does not attempt to increase the production of goods and services, except as a secondary objective."

Thailand's Encounter with Global Financial Capitalism

Through the 1980s the Thai economy was fueled by direct investment flows from Japanese corporations building production facilities there to produce goods destined for export to the United States. As the inflow of direct investment begin to level off, Thai economists came up with a scheme to keep foreign money flowing in to maintain the nation's high economic growth rate. They set a domestic interest rate above that of the US dollar and guaranteed a fixed exchange rate between the Thai baht and US dollar. This created a powerful incentive to borrow in dollars to invest in baht for a profit guaranteed by the Thai government.

Just as the Thai technocrats intended, foreign money poured in. The country's foreign debt escalated from $21 billion in 1988 to $89 billion in 1997—$66.2 billion of it private. Most of the money found its way into the purchase of real estate, existing stock shares in Thai companies, and increased consumer spending on imported goods. As the economy boomed and real estate in share prices headed for the sky, fortunes were made and the money poured in even faster as US and other foreign banks eager to profit from the Thai money machine competed with one another to create new dollars by lending to anyone who wanted to borrow dollars to convert to baht. The Thai government even invited the foreign banks to open branches in Bangkok to speed the process.

The agricultural and industrial sectors, Thailand's real productive sectors, couldn't compete for funds against the quick and easy high returns being generated by investments in stocks and real estate. Instead of upgrading their production facilities to maintain their international competitive position, industrialists diverted the cash flows from the industrial plants to more lucrative real estate or portfolio investments. This resulted in the seeming paradox that the faster foreign money flowed into Thailand, the faster money flowed out of the productive sector and into speculation. The country's actual productive base began to decline, and exports, which previously had grown vigorously, began to level off—undermining the country's ability to repay its rapidly growing foreign debt.

In the early stages, payments due to foreign loans had been easily covered by new inflows. In its 1996 World Development Report, the World Bank cited Thailand as "an excellent example of the dividends to be obtained through outward orientation, receptivity to foreign investment, and a market-friendly philosophy backed up by conservative macroeconomic management and cautious external borrowing policies."

The financial pyramid began to crumble at the beginning of 1997, when the consequences of the real estate overbuilding and a glut of unoccupied buildings and uncollectible loans forced two of Thailand's premier financial companies to default on interest payments to foreign lenders. The more astute portfolio investors started pulling out. Concern turned to panic and stock prices plummeted. The Bank of Thailand stepped in to cover the demand to convert baht to dollars with $9 billion of the country's foreign reserves. Currency speculators stepped in to profit from the inevitable devaluation. The government announced that as many as a million Thais would lose their jobs in three months' time, negotiated a $17.2 billion emergency loan from the IMF, and announced that the IMF fund would be used to guarantee the foreign debt of the Thai finance companies, local banks, and enterprises that were in default, thus providing a public bailout of the speculators, both foreign and domestic, at the expense of the Thai public.

Based on Walden Bellow, "The Rise and Fall of Southeast Asia's Economy," The Ecologist 28, no. 1, January/February 1990, 9-17; and Walden Bellow, "The End of the Asian Miracle," The Nation, January 12-19, 1998, 16-21.

In translation, the author is telling governments that they should no longer concern themselves with increasing the national output of goods and services that have real utility. Instead, they should favor policies that provide incentives for: (1) owners of productive assets to convert their ownership rights into freely tradable securities; (2) managers to give exclusive attention to short-term shareholder interests; and (3) investors to bid up share prices. Note that none of these actions makes any net addition to the output of any product or service, nor does it result in the investment of a single penny in the creation or enhancement of a productive asset.

The sole objective is to increase the total market value of traded securities, which serves only to create a temporary financial bubble that increases the claims of those who hold these securities against the society's real wealth. Forget production and the interests of working people, communities, and nature. Such is the flawed logic of finance capitalism that now drives policy making in the global economy and is bringing financial collapse to country after country.

As the logic serves their interests brilliantly, it is not surprising that the money world's insiders find it difficult to see its flaw. In 1997, the year of the Asia's financial crash, securities brokerages in the United States—firms that specialize in the trading of financial securities—yielded their investors a total investment return for the year of 83.6 percent—the highest of any industry category. Also in 1997, the senior partners of the Wall Street investment houses received annual bonuses of $5 to $7 million each. Even junior partners garnered on the order of $4 million for their year's labors. For the three years 1995 through 1997, US diversified financial services corporations produced an average return of 51 percent a year. The large money center banks averaged 47.1 percent a year. There can be no mistaking the fact that under finance capitalism the rewards go to those who make the money, not the wage laborers who actually make the things the money-makers hope to buy.

In a market economy, investment is about creating and renewing productive capacity to meet future needs. In the contemporary capitalist economy investment is about making money through financial manipulation. Whether productive capacity is created or destroyed in the process is purely incidental. Falsely equating the making of money with the creation of wealth, and oblivious to the consequences of what they doing to the rest of society, capitalists have proclaimed a new era of finance capitalism and congratulated themselves for having found the secret of creating wealth without the inconvenience of participating in any intervening productive activity. Far removed from the living world, the world of money has become their sole reality.

Underlying all the smoke and mirrors is the carefully cultivated cultural illusion that money is wealth and that making money creates wealth. In reality, most of the money currently in circulation is nothing but an accounting entry and most of the profits of Wall Street capitalists represent nothing more than the ill-gotten gains of deceptive accounting practices.

From Self-Organization to Central Planning

We have long been told of the self-organizing market's superiority to the stultifying central planning of socialism. It seems to follow therefore that to reap the full benefit of the market's invisible hand we must eliminate the barriers of regulation and economic borders to allow the market's free function. Only then, or so we are assured, can the market work its magic, allowing consumers to express their preferences and rewarding those producers who are most responsive to them.

Indeed, the last twenty to thirty years have seen major movement in the direction of deregulation and the opening of economic borders. We are coming to see that the result bears little resemblance, however, to Adam Smith's ideal of a socially efficient self-organizing market. What we have instead is a global economy centrally planned by corporations larger than most states, marching to the tune of financial speculators. It is yet another mark of capitalism's triumph over the market.

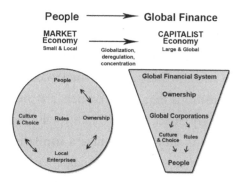

Figure 1: POWER SHIFT: The processes of economic globalization, market deregulation, and corporate concentration combine to transform the market economy into a capitalist economy. In so doing, they shift power from people to global finance.

Figure 1 sketches what happens as capitalism consolidates its hold over a market economy—shifting power and the lines of accountability away from people to the impersonal and detached institutions of global finance. In a functioning market economy comprised of small and medium scale locally owned enterprises, power is broadly distributed among local people who engage in reproducing the cultural values that shape their community, making purchasing decisions, setting the rules of local commerce through their democratically elected governments, and participating in the ownership of local enterprises. It is a dynamic and interactive system in which people participate in many roles and bring their human sensibilities to bear on every aspect of economic life.

In fact, what deregulation and economic globalization free is not the market, but rather the institutions of global capitalism. Freed from the constraints of regulation and national borders, financial markets become merged into a single electronic trading system and global corporations consolidate and concentrate their power through mergers, acquisitions, and strategic alliances beyond the reach of any state. Savings are aggregated into professionally managed retirement, trust, and mutual funds with a fiduciary responsibility to maximize financial returns commensurate with risk.

   The result is a capitalist economy in which the power to exercise owner-ship rights passes to the impersonal institutions of global finance. Money's power becomes delinked from human sensibility and people become captives of a system with no allegiance to their needs.

   The financial institutions that act as owners are themselves blind to all but the financial consequences of their actions. Expecting those respon-sible for the corporations they own to take a similarly narrow view, they send a powerful message to corporate management. A solid profit is not enough. Annual profits must be constantly *increased* at a rate sufficient to produce the 20 to 40 percent annual increase in share price the markets have come to expect. The CEO who fails to produce such increases risks losing credibility with the financial community and may invite a take-over bid or ejection by large shareholders. How it's done isn't the market's concern. Just do it. The global corporation responds by using its great power to reshape cultures, limit consumer choices, pass costs onto the public, and press governments to provide subsidies and rewrite the rules of commerce in their favor.

   Perhaps the most ironic twist is that the economy internal to a corpora-tion has far more in common with a centrally planned economy than with a self-organizing market economy. In the US system of corporate and financial libertarianism, which is rapidly infecting Europe, Japan, and the rest of the world, no matter what authority a CEO may delegate, he has the legal right to withdraw it at any time. He, or in the rare instance, she, can virtually hire and fire any worker, open and close any plant, change transfer prices, create and drop product lines almost at will—with no meaningful recourse by the persons or communities affected. Such centralized power and control would surely have been the envy of any central planner in the Soviet Union.

The scale of central planning under capitalism is also impressive. For example, if we take the gross sales of a corporation to be roughly the equiva-lent of the GDP of a country, we find that of the world's 100 largest econo-mies, 51 are economies internal to corporations. In addition, the largest corporations are actively engaged in planning relations among themselves through industrial associations, strategic alliances, and cartels; influencing economic policies through aggressive lobbying; and reshaping the rules of the global economy through their participation with their governments in the negotiation of trade and investment agreements. Step-by-step, through institutions such as the World Trade Organization and the International Monetary Fund, corporations have forged the instruments of a wholly undemocratic central economic planning process on a global scale.

In one critical respect, however, capitalism's central planners are quite unlike the Soviet planners who, at least in theory, sought to plan for the interests of all their country's citizens. The corporate central planners are legally obligated to devote their attention solely to maximizing the returns to their shareholders. Of course, they may reassure themselves and the public that the market's invisible hand will translate this self-seeking into a public good, but unfortunately they are operating not a market economy, but rather in a capitalist economy whose hand is neither hidden nor benevolent.

Of course we are also reassured that so many people now hold shares in pension and mutual funds that virtually everyone benefits directly from the increase in shareholder value that is capitalism's proud accomplishment. Again myth triumphs over reality. Of all the world's countries, the United States probably has the broadest participation in stock ownership. Even so, five percent of US households own 77 percent of US shareholder wealth. Seventy-one percent of households own less than $2,000 in stocks—including ownership through mutual funds and defined contribution retirement funds in which the employee benefits from stock appreciation. Globally the world's population that has a consequential participation in corporate ownership is most certainly far less than 1 percent.

This leads to a rather shocking conclusion. The triumph of global capitalism means that more than half of the world's 100 largest economies are centrally planned for the primary benefit of the wealthiest one percent of the world's people! It is a triumph of privatized central planning over markets and democracy. Even more it is the triumph of the extremely wealthy over the remainder of humanity.

Markets are remarkable human institutions for aggregating the choices of many individuals to achieve an efficient and equitable allocation of productive resources to meet human needs. Their function, however, depends on the presence of a number of critical conditions. Recognizing the power of the market ideal, capitalism cloaks itself in market rhetoric. Intent only on its own growth, its institutions set about systematically to destroy the market's healthy function. They eliminate regulations that protect the human and environmental interest, remove economic borders to place themselves beyond the reach of the state, deny consumers access to essential information, seek to monopolize beneficial technologies, and use mergers, acquisitions, strategic alliances, and other anti-competitive practices to undermine the market's ability to self-organize.

Step-by-step the institutional agents of the money world erode the conditions of healthy market function, using their control of the money creation process to concentrate the powers of the ownership of productive assets in their own hands. They in turn use their growing power to reshape cultures, rewrite the rules of commerce, and limit consumer choice. The purposes and the lines of accountability of a healthy market economy are thus turned upside down—leaving money as the master and demanding that its own reproduction be the defining purpose of economic life. People, who created economic life and institutions to serve their needs, are reduced to serving the needs of capitalism and the institutions of money for cheap labor and compliant consumers.

The end result and a chilling outcome of capitalism's triumph is the creation of a powerful and unfeeling global economic machine dedicated to the conversion of the real wealth of human, social, natural, and intellectual capital into phantom wealth financial capital. Capitalism is thus impoverishing us all even as it claims to be enriching us. Capitalism is neither inevitable nor our only alternative to socialism. There is a real wealth alternative based on valid market principles.

The Banker's Depression of the 1930s

In 1930 America did not lack industrial capacity, fertile farmland, skilled and willing workers or industrious farm families. It had an extensive and highly efficient transportation system in railroads, road networks, and inland and ocean waterways. Communications between regions and localities were the best in the world, utilizing telephone, teletype, radio, and a well-operated government mail system. No war had ravaged the cities or the countryside, no pestilence weakened the population, nor had famine stalked the land. The United States of America in 1930 lacked only one thing: an adequate supply of money to carry on trade and commerce.

In the early 1930's, Bankers, the only source of new money and credit, deliberately refused loans to industries, stores and farms. Payments on existing loans were required however, and money rapidly disappeared from circulation. Goods were available to be purchased, jobs waiting to be done, but the lack of money brought the nation to a standstill. By this simple ploy America was put in a "depression" and the greedy Bankers took possession of hundreds of thousands of farms, homes, and business properties. The people were told, "times are hard," and "money is short." Not understanding the system, they were cruelly robbed of their earnings, their savings, and their property.

Sheldon Emry

Good Witch/Bad Witch Scenarios

The Wicked Witch of the West rules over a dark fiefdom with a single private bank owned by the Witch. The bank issues and lends all the money in the realm, charging an interest rate of 10 percent. The Witch prints 100 witch-dollars, lends them to her constituents, and demands 110 back. The people don't have the extra 10, so the Witch creates 10 more on her books and lends them as well. The money supply must continually increase to cover the interest, which winds up in the Witch's private coffers. She gets progressively richer, as the people slip further into debt. She uses her accumulated profits to buy things she wants. She is particularly fond of little thatched houses and shops, of which she has an increasingly large collection. To fund the operations of her fiefdom, she taxes the people heavily, adding to their financial burdens.

Glinda the Good Witch of the South runs her realm in a more people-friendly way. All of the money in the land is issued and lent by a "people's bank" operated for their benefit. She begins by creating 110 people's-dollars. She lends 100 of these dollars at 10 percent interest and spends the extra 10 dollars into the community on programs designed to improve the general welfare—things such as pensions for retirees, social services, infrastructure, education, research and development. The $110 circulates in the community and comes back to the people's bank as principal and interest on its loans. Glinda again lends $100 of this money into the community and spends the other $10 on public programs, supplying the interest for the next round of loans while providing the people with jobs and benefits.

For many years, she just recycles the same $110, without creating new money. Then one year, a cyclone comes up that destroys many of the charming little thatched houses. The people asked for extra money to rebuild. No problem, says Glinda; she will just print more people's-dollars and use them to pay for the necessary labor and materials. Inflation is avoided, because supply increases along with demand. Best of all, *taxes are unknown in the realm.*

Ellen Hodgson Brown, *The Web of Debt*

3

HOW WE THE PEOPLE LOST THE MONEY POWER AND HOW WE CAN GET IT BACK

Ellen Hodgson Brown, JD
www.webofdebt.com

Although we have so foolishly allowed the field of circulating medium to be filched from us by private individuals, I think we may recover it.... The states should be asked to transfer the right of issuing paper money to Congress, in perpetuity.

Thomas Jefferson, Letter to John Eppes, 1813

Thomas Jefferson saw the problem in 1813—the power to create the national money supply had been usurped from the new country's leaders by a private banking cartel. The American colonists won the war but lost the financial freedom for which they fought. Jefferson also saw the solution—return the power to issue money to Congress and the people it represents. He spoke of "paper money," but today that power would have to include checkbook money, electronic money, and all those other forms of the national medium of exchange in popular use.

Jefferson saw the problem, but too late. The die had been cast, and his vision faded into history. The people struggled along, hampered by a scarcity of money. Yet few ever realized that what determined the abundance or scarcity of money was not some immutable law called *the business cycle* but was a simple political lever, and that the lever was and is in the exclusive control of private banks. That remains true in most of the world today. The banks use their Money Power to make loans and collect interest on them, siphoning profit from virtually every monetary transaction on the globe.

As a result, nations and individuals around the world now find themselves facing such crushing debts that they need new bank loans just to make good on old interest payments. The debt trap that has captured underdeveloped countries in sub-Saharan Africa, South-east Asia, and Latin America has now spread to European countries, including Latvia, Iceland and Greece. The United States may be the next domino to fall.

The US is now facing debt of catastrophic proportions. As of January 2014, the Treasury department put the national debt at around $17.3 trillion—nearly the country's entire annual gross domestic product. In fiscal year 2009, the Treasury spent $383 billion of taxpayer money on *interest payments alone*. By comparison, in 2009 the US government spent just $60 billion on education. All of this debt is combining with other economic clouds on the horizon to shape into a perfect storm that could blow the US economy into a long-term recession, despite the rosy predictions of mainstream market analysts.

Misguided Plans for "Recovery"

Since World War II, the US dollar has been the de facto global currency, and the US has been the investment center for much of the world's savings. But that status could soon change. Since 2005, the two largest foreign holders of US debt, China and Japan, have been cutting back on their purchases of US Treasury securities. In 2009, according to the United

Nations, foreign businesses slashed US investments by 57%, far above the average global downturn in foreign investment of 39%. In 2006, the Euro became the most important currency for the international bond and note trade. Observing these trends, countries worldwide met in 2009 to design new ways of shifting their businesses out of dollars.

In June 2009, officials from countries including Russia, China, Mongolia, Iran, India, Pakistan, Kazakhstan, Tajikistan, Kyrgyzstan, Uzbekistan, and Brazil met in Yakaterinburg, Russia, to discuss the creation of regional currencies to replace the dollar. With the express purpose of scaling down the dollar, nine leftist Latin American countries agreed in October 2009 to create a regional currency called the Sucre. Aims to launch a regional currency have been expressed by Saudi Arabia, Abu Dhabi, Kuwait and Qatar. Oil-producing countries are looking to create new currencies for the trade of oil, which was once exclusively traded in dollars. The move would remove a major incentive for foreign central banks to hold US government bonds. Arab nations have suggested that oil trade in a basket of currencies including the Euro, Yen, Yuan, and gold. The idea has received support from China and Russia and attracted the interest of Brazil, India, and Venezuela. Iran began accepting Euros for its oil back in mid-2003, even setting up its own stock market Oil Exchange in mid-2006 to trade oil exclusively in Euros.

These moves to seek dollar alternatives reveal an international scramble to secure investments and markets that will be unperturbed by a US economic decline, but they do not address the underlying causes of the economic crisis, and neither do the massive bank bailout schemes of the US Administration, Treasury and Federal Reserve. The mainstream policy options leave in place or even enhance the institutions that brought the system down in the first place. The 2008 US economic crash was the result of a swollen housing bubble that burst, along with the fallout from Wall Street's massive derivatives gambles.

Rather than fixing the problem, the government's solution has been to bail out the gamblers. Neil Barofsky, inspector general for the government's Troubled Asset Relief Program (TARP), said in July 2009 that government spending to bolster the economy and save financial companies could total $23.7 trillion. The inevitable result will be to plunge the US government much deeper into debt, while consolidating Wall Street's power and leaving Main Street high and dry.

Solutions being pursued at the international level are even less likely to achieve economic recovery for anyone except the financial sector. Poor countries have been struggling for decades to break the chains of debt owed to international lenders including the International Monetary Fund and the World Bank. The recent crisis is serving instead to strengthen those chains. At the April 2009 meeting of the G-20 nations, the IMF's funding was quadrupled, to $1 trillion. Much of this money is being used to provide emergency loans to nations ailing from the global recession, loans made contingent on conditions such as mandatory wage cuts and the downsizing of public services, including education and health care. The loans are designed not to rebuild these care-worn countries but to wring them of even more money to pay what economist Michael Hudson calls the "world's most predatory creditors." He writes:

> This G-20 agreement means that the world's leading governments are responding to today's financial crisis with "planned shrinkage" for debtors—a 10 per cent cut in wage payments in hapless Latvia, Hungary put on rations, and permanent debt peonage for Iceland.

Addressing the Real Problem

Current solutions are missing the mark because the problem itself is not understood by the politicians in charge of rectifying it. What Jefferson realized late in life even experts today generally miss, because it has been obscured by a financier-controlled media and educational system. Most people blame our economic ills on the government, which they think is printing money with reckless abandon, hyper-inflating the money supply and diluting the value of the dollar. In fact, the government could solve many of its problems if it *were* to simply print the money needed by the government and the economy; but that is not how the system works.

Except for coins, which compose only about one ten-thousandth of the total US money supply, *all* of our money is now created by *banks*. The government has to borrow this money like everyone else, and that is why it is sinking further and further into debt. Again, this holds true in most of the world. The Federal Reserve (the US central bank) is not actually federal; and today it keeps nothing in "reserve" except government bonds or I.O.U.s The Federal Reserve is a private banking corporation authorized to print and sell its own Federal Reserve Notes to the government in return for government bonds, putting the taxpayers in perpetual debt for money created privately with accounting entries. Moreover, Federal Reserve Notes and coins together compose less than 3 percent of the money supply. The other 97 percent is created by commercial banks as loans.

The dire result was underscored by Robert H. Hemphill, Credit Manager of the Federal Reserve Bank of Atlanta during the Great Depression, who wrote in 1934:

> We are completely dependent on the commercial Banks. Someone has to borrow every dollar we have in circulation, cash or credit. If the Banks create ample synthetic money we are prosperous; if not, we starve. We are absolutely without a permanent money system. When one gets a complete grasp of the picture, the tragic absurdity of our hopeless position is almost incredible, but there it is. It is the most important subject intelligent persons can investigate and reflect upon.

The archetype for the Federal Reserve was the Bank of England, which established the private central banking model in the late seventeenth century. That model involves credit issued by private bankers, backed by *reserves* that at one time consisted of gold but today are merely government securities (promises to pay). In the nineteenth century, the US government was constrained from issuing unbacked paper *fiat* money on the ground that it would produce dangerous inflation. The bankers insisted that paper money had to be backed by gold. What they failed to disclose was that there was not nearly enough gold in their own vaults to back the privately-issued paper notes laying claim to it. The bankers themselves were dangerously inflating the money supply based on a fictitious *gold standard* that allowed them to lend the same gold reserves many times over, collecting interest each time.

Economist John Kenneth Galbraith famously said, "The process by which banks create money is so simple that the mind is repelled." It is created by sleight of hand, by the shell game called *fractional reserve* lending. Banks are permitted to lend money equal to a multiple of their *reserves*. The website of the Federal Reserve Bank of Dallas explains:

> Banks actually create money when they lend it. Here's how it works: Most of a bank's loans are made to its own customers and are deposited in their checking accounts. Because the loan becomes a new deposit, just like a paycheck does, the bank…holds a small percentage of that new amount in reserve and again lends the remainder to someone else, repeating the money-creation process many times.

The fractional reserve ratio is determined by the Federal Reserve and has typically been set at 10%. At a 10% reserve requirement, banks collectively can turn $1 million in reserves into $10 million in loans. At 5% interest, with $1 million in reserves the banking system as a whole could create new loans of $9 million and collect $450,000 in interest, a 45% profit margin.

When banknotes were backed by gold, banks were subject to *bank panics* whenever their customers periodically figured out that there was not enough gold to go around and all came for theirs at once. The initial function of the Federal Reserve (or Fed) was to bail out banks that got caught in this fractional-reserve shell game, using money the Fed created in *open market* operations. When the Fed failed in that backup function, the Federal Deposit Insurance Corporation (FDIC) and then the International Monetary Fund were instituted, ensuring that mega-banks considered "too big to fail" would get bailed out no matter what unwarranted risks they took.

The United States went off the gold standard in the 1930s but the *fractional reserve* system continued, backed by *reserves* of government bonds. The federal debt these securities represent is never paid off but is continually rolled over, forming the basis of the national money supply. What *is* paid is just the interest; and to insure that those payments are made to the lenders, the federal income tax was instituted. Considered unconstitutional for over a century, it was legalized by the Sixteenth Amendment to the Constitution in 1913, the same year the Federal Reserve Act was passed.

If banks can simply create credit on their books, why are we suffering from a *credit crunch*? The answer is that the crisis is one not of *liquidity* but of *solvency*. It has been caused, not by the banks' inability to get credit (something they can create with accounting entries), but by their inability to meet the capital requirement imposed by the Bank for International Settlements, the private foreign head of the international banking system in Switzerland. That inability, in turn, has been caused by the derivatives virus, a subject that is too complicated to go into here; but suffice it to say that only a few big banks are seriously infected with it. By bailing out these big banks, the government is actually spreading the virus by furnishing the funds for them to take over smaller regional banks.

We the people and our representatives in Congress have allowed Wall Street to call the shots because we think we are dependent on their credit system, but we aren't. There are other ways to generate money and credit— ways that are fair, efficient, transparent, and don't encourage greed. A more effective solution to the credit crisis than trying to patch up the hopelessly imperiled derivatives positions of a few Wall Street mega-banks would be to simply create another credit system with a pristine set of books. We don't need to fix the Wall Street disease; we can bypass the whole problem and create a new, healthy, parallel system. A network of *publicly-owned* banks (federal and state) could create *credit* just as private banks do now. This credit could be extended at low interest rates to consumers and at very low interest to local governments, drastically reducing the cost of public projects by reducing the cost of funding them. And federal governments wouldn't need to borrow at all. They could create the money they needed directly, exercising the sovereign right of governments to create the national money supply.

Building on a Successful Tradition

Some of the best examples of the effective use of government-created money lie in our own suppressed US history. According to Benjamin Franklin, it was the colonists' homegrown paper *scrip* that was responsible for the remarkable abundance in the American colonies at a time when England was already beginning to suffer from the ravages of the Industrial Revolution. But this prosperity posed a threat to the control of the British Crown and the emerging network of private British banks, prompting the King to ban the colonists' paper money and require the payment of taxes in gold. Several historians of the period said it was these onerous demands by the Crown, and the corresponding collapse of the colonists' paper money supply, that actually sparked the Revolutionary War.

The colonists won the war, but they ultimately lost the Money Power to a private banking faction issuing another form of paper money called *banknotes*. The colonists' ingenious public money system was revived, however, by Abraham Lincoln, who devised the most far-reaching *economic stimulus plan* ever implemented by a US President.

In 1861, Lincoln stepped into the presidency of a country suddenly in a civil war. The bankers had his government over a barrel, just as Wall

Street has Congress in its vice-like grip today. The North needed money to fund the war, and the bankers were willing to lend it only under circumstances that amounted to extortion, involving staggering interest rates of 24 to 36 percent. Lincoln saw that this would bankrupt the North and chose instead to fund the war by printing paper notes called US Notes or Greenbacks backed by the credit of the government; these legal-tender notes were essentially receipts for labor and goods delivered to the government. They were paid to soldiers and suppliers and were tradable for goods and services of a value equivalent to their service to the community.

The greenbacks aided the Union not only in winning the war but in funding a period of unprecedented economic expansion. Lincoln's government created the greatest industrial giant the world had yet seen. The steel industry was launched, a continental railroad system was created, a new era of farm machinery and cheap tools was promoted, free higher education was established, government support was provided to all branches of science, the Bureau of Mines was organized, and labor productivity was increased by 50 to 75 percent. The greenback was not the only currency used to fund these achievements; but they could not have been accomplished without it, and they could not have been accomplished on money borrowed at the usurious rates the bankers were attempting to extort from the North.

Lincoln succeeded in restoring the government's power to issue the national currency, but his revolutionary monetary policy was opposed by powerful forces. In 1865, he was assassinated. According to historian W. Cleon Skousen:

> Right after the Civil War there was considerable talk about reviving Lincoln's brief experiment with the Constitutional monetary system. Had not the European money-trust intervened, it would have no doubt become an established institution.

The institution established instead was the Federal Reserve, a privately-owned central bank given the power to permanently indebt the government by printing its own Federal Reserve Notes and lending them to the government. The result was a federal debt that has grown exponentially ever since, to a staggering $17.3 trillion as this book goes to press.

Besides our own home-grown models, there are a number of examples in other countries of the successful funding of economic development simply with government-issued credit. In Australia and New Zealand in the 1930s, the Depression conditions suffered elsewhere were avoided by drawing on a national credit card issued by publicly-owned central banks. The governments of the island states of Guernsey and Jersey created thriving economies that carried no federal debt, just by issuing their own debt-free public currencies. China has also funded impressive internal development through a system of state-owned banks.

Here in the United States, the state of North Dakota has a wholly state-owned bank that creates credit on its books just as private banks do. This credit is used to serve the needs of the community, and the interest on loans is returned to the government. The state-owned Bank of North Dakota has been a credit engine for the state ever since 1919. In 2009, North Dakota had a $1.3 billion budget surplus at a time when 48 of 50 states were technically insolvent, an impressive achievement for a state of isolated farmers battling challenging weather. As of this writing (December 2013), twenty states have brought bills of one kind another for the creation of state-owned banks. The objection invariably raised to government-issued currency or credit is that it would create dangerous hyperinflation, but in none of the foregoing examples has that proven to be true. Price inflation results either when the supply of money goes up but the supply of goods doesn't, or when speculators devalue currencies by massive short selling, as in those cases of Latin American hyperinflation when printing-press money was used to pay off foreign debt. When new money is used to produce new goods and services, price inflation does not result because supply and demand rise together. Prices did increase during the American Civil War, but this was attributed to the scarcity of goods common in wartime rather than to the greenback itself. War produces weapons rather than consumer goods.

The struggle to generate humane and sustainable societies is thoroughly tangled up in the issue of money. When plentiful, money facilitates innovation, exchange, and employment. When scarce, it incites conflict, cultivates selfishness, and ensures deprivation. The credit crunch could be avoided and the dynamic potential of money could be released by returning to publicly-owned national and local systems of banking, money and credit; and this could be done not just in the United States but around the world. Countries that have been seduced or coerced into funneling their productive assets into serving foreign markets and foreign investors could become self-sustaining, using their own credit and their own resources to feed and serve their own people.

On the Federal Reserve

The basic plan for the Federal Reserve System was drafted at a secret meeting held in November 1910 at the private resort of J.P. Morgan on Jekyll Island off the coast of Georgia. Those who attended represented the great financial institutions of Wall Street and, indirectly, Europe as well. The reason for secrecy was simple. Had it been known that rival factions of the banking community had joined together, the public would have been alerted to the possibility that the bankers were plotting an agreement in restraint of trade—which, of course, is exactly what they were doing. What emerged was a cartel agreement with five objectives: stop the growing competition from the nation's newer banks; obtain a franchise to create money out of nothing for the purpose of lending; get control of the reserves of all banks so that the more reckless ones would not be exposed to currency drains and bank runs; get the taxpayer to pick up the cartel's inevitable losses; and convince Congress that the purpose was to protect the public. It was realized that the bankers would have to become partners with the politicians and that the structure of the cartel would have to be a central bank. The record shows that the Fed has failed to achieve its stated objectives. That is because those were never its true goals. As a banking cartel, and in terms of the five objectives stated above, it has been an unqualified success.

G. Edward Griffin, *The Creature from Jekyll Island*

Oh! what a tangled web we weave
When first we practice to deceive!

Sir Walter Scott

This act establishes the most gigantic trust on earth. When the president signs this bill, the 'invisible government' by monetary power will be legalized. The people may not know it yet, but the day of reckoning is only a few years removed…. The worst legislative crime of the ages is perpetrated by this banking bill.

Rep. Charles Lindbergh Sr.

Some people think the Federal Reserve Banks are US government institutions. They are not… they are private credit monopolies which prey upon the people of the US for the benefit of themselves and their foreign and domestic swindlers, and rich and predatory money lenders. The sack of the United States by the Fed is the greatest crime in history. Every effort has been made by the Fed to conceal its powers, but the truth is the Fed has usurped the government. It controls everything here and it controls all our foreign relations. It makes and breaks governments at will.

Congressman Louis T. McFadden, Chairman, House Banking and Currency Committee, 1932

The creation of money is a total mystery to probably 99 percent of the US population, and that most definitely includes the Congress and the Senate. The takeover of US money creation by the Fed is one of the most mysterious and ominous acts in US history…. The legality of the Federal Reserve has never been "tried" before the US Supreme Court.

Richard Russell

We have, in this country, one of the most corrupt institutions the world has ever known. I refer to the Federal Reserve Board. This evil institution has impoverished the people of the United States and has practically bankrupted our government. It has done this through the corrupt practices of the moneyed vultures who control it.

Congressman Louis T. McFadden, 1932

What is needed here is a return to the Constitution of the United States. We need to have a complete divorce of Bank and State. The old struggle that was fought out here in Jackson's day must be fought over again…. The Federal Reserve Act should be repealed and the Federal Reserve Banks, having violated their charters, should be liquidated immediately…. Unless this is done by us, I predict that the American people, outraged, robbed, pillaged, insulted, and betrayed as they are in their own land, will rise in their wrath and send a President here who will sweep the money changers out of the temple.

Congressman Louis T. McFadden

In the US today, we have in effect two governments. We have the duly constituted government, then we have an independent, uncontrolled and uncoordinated government of the Federal Reserve, operating the money powers which are reserved to the Congress by the Constitution.

Wright Patman, Chairman of the House Banking and Currency Committee, Speech on the House Floor, 1967

[The Federal Reserve Board] can cause the pendulum of a rising and falling market to swing gently back and forth by slight changes in the discount rate, or cause violent fluctuations by greater rate variation, and in either case it will possess inside information as to financial conditions and advance knowledge of the coming change, either up or down. This is the strangest, most dangerous advantage ever placed in the hands of a special privilege class by any Government that ever existed…. The financial system has been turned over to…a purely profiteering group. The system is private, conducted for the sole purpose of obtaining the greatest possible profits from the use of other people's money.

Representative Charles Lindbergh, Sr.

The Federal Reserve System is not Federal; it has no reserves; and it is not a system at all, but rather, a criminal syndicate.

Eustace Mullins, author of *Secrets of the Federal Reserve*, 1991

[The Great Depression] was no accident. It was a carefully contrived occurrence…. The international bankers sought to bring about a condition of despair here so that they might emerge as rulers of us all.

Congressman Louis T. McFadden

Most Americans have no real understanding of the operation of the international money lenders. The accounts of the Federal Reserve System have never been audited. It operates outside the control of Congress and manipulates the credit of the United States.

Senator Barry Goldwater

4

EUROPE'S TRANSITION FROM SOCIAL DEMOCRACY TO OLIGARCHY

First published in German in *Frankfurter Allgemeine Zeitung*

Michael Hudson, PhD

The easiest way to understand Europe's financial crisis is to look at the solutions being proposed to resolve it. They are a banker's dream, a grab bag of giveaways that few voters would be likely to approve in a democratic referendum. Bank strategists learned not to risk submitting their plans to democratic vote after Icelanders twice refused in 2010-11 to approve their government's capitulation to pay Britain and the Netherlands for losses run up by badly regulated Icelandic banks operating abroad. Lacking such a referendum, mass demonstrations were the only way for Greek voters to register their opposition to the €50 billion in privatization sell-offs demanded by the European Central Bank (ECB) in autumn 2011.

The problem is that Greece lacks the ready money to redeem its debts and pay the interest charges. The ECB is demanding that it sell off public assets—land, water and sewer systems, ports and other assets in the public domain, and also cut back pensions and other payments to its population. The *bottom 99%* understandably are angry to be informed that the wealthiest layer of the population is largely responsible for the budget shortfall by stashing away a reported €45 billion in Swiss banks alone. The idea of normal wage-earners being obliged to forfeit their pensions to pay for tax evaders—and for the general un-taxing of wealth since the regime of the colonels—makes most people understandably angry. For the ECB, EU and IMF *troika* to say that whatever the wealthy take, steal or evade paying must be made up by the population at large is not a politically neutral position. It comes down hard on the side of wealth that has been unfairly taken.

A democratic tax policy would reinstate progressive taxation on income and property and would enforce its collection—with penalties for evasion. Ever since the 19th century, democratic reformers have sought to free economies from waste, corruption and *unearned income*. But the ECB *troika* is imposing a regressive tax—one that can be imposed only by turning government policy-making over to a set of unelected technocrats.

To call the administrators of so anti-democratic a policy *technocrats* seems to be a cynical scientific-sounding euphemism for financial lobbyists or bureaucrats deemed suitably tunnel-visioned to act as useful idiots on behalf of their sponsors. Their ideology is the same austerity philosophy that the IMF imposed on Third World debtors from the 1960s through the 1980s. Claiming to stabilize the balance of payments while introducing free markets, these officials sold off export sectors and basic infrastructure to creditor-nation buyers. The effect was to drive austerity-ridden economies even deeper into debt—to foreign bankers and their own domestic oligarchies.

This is the treadmill on which Eurozone social democracies are now being placed. Under the political umbrella of financial emergency, wages and living standards are to be scaled back and political power shifted from elected government to technocrats governing on behalf of large banks and financial institutions. Public sector labor is to be privatized and de-unionized, while Social Security, pension plans and health insurance are scaled back.

This is the basic playbook corporate raiders follow when they empty out corporate pension plans to pay their financial backers in leveraged buyouts. It also is how the former Soviet Union's economy was privatized after 1991, transferring public assets into the hands of kleptocrats who worked with Western investment bankers to make the Russian and other stock exchanges the darlings of the global financial markets. Property taxes were scaled back while flat taxes were imposed on wages (a cumulative 59% in Latvia). Industry was dismantled as land and mineral rights were transferred to foreigners, economies driven into debt and skilled and unskilled labor alike was obliged to emigrate to find work.

Pretending to be committed to price stability and free markets, bankers inflated a real estate bubble on credit. Rental income was capitalized into bank loans and paid out as interest. This was enormously profitable for bankers, but it left the Baltics and much of Central Europe debt strapped and in negative equity by 2008. Neoliberals applaud their plunging wage levels and shrinking GDP as a success story, because these countries shifted the tax burden onto employment rather than property or finance. Governments bailed out banks at taxpayer expense.

It is axiomatic that the solution to any major social problem tends to create even larger problems—not always unintended! From the financial sector's vantage point, the *solution* to the Eurozone crisis is to reverse the aims of the Progressive Era a century ago—what John Maynard Keynes gently termed "euthanasia of the rentier" in 1936. The idea was to subordinate the banking system to serve the economy rather than the other way around. Instead, finance has become the new mode of warfare—less ostensibly bloody, but with the same objectives as the Viking invasions over a thousand years ago, and Europe's subsequent colonial conquests: appropriation of land and natural resources, infrastructure and whatever other assets can provide a revenue stream. It was to capitalize and estimate such values, for instance, that William the Conqueror compiled the

Doomsday Book after 1066, a model of ECB and IMF-style calculations today.

This appropriation of the economic surplus to pay bankers is turning the traditional values of most Europeans upside down. Imposition of economic austerity, dismantling social spending, sell-offs of public assets, de-unionization of labor, falling wage levels, scaled-back pension plans and health care in countries subject to democratic rules requires convincing voters that there is no alternative. It is claimed that without a profitable banking sector (no matter how predatory) the economy will break down as bank losses on bad loans and gambles pull down the payments system. No regulatory agencies can help, no better tax policy, nothing except to turn over control to lobbyists to save banks from losing the financial claims they have built up.

What banks want is for the economic surplus to be paid out as interest, not used for rising living standards, public social spending or even for new capital investment. Research and development takes too long. Finance lives in the short run. This short-termism is self-defeating, yet it is presented as science. The alternative, voters are told, is the road to serfdom: interfering with the *free market* by financial regulation and even progressive taxation.

There is an alternative, of course. It is what European civilization from the 13th-century Schoolmen through the Enlightenment and the flowering of classical political economy sought to create: an economy free of unearned income, free of vested interests using special privileges for *rent extraction*. At the hands of the neoliberals, by contrast, a free market is one free for a tax-favored rentier class to extract interest, economic rent and monopoly prices.

Rentier interests present their behavior as efficient *wealth creation*. Business schools teach privatizers how to arrange bank loans and bond financing by pledging whatever they can charge for the public infrastructure services being sold by governments. The idea is to pay this revenue to banks and bondholders as interest, and then make a capital gain by raising access fees for roads and ports, water and sewer usage and other basic services. Governments are told economies can be run more efficiently by dismantling public programs and selling off assets.

Never has the gap between pretended aim and actual effect been more hypocritical. Making interest payments (and even capital gains) tax-exempt deprives governments of revenue from the user fees they are relinquishing, increasing their budget deficits. And instead of promoting price stability (the ECB's ostensible priority), privatization increases prices for infrastructure, housing and other costs of living and doing business by building in interest charges and other financial overhead—and much higher salaries for management. So it is merely a knee-jerk ideological claim that this policy is more efficient simply because privatizers do the borrowing rather than government.

There is no technological or economic need for Europe's financial managers to impose depression on much of its population. But there is a great opportunity to gain for the banks that have gained control of ECB economic policy. Since the 1960s, balance-of-payments crises have provided opportunities for bankers and liquid investors to seize control of fiscal policy—to shift the tax burden onto labor and dismantle social spending in favor of subsidizing foreign investors and the financial sector. They gain from austerity policies that lower living standards and scale back social spending. A debt crisis enables the domestic financial elite and foreign bankers to indebt the rest of society, using their privilege of credit (or savings built up as a result of less progressive tax policies) as a lever to grab assets and reduce populations to a state of debt dependency.

The kind of warfare now engulfing Europe is thus more than just economic in scope. It threatens to become a historic dividing line between the past half-century's epoch of hope and technological potential to a new era of polarization as a financial oligarchy replaces democratic governments and reduces populations to debt peonage.

For so bold an asset and power grab to succeed, it needs a crisis to suspend the normal political and democratic legislative processes that would oppose it. Political panic and anarchy create a vacuum into which grabbers can move quickly, using the rhetoric of financial deception and a junk economics to rationalize self-serving solutions by a false view of economic history—and in the case of today's ECB, German history in particular.

A Central Bank that is Blocked from Acting Like One

Governments do not need to borrow from commercial bankers or other lenders. Ever since the Bank of England was founded in 1694, central banks have printed money to finance public spending. Bankers also create credit freely—when they make a loan and credit the customer's account, in exchange for a promissory note bearing interest. Today, these banks can borrow reserves from the government central bank at a low annual interest rate (0.25% in the United States) and lend it out at a higher rate. So banks are glad to see the government's central bank create credit to lend to them. But when it comes to governments creating money to finance their budget deficits for spending in the rest of the economy, banks would prefer to have this market and its interest return for themselves.

European commercial banks are especially adamant that the European Central Bank should not finance government budget deficits. But private credit creation is not necessarily less inflationary than governments monetizing their deficits (simply by printing the money needed). Most commercial bank loans are made against real estate, stocks and bonds— providing credit that is used to bid up housing prices, and prices for financial securities (as in loans for leveraged buyouts).

It is mainly government that spends credit on the *real* economy, to the extent that public budget deficits employ labor or are spent on goods and services. Governments could avoid paying interest by having their central banks print money on their own computer keyboards rather than borrowing from banks that do the same thing on their keyboards. (Abraham Lincoln simply printed currency when he financed the US Civil War with his Greenbacks.)

Banks would like to use their credit-creating privilege to obtain interest for lending to governments to finance public budget deficits. So they have a self-interest in limiting the government's *public option* to monetize its budget deficits. To secure a monopoly on their credit-creating privilege, banks have mounted a vast character assassination on government spending, and indeed on government authority in general—which happens to be the only authority with sufficient power to control their power or provide an alternative public financial option, as Post Office savings banks do in Japan, Russia and other countries. This competition between banks and government explains the false accusations made that government credit creation is more inflationary than when commercial banks do it.

The reality is made clear by comparing the ways in which the United States, Britain and Europe handle their public financing. The US Treasury is by far the world's largest debtor, and its largest banks seem to be in negative equity, liable to their depositors and to other financial institutions for much larger sums that can be paid by their portfolio of loans, investments and assorted financial gambles. Yet as global financial turmoil escalates, institutional investors are putting their money into US Treasury bonds—so much that these bonds now yield less than 1%. By contrast, a quarter of US real estate is in negative equity, and American states and cities are facing insolvency and must scale back spending. Large companies are going bankrupt, pension plans are falling deeper into arrears, yet the US economy remains a magnet for global savings.

Britain's economy also is staggering, yet its government is paying just 2% interest. But European governments are now paying over 7%. The reason for this disparity is that they lack a *public option* in money creation. Having a Federal Reserve Bank or Bank of England that can print the money to pay interest or roll over existing debts is what makes the United States and Britain different from Europe. Nobody expects these two nations to be forced to sell off their public lands and other assets to raise money to pay off debt (although they may do this as a policy choice). Given that the US Treasury and Federal Reserve can create new money, it follows that as long as government debts are denominated in dollars, they can print enough IOUs on their computer keyboards so that the only risk that holders of Treasury bonds bear is the dollar's exchange rate vis-à-vis other currencies.

By contrast, the Eurozone has a central bank, but Article 123 of the Lisbon treaty forbids the ECB from doing what central banks were created to do: create the money to finance government budget deficits or roll over their debt falling due. Future historians will no doubt find it remarkable that there actually is a rationale behind this policy—or at least the pretense of a cover story. It is so flimsy that any student of history can see how distorted it is. The claim is that if a central bank creates credit, this threatens price stability. Only government spending is deemed to be inflationary, but not private credit!

The Clinton Administration balanced the US Government budget in the late 1990s, yet the Bubble Economy was exploding. On the other hand, the Federal Reserve and Treasury flooded the economy with $13 trillion in credit to the banking system after September 2008, $800 billion more in 2011 in the Federal Reserve's Quantitative Easing program (QE2), and an additional $40 billion in 2012 (QE3). Yet consumer and commodity prices are not rising. Not even real estate or stock market prices are being bid up. So the idea that more money will bid up prices (MV=PT) is not operating today.

Commercial banks create debt. That is their product. This debt leveraging was used for more than a decade to bid up prices—making housing and buying a retirement income more expensive for Americans—but today's economy is suffering from debt deflation as personal income, business and tax revenue is diverted to pay debt service rather than to spend on goods or invest or hire labor.

Much more striking is the travesty of German history that is being repeated again and again, as if repetition somehow will stop people from remembering what actually happened in the 20th century. To hear ECB officials tell the story, it would be reckless for a central bank to lend to government because of the danger of hyperinflation. Memories are conjured up of the Weimar inflation in Germany in the 1920s. But upon examination, this turns out to be what psychiatrists call an implanted memory—a condition in which a patient is convinced that they have suffered a trauma that seems real, but which did not exist in reality.

What happened back in 1921 was not a case of governments borrowing from central banks to finance domestic spending such as social programs, pensions or health care as today. Rather, Germany's obligation to pay reparations led the Reichsbank to flood the foreign exchange markets with deutsche marks to obtain the currency to buy pounds sterling, French francs and other currency to pay the Allies—which used the money to pay their Inter-Ally arms debts to the United States. The nation's hyperinflation stemmed from its obligation to pay reparations in foreign currency. No amount of domestic taxation could have raised the foreign exchange that was scheduled to be paid.

By the 1930s this was a well-understood phenomenon, explained by Keynes and others who analyzed the structural limits on the ability to pay foreign debt imposed without regard for the ability to pay out of current domestic-currency budgets. From Salomon Flink's *The Reichsbank and Economic Germany* (1931) to studies of the Chilean and other Third World hyperinflations, economists have found a common causality at work, based on the balance of payments. First comes a fall in the exchange rate. This raises the price of imports, and hence the domestic price level. More money is then needed to transact purchases at the higher price level. The statistical sequence and line of causation leads from balance-of-payments deficits to currency depreciation to raising import costs, and from these price increases to the money supply, not the other way around.

Today's *free marketers* writing in the Chicago monetarist tradition (basically that of David Ricardo) leaves the foreign and domestic debt dimensions out of account. It is as if *money* and *credit* are assets to be bartered against goods. But a bank account or other form of credit means debt on the opposite side of the balance sheet. One party's debt is another party's saving—and most savings today are lent out at interest, absorbing money from the non-financial sectors of the economy. The discussion is stripped down to a simplistic relationship between the money supply and price level—and indeed, only consumer prices, not asset prices. In their eagerness to oppose government spending—and indeed to dismantle government and replace it with financial planners—neoliberal monetarists neglect the debt burden being imposed today from Latvia and Iceland to Ireland and Greece, Italy, Spain and Portugal.

If the euro breaks up, it is because of the obligation of governments to pay bankers in money that must be borrowed rather than created through their own central bank. Unlike the United States and Britain which can create central bank credit on their own computer keyboards to keep their economy from shrinking or becoming insolvent, the German constitution and the Lisbon Treaty prevent the central bank from doing this.

The effect is to oblige governments to borrow from commercial banks at interest. This gives bankers the ability to create a crisis—threatening to drive economies out of the Eurozone if they do not submit to *conditionalities* being imposed in what quickly is becoming a new class war of finance against labor.

Disabling Europe's Central Bank to Deprive Governments of the Power to Create Money

One of the three defining characteristics of a nation-state is the power to create money. A second characteristic is the power to levy taxes. Both of these powers are being transferred out of the hands of democratically elected representatives to the financial sector as a result of tying the hands of government.

The third characteristic of a nation-state is the power to declare war. What is happening today is the equivalent of warfare—but against the power of government! It is above all a financial mode of warfare—and the aims of this financial appropriation are the same as those of military conquest: first, the land and subsoil riches on which to charge rents as tribute; second, public infrastructure to extract rent as access fees; and third, any other enterprises or assets in the public domain.

In this new financialized warfare, governments are being directed to act as enforcement agents on behalf of the financial conquerors against their own domestic populations. This is not new, to be sure. We have seen the IMF and World Bank impose austerity on Latin American dictatorships, African military chiefdoms and other client oligarchies from the 1960s through the 1980s. Ireland and Greece, Spain and Portugal are now to be subjected to similar asset stripping as public policy making is shifted into the hands of supra-governmental financial agencies acting on behalf of bankers—and thereby for the top 1% of the population.

When debts cannot be paid or rolled over, foreclosure time arrives. For governments, this means privatization sell-offs to pay creditors. In addition to being a property grab, privatization aims at replacing public sector labor with a non-union work force having fewer pension rights, health care or voice in working conditions. The old class war is thus back in business—with a financial twist. By shrinking the economy, debt deflation helps break the power of labor to resist.

It also gives creditors control of fiscal policy. In the absence of a pan-European Parliament empowered to set tax rules, fiscal policy passes to the ECB. Acting on behalf of banks, the ECB seems to favor reversing the 20th century's drive for progressive taxation. And as US financial lobbyists have made clear, the creditor demand is for governments to re-classify public social obligations as *user fees*, to be financed by wage withholding turned over to banks to manage (or mismanage, as the case may be). Shifting the tax burden off real estate and finance onto labor and the *real* economy thus threatens to become a fiscal grab coming on top of the privatization grab.

This is self-destructive short-termism. The irony is that the PIIGS (Portugal, Italy, Ireland, Greece & Spain) budget deficits stem largely from un-taxing property, and a further tax shift will worsen rather than help stabilize government budgets. But bankers are looking only at what they can take in the short run. They know that whatever revenue the tax collector relinquishes from real estate and business is *free* for buyers to pledge to the banks as interest. So Greece and other oligarchic economies are told to *pay their way* by slashing government social spending (but not military spending for the purchase of German and French arms) and shifting taxes onto labor and industry, and onto consumers in the form of higher user fees for public services not yet privatized.

In Britain, Prime Minister Cameron claims that scaling back government even more along Thatcherite-Blairite lines will leave more labor and resources available for private business to hire. Fiscal cutbacks will indeed throw labor out of work, or at least oblige it to find lower-paid jobs with fewer rights. But cutting back public spending will shrink the business sector as well, worsening the fiscal and debt problems by pushing economies deeper into recession.

If governments cut back their spending to reduce the size of their budget deficits—or if they raise taxes on the economy at large, to run a surplus—then these surpluses will suck money out of the economy, leaving less to be spent on goods and services. The result can only be unemployment, further debt defaults and bankruptcies. We may look to Iceland and Latvia as canaries in this financial coalmine. Their recent experience shows that debt deflation leads to emigration, shortening life spans, lower birth rates, marriages and family formation—but provides great opportunities for vulture funds to suck wealth upward to the top of the financial pyramid.

Today's economic crisis is a matter of policy choice, not necessity. As President Obama's former chief of staff Rahm Emanuel quipped: "A crisis is too good an opportunity to let go to waste." In such cases the most logical explanation is that some special interest must be benefiting. Depressions increase unemployment, helping to break the power of unionized as well as non-union labor. The United States is seeing a state and local budget squeeze (as bankruptcies begin to be announced), with the first cutbacks coming in the sphere of pension defaults. High finance is being paid—by not paying the working population for savings and promises made as part of labor contracts and employee retirement plans.

Big fish are eating little fish.

This seems to be the financial sector's idea of good economic planning. But it is worse than a zero-sum plan in which one party's gain is another's loss. Economies as a whole will shrink—and change their shape, creating polarization between creditors and debtors. Economic democracy will give way to financial oligarchy, reversing the trend of the past few centuries.

Is Europe really ready to take this step? Do its voters recognize that stripping the government of the public option of money creation will hand the privilege over to banks as a monopoly? How many observers have traced the almost inevitable result: the shifting of economic planning and credit allocation to the banks?

Even if governments provide a *public option*, creating their own money to finance their budget deficits and supplying the economy with productive credit to rebuild infrastructure, a serious problem remains: how to dispose of the existing debt overhead which now acts as a deadweight on the economy. Bankers and the politicians they back are refusing to write down debts to reflect the ability to pay. Lawmakers have not prepared society with a legal procedure for debt write-downs—except for New York State's Fraudulent Conveyance Law, calling for debts to be annulled if lenders made loans without first assuring themselves of the debtor's ability to pay.

Bankers do not want to take responsibility for bad loans. This poses the financial problem of just what policy-makers should do when banks have been so irresponsible in allocating credit. But somebody has to take a loss. Should it be society at large, or the bankers?

It is not a problem bankers are prepared to solve. They want to turn the problem over to governments—and define the problem in terms of how governments can *make them whole*. What they call a *solution* to the bad-debt problem is for the government to give them good bonds for bad loans ("cash for trash")—to be paid in full by taxpayers. Having engineered an enormous increase in wealth for themselves, bankers now want to take the money and run—leaving economies debt ridden. The revenue debtors cannot pay will now be spread over the entire economy to pay—vastly increasing everyone's cost of living and doing business.

Why should they be *made whole* at the cost of shrinking the rest of the economy? The bankers' answer is that debts are owed to labor's pension funds, to consumers with bank deposits, and the whole system will come crashing down if governments miss a bond payment. When pressed, bankers admit they have taken out risk insurance—collateralized debt obligations and other risk swaps. But the insurers are largely US banks, and the American Government is pressuring Europe not to default and thereby hurt the US banking system. So the debt tangle has become politicized internationally.

So for bankers, the line of least resistance is to foster an illusion that there is no need for them to accept defaults on the unpayably high debts they have encouraged. Creditors always insist that the debt overhead can be maintained—if governments will simply reduce other expenditures, while raising taxes on individuals and non-financial business.

The reason why this won't work is that trying to collect today's magnitude of debt will injure the underlying *real* economy, making it even less able to pay its debts. What started as a financial problem (bad debts) will now be turned into a fiscal problem (bad taxes). Taxes are a cost of doing business just as paying debt service is a cost. Both costs must be reflected in product prices. When taxpayers are saddled with taxes and debts, they have less revenue free to spend on consumption. So markets shrink, putting further pressure on the profitability of domestic enterprises. The combination makes any country following such policy a high-cost producer and hence less competitive in global markets.

This kind of financial planning—and its parallel fiscal tax shift—leads toward de-industrialization. Creating ECB or IMF inter-government fiat money leaves the debts in place, while preserving wealth and economic control in the hands of the financial sector. Banks can receive debt payments on overly mortgaged properties only if debtors are relieved of some real estate taxes. Debt-strapped industrial companies can pay their debts only by scaling back pension obligations, health care and wages to their employees—or tax payments to the government. In practice, *honoring debts* turns out to mean debt deflation and general economic shrinkage.

• This is the financiers' business plan. But to leave tax policy and centralized planning in the hands of bankers turns out to be the opposite of what the past few centuries of free market economics have been all about. The classical objective was to minimize the debt overhead, to tax land and natural resource rents, and to keep monopoly prices in line with actual costs of production (value). Bankers have lent increasingly against the same revenues that free market economists believed should be the natural tax base.

So something has to give. Will it be the past few centuries of liberal free-market economic philosophy, relinquishing planning the economic surplus to bankers? Or will society re-assert classical economic philosophy and Progressive Era principles and re-assert social shaping of financial markets to promote long-term growth with minimum costs of living and doing business?

At least in the most badly indebted countries, European voters are waking up to an oligarchic coup in which taxation and government budgetary planning and control are passing into the hands of executives nominated by the international bankers' cartel. The result is the opposite of what the past few centuries of free market economics has been all about.

Our Banker Overlords

The fact is that there is a serious danger of this country becoming a Pluto-democracy; that is, a sham republic with the real government in the hands of a small clique of enormously wealthy men, who speak through their money, and whose influence, even today, radiates to every corner of the United States.

William McAdoo, 1912—President Wilson's national campaign vice-chairman

Capital must protect itself in every way, through combination [monopoly] and through legislation. Debts must be collected and loans and mortgages foreclosed as soon as possible. When through a process of law, the common people have lost their homes, they will be more tractable and more easily governed by the strong arm of the law applied by the central power of wealth, under control of leading financiers. People without homes will not quarrel with their leaders. This is well known among our principal men now engaged in forming an imperialism of capital to govern the world.

The Bankers Manifesto of 1934, privately circulated to leading bankers

A fiat monetary system allows power and influence to fall into the hands of those who control the creation of new money, and to those who get to use the money or credit early in its circulation. The insidious and eventual cost falls on unidentified victims who are usually oblivious to the cause of their plight. This system of legalized plunder (though not constitutional) allows one group to benefit at the expense of another. An actual transfer of wealth goes from the poor and the middle class to those in privileged financial positions

Congressman Ron Paul

The foundation of classical monetary theory…held that inflation is caused by "too much money chasing too few goods."… A corollary to that theory was the classical maxim that the government should balance its budget at all costs. If it ran short of money, it was supposed to borrow from the bankers rather than print the money it needed, in order to keep from inflating the money supply. This argument was a "straw man" argument, one easily knocked down because it contained a logical fallacy, but the fallacy was not immediately obvious, because the bankers were concealing their hand. The fallacy lay in the assumption that the money the government borrowed from the banks already existed and was merely being recycled. If the bankers themselves were creating the money they lent, the argument collapsed in a heap of straw. The money supply would obviously increase just as much from bank-created money as from government-created money. In either case, it was money pulled out of an empty hat. Money created by the government had the advantage that it would not plunge the taxpayers into debt; and it provided a permanent money supply, one not dependent on higher and higher levels of borrowing to stay afloat.

Ellen Brown

There is an obvious alternative to allowing our money, credit and public finances to be controlled by a corrupt and rapacious private banking cartel: public control. And it will fall to the American people to make it a reality.

States, municipalities, unions, school districts, foundations, churches and charities control perhaps trillions of dollars, much on deposit with Wall Street. That money needs to be moved to Main Street, into local banks, and a significant portion set aside to capitalize the public banks which can guarantee the sustainable and affordable credit required to rebuild American prosperity, and re-establish the accountability and transparency necessary to the finances of a democracy.

But more is needed. While the scale of the fraud is international, the impacts are local—touching your family, your neighbors and your community. It is time for state and municipal officers to take action to begin to recover the stolen wealth of their citizens.

Mike Krauss

ENDING THE
WORLD FINANCIAL CRISIS

Paul Hellyer, PC

Banking was conceived in iniquity and was born in sin. The Bankers own the earth. Take it away from them, but leave them the power to create money, and with the flick of the pen they will create enough money to buy it back again. However, take that power away from them and all the great fortunes like mine will disappear, and they ought to disappear, for this would be a happier and better world to live in. But if you wish to remain the slaves of Bankers, and pay the cost of your own slavery, let them continue to create money.

Sir Josiah (later Baron) Stamp, Director, Bank of England 1928-1941

The World Needs a Massive Real Money Reflation

"Never again!" should be the rallying cry of real reformers all around the world. Never again should we have a banking system where a combination of greed and incompetence can doom billions of people to lives of misery and hopelessness. So the real issue is who is going to run the world? Will it be the politicians we elect and pay to look after our health and welfare? Or will it be unelected, unaccountable bankers at all levels who have pretended to know what was best for us when in fact they were only interested in their own welfare, without concern for the money supply that they have been diluting indiscriminately.

Under the existing *capital adequacy* system banks are not only allowed to lend or invest their own money (capital), the rules (as interpreted) permit them to multiply the process nineteen (or more) times by simply creating the credit (virtual money) to do it. So when the market value of their total assets drops 5% or more, on average, their original capital is wiped out, and they are bankrupt. It is as simple as that.

An everyday life experience may be easier to understand. You buy a house for $200,000 and use your life savings of $10,000 as a 5% down payment. You assume a mortgage of $190,000 to cover the balance. Sometime later you have to move to another city. Meanwhile the market value of your house has fallen below $190,000. When you sell the house you lose your entire capital of $10,000 and may not receive enough to pay off the outstanding mortgage. That is the position in which many banks found themselves.

In this latest meltdown there were some dramatic declines in the values of mortgages, and mortgage-backed financial instruments. Stock markets tanked, and the ensuing days of roller-coaster rises and declines wiped off as much as forty percent or more of their previous values when they reached their November 2008 and March 2009 lows. With losses on this scale some of the largest banks lost their entire capital base, or more, and that is the reason the whole unstable system teetered on the brink of disaster.

The patchwork solutions that have been applied have at least restored some sense of order. Although banks are now being more selective in their risk assessments, and several are cracking down on their credit card customers, their doors are open again to credit-worthy borrowers. That will help some established businesses but will provide little relief to the people who need it most. Struggling entrepreneurs and undercapitalized initiatives of various kinds will be ignored and allowed to wither on the vine. So the availability of credit is welcomed by a small minority but provides no comfort to the vast majority.

A front-page story in the Toronto *Globe and Mail* of November 2, 2008 read as follows: "Universities eye 'painful cuts' in wake of crisis. With endowment funds taking a beating, student aid, scholarships, hiring and academic programs could all be on the chopping block."[1] Another headline in *The New York Times* of November 17, 2008 read "Facing Deficits, States Get out Sharper Knives—HUGE REVENUE DECLINE—Deep Cuts, US Loans, Hiring Freezes, Taxes are All on Table."[2] While the specific items vary from institution to institution, these headlines captured the essence of the road ahead when city, state and provincial governments will be cutting back programs. Each of these actions tends to exacerbate and prolong the recessionary period.

To end the recession quickly all of these types of decisions that are a consequence of the meltdown have to be reversed. The common denominator in each decision is money—cash money. But where will it come from? In the case of universities, tuition fees, on average, are already too high for many middle class and working class students. So, too, are municipal, state and provincial taxes judged by what is politically tenable.

The only hope, then, lies with federal governments that have authority over money and banking and bear overall responsibility for the welfare of their citizens, and the economic climate that affects them so directly. Should governments incur deficits if they have none, or increase them if they are already in deficit as recommended by the late, great English economist John Maynard Keynes? Or are there other alternatives?

This dilemma leads to two more fundamental questions. Are recessions a fundamental facet of the system, and therefore we should expect our economic tsunami every so often as suggested by former Chairman of the Federal Reserve System Alan Greenspan? Or are they the result of faulty economic theory, as I will argue? Two other questions are related to the first. What is money? And where does it come from?

But first, the multi-trillion dollar question. Why should a national or world economy that has all of the machinery and labor required to run smoothly and produce as much as it had done previously, suddenly start producing less? It doesn't make any sense! The problem, on analysis, is insufficient gas—gas in this case being money.

What is Money?

What is money? It is a good question for which there is no easy answer. It has meant different things to different people in different cultures at different times. In early cultures money usually meant copper, iron, silver or gold coins, although there were many innovative exceptions such as cattle, sea shells, beads and playing cards to meet extenuating circumstances.

A dual system of metallic coins and barter acted as the principal financial instruments worldwide for centuries. With the advent of the Industrial Revolution, however, the volume of commerce became so great that the widespread use of paper money became essential. Sometimes the paper money was convertible into gold or silver and sometimes it was not, but that is too long a story to include here.

In any event the practice of convertibility into gold was ended by US President Richard Nixon in 1971 when the market value of gold rose above the exchange rate and some foreign governments were taking advantage of a profit-making opportunity. Incidentally, of all the ideas being floated around today perhaps the worst is a return to some kind of gold standard. It would be one more millstone around the neck of international commerce.

Besides, most of us don't really care how much gold we can buy with our money. We do care very much, however, how many groceries, and other goods and services of all kinds that we can purchase. It is the *basket* of our day-to-day needs that concerns us—our total range of needs and wants as measured in the consumer price index.

Our current monetary system is quite complex. In addition to a few coins we have three major sources of *money*. The bills we carry are known as *fiat money* that Webster's Dictionary defines as "paper currency that has value only by law and is not backed by gold or silver." This kind of money is created by governments or their agents—usually a central bank—and can be called government-created money, or GCM, for short.

Another kind of money is virtual money, or phantom money, as I call it. This money is created by privately owned banks and can be called bank-created money, or BCM. A third important source is the money that is *created* by the issuance of credit cards. Let's call it CCM. A retired chief economist of one of Canada's largest banks summed it all up this way. "Money is what is generally accepted in exchange for goods and services." That is as good a definition as any.

Without in any way underestimating the importance of credit card money for which some kind of regulation appears to be highly desirable, my examination relates primarily to government-created money and bank-created money, and especially the quantity of each that determine our financial destiny. It is essential to take a closer look at the relationship between the two, and the advantages and disadvantages of each. If readers are similar to most of my friends, these are matters that have not been given as much thought as they deserve.

Where Does Money Come From?

When I was writing my first book on the subject, which was called *Funny Money*, even though there wasn't anything very funny about it, I asked scores of my friends and acquaintances—not including my circle of economist friends, some of whom are well versed in the subject, while the majority is not—the leading question that is the heading for this section.

My sample included doctors, lawyers, dentists, accountants, a newspaper editors-in-chief, newspaper publishers, financial page columnists and scores of ordinary common-sense people. I asked each one the same question. "Do you know where money comes from?" Some were a little hesitant about the question but, when pressed, they all said that the government prints it. When I asked the follow-up question of what percentage of the new money *printed* each year the government created, the answers ranged from 60% to 100 percent. No one came up with a number smaller than 60 percent. If that were true we would have a very different system from the one that actually exists. Not one of my samples had what you might call a working knowledge of the monetary system, yet these are the kinds of people who tell governments how they should be running things.

In fact, most of the new money added to the money supply each year (printed, manufactured or put into circulation, if you prefer—it's all the same) is created by privately owned banks. In his book *Money, Whence it Came, Where it Went*, the late economist John Kenneth Galbraith said, "The process by which banks create money is so simple the mind is repelled. When something so important is involved, a deeper mystery seems only decent."[3]

The fact that private banks *print* money is extremely difficult for many of my friends to accept. Most of them believe the bankers' myth that the money they lend you today is money I or someone else deposited yesterday. The odds of that being true are infinitesimal. Usually banks are fully lent so when you go in for a loan they have to create the money for you.

This is the way it works. Suppose that you want to borrow $35,000 to buy a new car. So you visit your friendly banker and ask for a loan. He/ she will ask you for collateral—some stocks, bonds, a second mortgage on your house or cottage or, if you are unable to supply any of these, the co-signature of a well-to-do friend or relative. When the collateral require-ment is satisfied you will be asked to sign a note for the principal amount with an agreed rate of interest.

When the paperwork is complete, and the note signed, your banker will make an entry on the bank's computer and, presto, a $35,000 credit will appear in your account which you can use to buy your car. The important point is that seconds earlier that money did not exist. It was created out of thin air, so to speak.

The banking equation is a kind of double-entry bookkeeping where your note becomes an asset on the bank's books, and the new money that was deposited to your account is a liability. The profit for the bank comes from the difference between the low rate of interest, if any, you would be paid on your deposit if you didn't spend the borrowed money immediately, and the much higher rate you would be obliged to pay on your note—the technical term is *the spread*.

An even more striking illustration of how the system works is to consider someone in the building business who borrows $200,000 to build a house. This money is used to pay the people who dig clay from a pit and make bricks, the bricklayers who lay the bricks, the woodsmen who cut trees to make lumber, the carpenters who use it to build the frame, the miners who extract the metals for the hardware, and the manufacturers who turn out the plumbing, wiring and fixtures. But when they are all finished, it is the bank that owns the house.

The bank did little more than create the *money* which acted as the intermediary to facilitate construction. Nevertheless, because it was created as debt, all of the money has to be repaid when the house is sold because there may be the equivalent of a lien on it that has to be discharged by the bank. Consequently, the builder has to sell the house at a price that will allow him to repay the bank and, if he is lucky, leave a little over to reward him for the work he has done and the risk he has taken. If he can't, and there is a shortfall, he will have to make up the difference to prevent the bank from liquidating part or all of the collateral pledged to get the loan.

In reality, the banks have turned the world into one humongous pawn shop. You hock your stocks, bonds, house, business, rich mother-in-law or country and the bank(s) will give you a loan based on the value of the collateral. Still there is an element of uncertainty in dealing with the banks that doesn't apply with legitimate pawn shops. The latter don't phone you and ask for their money back if the price of silver or gold goes down after they have given you cash for your gold watch or silver candlesticks.

The banks, on the other hand, often change the terms of the deal with little warning. If the market value of your collateral goes down, they phone and insist that you either provide additional collateral, which you may not have, or give them their money back. That isn't always easy or convenient for you to do—especially on short notice.

That is exactly what happened when the crisis began in the fall of 2007. As the market value of assets banks were holding as collateral for loans began to fall, the banks demanded increased collateral or the repayment of part or all of their loans. Many borrowers had to sell stocks into a falling market—a dizzying downward spiral that the economists call de-leveraging. This would not have been necessary if the banks themselves were not so highly leveraged. They have loaned or invested twenty times as much money as they actually have on the basis of collateral that was no longer adequate for the amount that was loaned.

Bank Leverage: The Banks are Never Satisfied!

I believe that banking institutions are more dangerous to our liberties than standing armies. If the American people ever allow private banks to control the issue of their currency, first by inflation, then by deflation, the banks and corporations that will grow up around the banks will deprive the people of all property until their children wake-up homeless on the continent their fathers conquered.

Thomas Jefferson, 1802

Although European banking can be traced back to Roman times, I will begin my story of the gradual increase of bank leverage with the creation of the Bank of England over three hundred years ago. The Bank of England was conceived as a solution to a dilemma. King William's War, 1688-1697, had been extremely costly and this resulted in much of England's gold and silver going to the continent in payment of debt. As a result the money supply was sorely depleted and something had to be done to keep the wheels of commerce turning. Someone got the bright idea that establishing a bank might help to fill the void.

At the time the Bank was chartered the scheme involved an initial subscription by its shareholders of £1,200,000 in gold and silver which would be lent to the government at 8 percent. That seems fair enough, although the interest rate was more than ample for a government-guaranteed investment. It was only the beginning, however, because in addition to a £4,000 management fee, the Bank of England was granted an advantage only available to banks and bankers. It was granted authority to issue *banknotes* in an amount equal to its capital and lend the notes into circulation. This was not the first case of paper money issued by private banks in the modern era, but it was the first of great and lasting significance in the English-speaking world.[4] It was the same system that had been developed by the goldsmiths of Lombard Street, in London. By lending the same money twice the Bank could double the interest received on its capital. Nice work if you can get it and you can get it with a bank charter. It is not too surprising, then, that discussions of this advantage encouraged some members of parliament to become shareholders in the Bank. Money lenders learned early, and have never forgotten, that it pays to have friends in parliament.[5]

In the slightly over three hundred years since the Bank of England began with a leverage of two-to-one (in effect, lending twice the amount of its subscribed capital), the deal has been sweetened many times. In the early years of the 20th century, federally chartered US banks were required to have a gold reserve of 25 percent. They could lend four times as much as they had gold in their vaults, though they always required some redeemable asset as collateral. State chartered banks were subject to less restraint and there were some shocking examples of excess.

With the introduction of Central Banks, the Federal Reserve System in the US and the Bank of Canada north of the border, the system changed in form though not in substance. Banknotes issued by private banks were phased out and replaced by a uniform, legal tender currency. In the US, Federal Reserve Notes became predominant, while in Canada, the Bank of Canada was given a monopoly on the creation of legal tender paper money. In the process banks were required to keep cash, legal tender, reserves against deposits instead of gold.

Consequently, in Canada, when I was younger, the cash reserve require-ment for banks was 8% which allowed them to lend up to twelve and a half times that amount. Today the cash reserve requirements in the US are 3% for current accounts, 0% for savings accounts and 0% for Eurodollar accounts. In Canada, the reserve requirement is 0%, period! You are lucky if your bank has a cent, or a cent-and-a-half, in cash, for every dollar you think you have in the bank. The only reason they can get away with this is the time-honored one of knowing from experience that only a handful of depositors are likely to ask for cash at any one time. If for any reason depositors' confidence was shaken, and they began a *run* on the bank, they would be out of luck because their *money* doesn't exist in real form. Their only hope would be a massive intervention by the Federal Reserve in the US or the Bank of Canada in Canada to monetize (print legal tender money to buy) the bonds and other assets held by the banks.

It was Prime Minister Brian Mulroney who eliminated the requirement for Canadian banks to hold cash reserves. The Bank Act of 1991 phased them out. This was a gift worth several billion dollars a year to the banks, at taxpayers' expense. The banks were allowed to spend their reserves to purchase bonds and treasury bills on which we, the taxpayers, pay several billions a year in interest payments.

A Change in System

In effect the phasing out of cash reserve requirements marked the beginning of an entirely new system known as *capital adequacy*. Banks are allowed to own assets that are equal to several times their paid up capital. Regulations have varied, but for Canadian banks the permitted limit has been twenty times and most large US banks have been operating at similar multiples, while some merchant banks have scaled the heights to much higher numbers.

The new system is quite inferior to the old one of cash reserves because in practice it is pretty well tantamount to total deregulation. It is a system that the Bank for International Settlements (BIS), with its headquarters in Basel, Switzerland, has foisted upon an unsuspecting world. It is a part of the plan to switch the world banking system to 0% reserves in accord with the theories of the late Professor Milton Friedman.

The Current Chaos is the Legacy of Milton Friedman and the Chicago School

In 1996, the first chapter of my book, *Surviving the Global Financial Crisis: The Economics of Hope for Generation X*, was entitled "Monetarists and the Chicago School Blew It!" The first two paragraphs read as follows.

"Let's face it; the monetarist counter-revolution of the last twenty years has been one monumental flop. This was inevitable because monetarism is a hothouse plant bred and nurtured in the esoteric garden of the Academy. It was never suitable for transplanting directly into the real economy where, despite its cosmetic innocence, it would have the same smothering effect demonstrated by the purple loosestrife when transported from Europe to the swamps of North America. It crowded out everything traditional and worthwhile.

"It is true that 'practical monetarism,' as former Federal Reserve Board Chairman Paul Volcker called the variety that he planted in the real world, reduced the level of inflation substantially and dampened the inflationary expectations that had raised their ugly head. But at what cost? The implementation of monetarism has created more financial turbulence than we have seen at any time since World War II. It has induced two horrendous recessions, slowed economic growth, produced unconscionable levels of unemployment and raised the debt burden to the point where the world economy is set on a collision course with disaster. Thanks to 'practical monetarism' the world financial system is headed for a meltdown."[6]

It would have been nice if that prediction had proved to be wrong. But the cards were stacked from the beginning. Professor Milton Friedman and his colleagues made several cardinal errors in their analyses. The first was the attempt to make a science of something that is really more of a combined art and science that used to be described as political economy. In the process Friedman and his colleagues produced complex mathematical models that are good fun for mathematicians, but which don't relate to the real world where there are an almost infinite number of variables.

Another fundamental error was Friedman's misdiagnosis of the inflation of the late '60s and early '70s. He claimed that it was classic inflation, defined as "too much money chasing too few goods." He couldn't have been more wrong. The supermarkets were crammed with goods, and small stores were going bankrupt every day for lack of customers for their wares. The facts refuted Friedman's thesis, but that didn't matter to the Chicago School.

Friedman sold his theory to thousands of students on the basis of his research which had showed that for a hundred years in a hundred countries prices had risen in direct proportion to the amount of money created. While it may be true that figures don't lie, they don't always reveal the whole truth either. In this case Friedman's observations are about as helpful as the discovery that for a hundred years in a hundred countries summer followed winter.

That, too, is true but it doesn't tell you whether the summers were too hot and dry, too cool and wet, or just about the right balance for abundant crops. The devil is in the details and Friedman completely overlooked a *!!* new phenomenon that had profoundly influenced prices in the '60s and '70s. For the first time in recorded economic history nominal wages in Western countries had risen two or more times faster than productivity for twenty-five consecutive years.

It had been this disconnect between wages and productivity that had been primarily responsible for the inflation of those years. True, there were a couple of blips caused by increases in oil prices when the Organization of Petroleum Exporting Countries (OPEC) got its act together. But this was never responsible for more than a small fraction of the inflation of that period. Nor was the Vietnam War the culprit, as most orthodox economists insisted.

The data from fifteen Organization for Economic Co-operation and Development (OECD) countries shows clearly that the principal cause of inflation in the '50s, '60s and '70s was nominal wages rising faster than productivity. The average of averages for fifteen countries showed that prices rose by the difference between the average increase in nominal wages, and the average increase in real output per member of the labor force, within one-quarter of one percent, which is about as close as you can get in economics.

The arithmetic is simple. If each of us, on average, produces less than 2% more goods and services than we did the year before, as was the case in the United States and Canada from 1964 to 1991, how large a real wage increase can we have? The answer is, less than 2%, on average. Anything more than that creates inflation—of the cost-push variety.

The problem with misdiagnosis in economics, as in medicine, is that prescribing the wrong medication can produce excruciatingly painful results. So when Friedman's disciple Paul Volcker, Chairman of the Federal Reserve Board in the United States, Gerald Bouey, Governor of the Bank of Canada, and other central bankers restricted the money supply in 1981-82, their actions caused the worst recession since the Great Depression of the 1930s. Economies were strangled, growth rates plummeted, government revenues fell dramatically and deficits soared; these were rolled over into debt which compounded at the artificially high interest rates, and headed to heights that put the world in hock to the money lenders.

The ratio of total public and private debt to GDP in the United States had fallen from slightly above 165% in 1946, to a low of 134% in 1951, and then remained more or less constant in the 135-145% range for thirty years until 1981. It was only when the Fed adopted the monetarist *theology*, and its consequent high interest rates, that the ratio began to rise again to a level of approximately 200% of GDP—well above the 1946 peak.[7]

The totally disastrous recession of 1981-82 not only put millions of people out of their jobs, their homes, their businesses, and off their farms, it was the beginning of a new era of high debt for governments, both domestic and foreign, that has never been brought under control, and never will be as long as the present system continues. About 95% of all the new money created every year is created as debt. The debt load just keeps getting bigger and bigger until the balloon bursts and recession sets in.

Sadly, just as we were beginning to recover from that smashing blow, the central bankers induced another recession in 1990-91, and the world economy is still reeling from the cumulative effects.

Perhaps the saddest commentary of all is that almost twenty years later central bankers, steeped in the Friedman dogma, still don't see the real nature of the problem or the appropriate policy mix necessary to cope.

The third and probably most disastrous of Friedman's errors related to his views on the necessity for banks to maintain cash reserves against deposits.

The Bank for International Settlements (BIS)

In 1974 the Bank for International Settlements, the central bankers' bank, endorsed Friedmanism. As a result, the central banks of the western world changed the rules which, however inadequate, had kept the system afloat since the end of World War II. It has been downhill for the world system ever since.

Central banks drastically reduced their holdings of government bonds that had filled the function of interest-free loans. This was a big loss to taxpayers because their governments then had to borrow from private banks and pay interest at market rates. More subtle, yet more profound, the economy began to split into two parts—an increasingly complex financial economy and an increasingly neglected real economy. The financial economy was soon recognized as the place where easy money could be made. The people who printed money and played with money became the exorbitantly paid high rollers who eclipsed most—though not all—of the visionaries who developed new products and new services.

Bright mathematicians created exotic financial instruments that were so complex that they were not fully understood even by financial managers charged with assessing the risk. There were significant underlying unknowns that were downplayed in order to keep the risk within the limits imposed by *capital adequacy*, the new regulatory jargon adopted by the BIS that proved to be *capital inadequacy*.

Inevitably, in an industry that was to all intents and purposes self-regulated, greed that knew no bounds trumped both prudence and common sense. The system collapsed once again in 2008 and taxpayers were asked to ride to the rescue one more time.

Periodic meltdowns are integral to a system that is so heavily dependent on bank-created credit. It's like blowing up a balloon. The balloon keeps getting bigger and bigger until someone sticks a pin in it. Then the system looks like a deflated balloon and it takes a long while to reflate it.

It should be self-evident that the boom-bust system that has plagued humankind for so long must end. Propping up the existing system must be what Albert Einstein had in mind when he wrote, *"The definition of insanity is doing the same thing over and over again and expecting different results."*

My Proposal: A New Economics

There is one thing stronger than all the armies of the world, and that is an idea whose time has come.

Victor Hugo

First, I would like to list just a few important points for you to think about as you contemplate the major change in direction that national economies must take in order to secure your future and that of your children and their children.

In former times monarchs exercised the sovereign right to issue the currency of the realm.

In modern times federal politicians have inherited the sovereign control of money and banking on behalf of all the people.

Instead of exercising that right on behalf of the people, federal politicians, except in a few rare cases, have granted licenses to privately-owned banks and allowed them to create most of the nation's money supply.

These same politicians, when they are short of money, often borrow from the private banks and pay them interest on money that they could have created for themselves, interest free. Can you think of anything more ridiculous?

The chartered (privately-owned) banks now create approximately ninety-five percent of all the new money created each year.

All of this money is created as debtmoney on which interest must be paid.

No one creates any money with which to pay that interest.

Consequently the only way we can collectively pay the interest on bank-created money is to borrow more and go deeper in debt in the process.

If the average interest rate on the debt is higher than the growth in gross domestic product the debt rises faster than GDP until eventually the debt burden is too heavy for the system to sustain.

The system collapses!

Everyone scurries around trying to repair the unseaworthy ship so the cycle can start all over again.

What I am proposing is a new economic regime based on a fairer and more stable sharing of the money-creation function between governments, who control the patents on behalf of the people, and the private banks, the licensees who have benefited so enormously as a result of their right to *print* money.

In theory governments should create all the new money as a function of their sovereignty. If they did, however, they would have to set up new institutions to ration some of it out to meet the needs of industry and commerce and that is a function that is more suitable to privately-administered enterprise. So any long-term solution should be designed to meet the needs of governments, on the one hand, and business enterprise on the other.

In a couple of my earlier books, including one in the Jubilee year at the turn of the century, I proposed that private bank leverage allowing them to own assets equal to twenty or thirty times their invested capital be reduced to assets equal to twice their paid up capital including retained earnings.

On reflection, however, I think that may be a bit Draconian. In addition it should be self-evident that the system of capital adequacy should be abandoned altogether as a principal control mechanism. It is time to turn our backs on an experiment that didn't work satisfactorily in favor of one that definitely will and that results in the transfer of power over the economy from private banks to duly elected officials.

So I am now proposing a return to the cash reserve system as the regulator of private banks money creation. It is not really a new system but rather a re-introduction of the one that existed prior to 1974 when central banks adopted Friedmanism. What would be new is that banks, near banks and deposit-taking institutions of all kinds would not be allowed to create assets in excess of three times the cash reserves in their vaults or on deposit with the central bank. It will take time to implement the changeover as I will explain later. It is a solution, however, that meets three important criteria.

First, it allows banks about the same maximum ratio of debt that a bank would consider prudent in making a commercial loan to industry. (Bank deposits are debts that banks owe to their depositors.)

Second, there would be virtually no chance that a bank could fail and, consequently, the need for a periodic government (taxpayer) bailout would be eliminated.

Third, and most important from a humanitarian and world view, governments of nation states would be able to create enough new money each year to balance any kind of realistic budget without resort to excessive taxation.

The figures are really impressive. For the years 2004 and 2005 in Canada, the average increase in the money supply (M2+) was about $43.3 billion. The government's share under the proposed formula would have been $14.29 billion a year. In 2006 and 2007 the gross increase was much higher and averaged $76.9 billion. The government's share would have been just over $26 billion.[8] Extrapolating to the United States the figures would be more than ten times greater. In both cases the extra cash available without resorting to higher taxation would be enormously helpful.

The banks would still have ample capacity to meet the core needs of business, industry and consumers—the sole justification for their licenses to print (create) money. Commercial banks should not be allowed to finance leveraged buyouts, the purchase of stocks on margin (a major cause of instability in times of crisis), to lend money to hedge funds or play Russian roulette with exotic derivatives. In other words, the divorce between the financial and real economies should end with reconciliation and remarriage.

Implementation Phase I: Jump Start the World Economy

How much government-created money will be required to jump start the world economy? A lot of it! Any number is just a guess because there is no formula for a rescue operation of this magnitude, but let's say ten trillion dollars, or equivalent, worldwide, to start, and more as needed until the desired result is achieved.

The cash infusion could be coupled with a short-term tax holiday for families of low and medium incomes and/or a modest across the board tax cut for those same income groups. Once the augmented source of government funds is established, the number of permutations and combinations is very large.

It would be nice if the G20 group of nations agreed to implement the policy simultaneously. But this is not essential and any country or group of countries can act on their own. It is highly desirable, however, that the United States take the lead because it was the meltdown of US institutions that spread like a virus around the world.

The Obama administration's opening salvo of close to a trillion was probably appropriate at the outset. Experience has shown it was just a start. The situation demands vast amounts of additional stimulus until the sleeping giant shows unmistakable signs of resuscitation, followed by a quick return to full health and vigor. Much of the new money should be made available for under-funded projects at every level, including health care, education and infrastructure. In the case of the latter, however, commitments should be of an order that can be guaranteed for a three or preferably four-year minimum. There are few experiences more frustrating than making plans and then having to cancel before the construction or installation is complete as a result of changing economic conditions.

* Each country or union of countries will have to work out the legalities of its own solution. All will be required to establish or re-establish cash reserve requirements for privately-owned banks. This is the answer to a former governor of the Bank of Canada who, when it was suggested that government-created money be used to escape from a particularly bad economic situation, said "But who will hold the government-created cash? Will people keep it under their mattresses or in their attics?" The banks will hold it governor; that should be an essential part of their mandate.

Implementation Phase II: A Permanent Stable System

Before this essay was written I talked to an American banker who had been referred to me by a mutual friend. I asked him how long he thought the current recession might last and he replied two or three years but it could be as long as six or eight. I offered to send him a copy of one of my old books where I argue that recessions are unnecessary and that there is a simple answer to the instability.

I become very upset when I hear former Fed Chairman Alan Greenspan and former Secretary of the Treasury Henry Paulson make it sound as though the 2008 experience has been a very rare event and, by implication, we should just accept it as inherent to the system and be prepared to muddle through. They remind me of my economics professors who could never give me a straight answer when I asked them if recessions and depressions were necessary.

Economic history tells us there have been a number of *panics*, more than we recall. And for sixty years since I first discovered what went wrong I have been of the strongly held view that none of them was necessary. Not one! Furthermore, even one more is one too many!

So what I am proposing is a system where bank leverage is so sensibly limited that it will be almost impossible for them to get in trouble; and where federal governments everywhere will have enough debt free income that they will be able to balance their budgets without taking on additional debt. In fact, changing the system would be a heaven-sent opportunity to reduce their debt somewhat and perhaps pay off most or all of Third World debt as well.

The money (cash) required to revitalize the US and other national economies will be insufficient to allow banks to meet their 34% reserve requirements, so governments should take advantage of the opportunity to monetize enough of their debt (buy back their bonds with cash they print) to achieve that goal. It would also be the opportunity for the industrialized world, collectively, to use some of the proceeds to pay off most, if not all Third World and developing world debt and still have enough left over to reduce their own indebtedness significantly.

There has been much talk of paying off Third World debt, a great deal of which can be considered *odious* by any just and moral standard.[9] So far, however, that is almost all it has been—just talk. And to be fair to political leaders, it would be virtually impossible for them to increase taxes to the extent necessary to accomplish the job that must be done.

To give the banks the privilege of financing it, however, as part of the de-leveraging process, would be a kind of just penance—a kind of reparations—for the part they have played in the whole dismal game of debt accumulation as well as the multi-trillion dollar losses due to the 2008 meltdown. This is not only politically desirable, it would be applauded by millions who want to see the poorest of the poor given a bit of a leg up in their struggle to achieve the most basic of needs.

This massive de-leveraging is just what the world desperately needs. Leverage has been the key contributor to the increasing gap between rich countries and poor countries and to the widening income spread between rich and poor within countries.

Even the banks will win in the long run because they will be perceived more favorably by most of us, their dutiful customers; and they will become more stable, reliable members of the world economic family to boot.

In *Funny Money* and its US version, *Surviving the Global Financial Crisis: The Economics of Hope for Generation X*, I referred to econometric simulations that had produced amazing results. The most significant new input, of course, was the addition of modest amounts of government-created money to federal government revenues. There was another assumption that contributed positively. It was the imposition of mandatory wage and profit guidelines in cases where monopoly or market power resulted in arbitrary wage and price increases. The policy only applied to monopolies and oligopolies, but it did theoretically limit the wage price spiral that had led to inflation and then stagflation.

The principle is based on the philosophy of the English political philosopher John Stuart Mill, who stated that the freedom of any person or group ends at the point where it trespasses on another person or group. If the new money created each year is distributed vertically, through higher wages for the already employed and consequently higher prices for existing output, it will not be available to finance additional employment and increased output. If there is any one thing that must be learned in order to understand the failure of monetarism it is this. To the extent that the increase in the money stock—translated into income—is distributed vertically, in excess of increases in productivity, it contributes to higher wages and prices rather than increased output. Unless wage increases to the already employed are limited to the average increase in real output, inflation will continue; and if inflation continues interest rates will be higher than necessary because lenders will continue to demand a premium as a hedge against the anticipated inflation. This has negative implications for governments and for the economy as a whole. It is the people who must bear the extra burden.

The other great advantage of continuous low inflation is that it permits a significantly higher level of employment. If there is one benefit which tops the list from a humanitarian point of view it is the availability of jobs for people who want to work. This has been the over-riding motive in my life-long obsession with economics because I think the need to contribute to the common well-being is fundamental to one's feeling of self-worth. Finally, it should be noted, negligible inflation protects the value of savings for everyone.

There are alternatives for anyone for whom any type of regulation is anathema. One is a social contract—an agreement by both big business and big labor to accept voluntary restrictions. Another is to use taxing power to make it unprofitable to exceed voluntary guidelines. Either is theoretically workable but experience would lead one to believe there is no long-term substitute for guidelines as a substitute for rigorous enforcement of anti-trust principles.

The Fed Must Be Replaced by a Publicly Owned Central Bank of the United States

Anyone familiar with the history of the Fed and the real reasons for its birth would shout Halleluiah at its demise. The whole sordid story of its beginning is told in *The Creature from Jekyll Island* by G. Edward Griffin where the summary of the first chapter begins as follows.

"The basic plan for the Federal Reserve System was drafted at a secret meeting held in November 1910 at the private resort of J.P. Morgan on Jekyll Island off the coast of Georgia. Those who attended represented the great financial institutions of Wall Street and, indirectly, Europe as well. The reason for secrecy was simple. Had it been known that rival factions of the banking community had joined together, the public would have been alerted to the possibility that the bankers were plotting an agreement in restraint of trade—which, of course, is exactly what they were doing. What emerged was a cartel agreement with five objectives: stop the growing competition from the nation's newer banks; obtain a franchise to create money out of nothing for the purpose of lending; get control of the reserves of all banks so that the more reckless ones would not be exposed to currency drains and bank runs; get the taxpayer to pick up the cartel's inevitable losses; and convince Congress that the purpose was to protect the public. It was realized that the bankers would have to become partners with the politicians and that the structure of the cartel would have to be a central bank. The record shows that the Fed has failed to achieve its stated objectives. That is because those were never its true goals. As a banking cartel, and in terms of the five objectives stated above, it has been an unqualified success."[10]

Griffin goes on to explain in great detail how the wool was pulled over the eyes of the politicians who ultimately approved the scheme very much as it was first drafted by its promoters. Little did they realize they were enshrining into law a Machiavellian plot to legalize one of the biggest heists in history.

William Jennings Bryan, who acted as Democrat whip, and is credited with a major effort in getting the Federal Reserve Act of 1913 passed, later said: "In my long political career, the one thing I genuinely regret is my part in getting the banking and currency legislation (FR Act) enacted into law."[11] Senator Carter Glass, one of the original sponsors of the Act of 1913, said on June 7, 1938: "I never thought the Federal Bank System would prove such a failure. The country is in a state of irretrievable bankruptcy."[12]

An early view from the Oval Office sounds the same note. President Woodrow Wilson, just three years after passage of the Act wrote: "A great industrial nation is controlled by its system of credit. Our system of credit is concentrated (in the Federal Reserve System). The growth of the nation, therefore, and all our activities are in the hands of a few men.... We have come to be one of the worst ruled, one of the most completely controlled and dominated governments in the civilized world."[13] It is a moot point as to why succeeding presidents and congresses have not remedied the mistake.

No one who is familiar with the Fed's dismal record of failures that include the Great Depression of the 1930s and every recession since, including the most recent disastrous one, could possibly justify giving it additional powers as some have suggested. On the contrary, it is beyond redemption and must either be converted into or replaced by a new Bank of the United States (BUS), a publicly owned central bank to be responsible for the day to day implementation of federal government policy. The governor of the Bank should be directly responsible to the secretary of the treasury and take direction from him or her. There should be a provision in the law that in the event of a disagreement between the two, the secretary, or minister of finance as the case may be, takes precedence but is required to make his or her instructions to the governor public.

This should effectively end the spectacle of central banks pursuing monetary policies that are totally at odds with the fiscal stance of the government of the day. I still burn when I recall the recession of 1980-81 when Paul Volcker in the US and Gerald Bouey in Canada adopted policies that resulted in putting hundreds of thousands of people on the breadlines while governments struggled valiantly to re-employ a few of them.

It was especially annoying when there was a better alternative. A twelve month freeze of wages and prices—except for the harvests of farm and sea and internationally traded commodities—would have reduced inflation much closer to zero than the monetarily-induced recession achieved, and the lower inflation would have been possible without a single job being lost.

Then if an incomes policy had followed the freeze, inflation would have remained low and we would have been spared the spectacle of central bankers following interest rate policies that made them look like neophyte pilots. First they would pull the stick back too far too fast and then overcorrect in the opposite direction when the economy began to stall.

The notion that there are no measures available to fight inflationary tendencies other than a universal increase in interest rates is both shortsighted and erroneous. If real estate prices are escalating too fast in one area, minimum equity requirements can be raised to cool the market before a bubble forms. If a general inflation appears on the horizon, minimum monthly payments on credit cards can be increased to dampen consumption. The bottom line is that there are options other than a high interest rate policy.

The era when ultimate control over the economic welfare of a nation is exercised by unelected, unaccountable bankers must end. Control must be exercised by the people who are elected for that purpose. If their policies fail they can be held accountable at the next available election.

One final consideration is only relevant when the Bank of the United States is up and running. It is a technical point of primary interest to economists and bankers who fret about such matters. It should interest politicians too.

It is quite a while since I read the story of how the Fed assisted the US government in financing World War II. I think it was similar to the Canadian system that I remember well. The Bank of Canada deposited cash to the government account in exchange for Government of Canada interest-bearing bonds that the Bank booked as assets against the liability of the money created.

The government paid the BOC interest on the bonds. Then the Bank gave it back in the form of dividends—deducting only enough to pay for the cost of administration. To all intents and purposes, however, they were interest-free loans. Still the bonds appeared on the government's books as debt.

Today, however, in a world overwhelmed in debt, cosmetics are important and what every country needs is an infusion of *debt free* money. So instead of governments giving central banks bonds to fill the function of assets on their books, they should use non-convertible, non-transferable shares in the country. The shares could be given a nominal value of, say, one share equals $10 billion in the US. For a smaller country like Canada, perhaps one share equals $1 billion would be more appropriate. But these are details. The aim is to provide governments with some cash that does not wind up on their books as debt. They all have much too much of that already.

The Pros and Cons

Whenever government-created money (GCM) is mentioned in polite circles you can expect the knee-jerk reaction, "It would be inflationary." This is a substitute for reasoned analysis on the part of economists and editorial writers who put it forward in all seriousness. In fact government-created money is no more inflationary than bank-created money if the amount is not excessive and the private banks' share is reduced proportionately. It is the total amount of money created that influences prices, not who creates it.

What the objectors are really saying is that they don't trust politicians and would prefer to leave the most powerful of all economic tools in the exclusive hands of unelected, unaccountable bankers. They won't come clean and say they don't believe in democracy, because that would be politically incorrect! Still, that is the inevitable, hard rock, core of their beliefs.

One of America's genius inventors, Thomas Edison, put the whole question of bonds, bills and national credit in perspective. "If the nation can issue a dollar bond it can issue a dollar bill. The element that makes the bond good makes the bill good. The difference between the bond and the bill is that the bond lets money brokers collect twice the amount of the bond and an additional 20 percent. (Total of principal and interest by the time the bond is paid off.) Whereas the currency of the honest sort provided for by the constitution pays nobody but those who contribute in some useful way. It is absurd to say our country can issue bonds but cannot issue currency. Both are promises to pay, but one fattens the usurers and the other helps the people. If the currency issued by the people were no good, then the bonds would be no good, either."[14] Edison said it well.

Graham Towers, the first and in my opinion the brightest of Bank of Canada governors, said: "Banks manufacture money the same way that steel companies manufacture steel, that is their business." He made no attempt to disguise the nature of money. "It is nothing but a book entry; that is all it is," he said. If he were alive today he would say: "Money is nothing but a computer entry; that is all it is."

More than half-a-century ago I raised the subject of GCM with Governor Towers during a recess when he was appearing as a witness before the House of Commons Finance and Commerce Committee. His reply explained both the advantages and the dangers in a nutshell. "It would be something like this," he said, "Drinking a bottle or two of Coca Cola from time to time can be quite refreshing. If you were to drink a whole case at one time it would kill you."[15] Towers analogy was his way of saying that judicious use of government-created money could be a good thing, whereas too much would be highly inflationary. Can you think of a more intelligent approach to the use of government-created money?

This is about the point during my lectures on the subject when someone will ask if there is anywhere in the world where the theory has been successfully translated into practice. "Not often enough," I reply, "but there are some noteworthy examples." The ideas are not new! They have been around for generations but they have been too long ignored at inestimable cost in human wellbeing.

As Curtis P. Nettles points out: "Paper currency issued under government auspices originated in the thirteen colonies; and during the 18th century they were the laboratories in which many currency experiments were performed."[16] There were no banks at that time in any of the thirteen colonies, so all the paper money was created under the authority of the colonial legislatures. In all there were about 250 separate issues of colonial notes between 1690 and 1775 and the system worked just fine when they avoided over or under issue. It also had distinct advantages over bank or coin money. The legislature could spend, lend or transfer the money into circulation, while banks could only lend (or spend their interest earnings back into circulation) and the coin money was always leaving the colonies to pay for imports.

There is no doubt that the thirteen colonies were the Western pioneers in the creation of *funny money*, the label many skeptics and cynics apply to government-created money. Why they consider it any funnier than the phantom money banks create I will never understand. Perhaps they just suffer from a peculiar sense of humor.

A more recent and continuing case is the Guernsey Experiment. When skeptics ask for an example in real life where government-created money has been utilized consistently and effectively for an extended period it is only necessary to look at the history of the Isle of Guernsey, beginning in the early 19th century. At that time the island boasted natural beauty but little else. There was nothing to attract visitors or to keep residents from moving to the mainland. There was no trade or hope of employment for the poor. The market was open to the elements and needed a roof, and the shores were eroding due to the sorry state of the dykes. What to do? Why set up a committee, of course.

"Finally," as Olive and Jan Grubiak report in *The GUERNSEY Experiment*, "after grave deliberation, the Committee reported in 1816 with this historic recommendation—that property should be acquired and a covered market erected; the expenses to be met by the Issue of States Notes to the value of £6000."[17] The story, as related by the Grubiaks in their well-documented pamphlet, is well worth reading for anyone interested in the subject.

The experiment had its ups and downs as the banks made an intense, but in the end unsuccessful, effort to put an end to the practice. Consequently, it has persisted to this day with the result that the island has modern infrastructure, no unemployment to speak of, very low taxes and no debt. If you contrast this extremely successful policy with that of the United Kingdom with its enormous debt, and taxpayers still paying interest on money borrowed to fight the American colonists in the War for Independence more than 200 years ago, it will be hard to escape the conclusion that there is a better system and that we should be well advised to adopt it.

Lincoln and Government-Created Money

Although Abraham Lincoln was not a proponent of government-created money, he certainly recognized its usefulness in time of emergency. In his December 1862 message to Congress, Lincoln made the following reference to greenbacks: "The suspension of specie payments by banks soon after the commencement of your last session, made large issues of

United States Notes [greenbacks] unavoidable. In no other way could the payment of the troops, and the satisfaction of other just demands, be so economically or so well provided for. The judicious legislation of Congress, securing the receivability of these notes for loans and internal duties, and making them a legal tender for other debts, has made them a universal currency; and has satisfied, partially, at least, and for the time, the long-felt want of a uniform circulating medium, saving thereby to the people immense sums in discounts and exchanges."[18]

There was some Congressional support for adopting the system on a permanent basis. Representative Thaddeus Stevens, first elected to Congress as a Whig and later as a Republican, in speaking during the spirited debates over the first of the Legal Tender Acts prior to the enactment of the legislation authorizing the printing of greenbacks, said: "The government and not the banks should have the profit from creating a medium of exchange."[19]

Another booster was Alexander Campbell, a mining engineer and entrepreneur, elected to Congress from Illinois in 1874 for a single term on a Democrat-Independent ticket. In *The True Greenback* he wrote: "The war has resulted in the complete overthrow and utter extinction of chattel slavery on this continent, but it has not destroyed the principle of oppression and wrong. The old pro-slaver serpent, beaten in the South, crawled up North and put on anti-slavery clothes, and established his headquarters in Wall Street where...he now, through bank monopolies and non-taxed bonds, rules the nation more despotically than under the old regime.... I assert... that an investment of a million dollars under the National Banking Law, or in non-taxed government securities, will yield a larger net income to its owner than a like amount invested in land and slaves employed in raising cotton and sugar did in the South in the palmiest days of the oligarchy."[20]

A Time for Statesmanship

It is a crime against humanity in the literal sense of those words for millions of people to suffer due to the lack of something that can be manufactured in twenty-four hours or less.

That is the truth! Worse, we are all guilty of being accessories after the
fact. Over the generations we have allowed the private banks to connive,
manipulate, bribe and cajole us into allowing them to usurp our heritage—the right to create our own money. The process has been incremental so very few of us were aware of what was actually taking place.
Like the proverbial camel that first stuck its nose into the tent to get warm
and then wriggle its way in bit by bit until it took over the whole tent,
the banking fraternity has managed to acquire a virtual monopoly in the
exercise of one of our most fundamental of rights. The result has been that
it has become our master and we have become its slaves.

The banking fraternity was responsible for the crash of 1929! During
the Great Depression it exercised its powers ruthlessly in foreclosing on
farms and homes. Its rights always superseded any human rights. The
great recessions of 1981-82 and 1990-91, while not on a scale comparable
to the Great Depression, again put vast numbers of people off their farms
after many generations, bankrupted many promising businesses, and put
millions of people out of work and on the bread lines.

This latest example of the meltdown of 2007 and 2008 is but the latest
and most horrendous since the Great Depression. By right, the people of
the world should be launching a class action suit for trillions of dollars
against the banks responsible for the meltdown. Instead, due to the
economic pickle (dependency) in which we have found ourselves, we are
in the unhappy position of having to lend the banks money, and buy their
questionable assets, in order to restore their ability to continue the scam
which can only be properly described as legal grand larceny.

This latest disaster, because that is what it is, has caused indescribable
hardship in poor countries around the world, as well as unnecessary and
unacceptable hardship in the more advanced countries that have developed safety nets in response to the earlier cases of banking system failure.
So we absolutely must take back at least part of our inalienable right to
create money and start undoing some of the damage that has been done
to the human species worldwide.

‼ This will not be easy because, in an earlier book entitled *Surviving the Global Financial Crisis: The Economics of Hope for Generation X*, I said the next world war would be a war between the people and the banks. They will fight ferociously to safeguard their monopoly in the hope of keeping us all on a short leash in perpetuity. Should they succeed, they will do it to us again sometime down the road. That must never happen!

‼ The final straw was an article in the July 31, 2009 edition of the *New York Times* entitled "Bankers Reaped Lavish Bonuses During Bailouts." According to the article "Nine of the financial firms that were among the largest recipients of federal bailout money paid about 5,000 of their traders and bankers bonuses of more than $1 million apiece for 2008."[21] It is particularly galling that they take such a large slice of the financial pie when their contribution to the production of real wealth is so small.

‼ As I said at the beginning of the chapter the world needs a massive infusion of real money, and quickly, to speed the recovery. At the same time the system must be changed fundamentally, and forever. Already we see the monstrous situation where banks that have been bailed out with taxpayers' money have regained the strength to buy government bonds and reward taxpayers by charging interest. If that isn't the most blatant case of double-dipping possible I don't know the meaning of those words.

‼ To end this nonsense America needs a man who can stand tall in the shoes of Abraham Lincoln, print the money necessary to free the slaves—black and yellow, red and white—from the helplessness and hopelessness of an economic collapse due entirely to a faulty banking system long entrenched for the benefit of an elite minority.

The world will salute the man brave enough to confront the elitists and win the victory of economic freedom on behalf of all people everywhere!

The Challenge We Face

Every advance in history, from ending slavery and establishing democracy to ending formal colonialism, has had to conquer the notion at some point that it was impossible to do because it had never been done before.

Robert W. McChesney

Capitalism is a cult. It is devoted to the ideals of privatization over the common good, profit over social needs, and control by a small group of people who defy the public's will. The tenets of the cult lead to extremes rather than to compromise.

Paul Buchheit

National Banks are privileged to either increase or contract their circulation at will and, of course, grant or withhold loans as they see fit. As the banks have a national organization and can easily act together in withholding loans or extending them it follows that they can by united action in refusing to make loans, cause a stringency in the money market and in a single week or even in a single day cause a decline in all the products of the country. The tremendous possibilities of speculation involved in this control of the money of a country like the United States will be at once understood by all bankers.

**Bank Circular from Ikleheimer, Morton, and Vandergould
3 Wall Street, New York City, July 6, 1863**

Capitalism is the astounding belief that the most wickedest of men will do the most wickedest of things for the greatest good of everyone.

John Maynard Keynes

As long as Christ confined his teachings to the realm of morality and righteousness, He was undisturbed; it was not till He assailed the established economic system and "cast out" the profiteers and "overthrew the tables of the money changers," that He was doomed. The following day He was questioned, betrayed on the second, tried on the third and on the fourth crucified.

F. R. Burch

As little as the world may yet realize it, the driving of the "money changers" from the temple of man is the last great act which must precede the resurrection of humanity out of the tomb of materialism and into the greater light of "life more abundant". Only then will the true heart of humanity shine forth and the glorious future which awaits us begin to manifest.

Finley Eversole

6

ROADMAP TO A NEW ECONOMICS: BEYOND CAPITALISM AND SOCIALISM

Economics as if women, men, children, and their future actually mattered

Riane Eisler, PhD

When thinking of a new economics, let's not think of stocks, bonds, derivatives, or other financial instruments. Let's think of children. Let's ask what kind of economic policies and practices are good for children. Let's ask what's needed so all children are healthy, get a good education, and are prepared to live good lives. More fundamentally, let's ask what kind of economic system helps, or prevents, children from realizing their great potentials for consciousness, empathy, caring, and creativity— the capacities that make us fully human.

Once we address these questions, we can start designing the road map to the economic system we want and need: one that not only promotes human survival but full human development.

We must design such a system, not only because it is the right thing to do, but because it is the economically sensible thing to do, particularly as we move into the postindustrial knowledge-information era where the most important capital is what some economists call "high quality human capital." Indeed, Nobel prize-winning economist Amartya Sen concurs that the aim of sound economic policy must be human capacity development.

This I agree with. But I want to add that for a truly new economic system, we need a broader definition of human capacity development than a purely economic one. Which brings us back to the children and to our human capacities for caring, empathy, consciousness, and creativity.

When children are the starting point for a new economic paradigm, the first step is to go beyond the tired debate of capitalism versus socialism and all the other old isms. Both capitalist and socialist theory ignore a fundamental truth: the real wealth of nations—and the world—consists of the contributions of people and nature.

Adam Smith and Karl Marx ignored the vital importance of nature's life-sustaining activities. For them, nature exists to be exploited, period. As for the life-sustaining activities of caring for people starting in childhood, they considered this merely *reproductive* labor, and not part of their *productive* economic equation.

In other words, their focus was on the market—for Smith to extol it and for Marx to excoriate it. Neither included in his economic model the life-sustaining sectors without which there would be no market economy: the household economy, the natural economy, and the volunteer economy.

The first step toward building a truly new economics is a *full-spectrum* economic model that includes these sectors and gives real visibility and value to the most essential human work: the work of caring for people and for our natural environment.

The move to this comprehensive economic model in turn requires understanding something else ignored in conventional economic discussions. This is that economic systems don't arise in a vacuum: they are influenced by, and in turn influence, the larger cultural system in which they are embedded.

The Failures of Capitalism and Socialism

In the wake of the global economic meltdown that began in 2008 has
come an outcry against capitalism, especially against its latest stage of
neoliberalism with its massive deregulation of powerful moneyed interests.
Critics point not only to the havoc wreaked by deregulating banks and
other financial institutions but also to the gargantuan size and power of
multinational corporations, the widening gap between haves and have-
nots both between and within nations caused by the globalization of *free
markets*, and the decimation of our natural environment by irresponsible
business practices. Some argue that capitalism must be replaced with
socialism because historically capitalism has been unjust, violent, and
exploitive of both people and nature.

But this argument reflects yet another old way of thinking we must
re-examine and transcend: classifying societies in terms of conventional
categories such as socialist vs. capitalist, religious vs. secular, rightist vs.
leftist, Eastern vs. Western, industrial vs. postindustrial, and so forth.
None of these categories describe the totality of a society's beliefs and
institutions—from the family, education, and religion to politics and
economics. Since they only focus on particular aspects of a society, these
old categories are useless for understanding what a more equitable, sustainable, and caring system really looks like.

The social categories of *partnership system* and *domination system* reveal
the core configurations of societies that support two very different kinds
of relations. The domination system supports relations of top-down
rankings: man over man, man over woman, race over race, religion over
religion, nation over nation, and man over nature. The partnership system
supports the relations we want and urgently need at this critical juncture
of history: relations of mutual respect, accountability, and benefit.

If from this perspective we re-examine the critique of capitalism as
unjust, violent, and exploitive, we see that it is in reality a critique of the
structures, relationships, and values inherent in domination systems—be
they ancient or modern, Western or Eastern, feudal, monarchic, or totali-

tarian. Long before capitalist billionaires amassed huge fortunes, Egyptian pharaohs and Chinese emperors hoarded their nations' wealth. Indian potentates demanded tributes of silver and gold while lower castes lived in abject poverty. Middle Eastern warlords pillaged, plundered, and terrorized their people. European feudal lords killed their neighbors and oppressed their subjects.

A domination system of top-down rankings has also characterized the two large-scale modern applications of socialism: the former Soviet Union and China. Both turned out to be authoritarian and violent. And while they alleviated some economic disparities, they were hardly egalitarian.

In 1984, I visited the Soviet Union as one of two US delegates with Nordic Women for Peace, which marched on both Washington, DC and Moscow to enlist support for nuclear disarmament. While ordinary Russians lived in overcrowded quarters, often with two families crammed into a small flat, we were put up in a luxury hotel's royal suite with gilded furniture and a grand piano in its foyer. And while most Russians lacked even the most basic consumer goods, we and the Soviet officials hosting us drank champagne and ate caviar and other delicacies.

Nor did these regimes protect our environment any more than capitalist nations did. In fact, their record is just as abysmal—as evidenced by disasters such as Chernobyl and Lake Baikal in the USSR and the strip mining, air pollution, and other environmental calamities of China.

In short, neither the historic records of capitalism or socialism hold real promise for a new, more sustainable and equitable economic system. Since capitalism has gained ascendancy, its failures are more evident. And it is true that at this point we need to leave the destructive aspects of capitalism behind.

This does not mean we should discard everything from capitalism and socialism. We need both markets and central planning. But to effectively address our problems, we have to go much deeper, to matters that conventional economic analyses and theories ignore.

To construct a more equitable and sustainable economic system, we have to take into account the larger social contexts out of which economics derive—specifically, the degree to which these orient to either a partnership system or a domination system.

Economics, Societies, and Values

Economics is above all about *values*. So to change economics, we must also look at cultural beliefs about what is valuable or not valuable. And one of the distinctions between partnership and domination systems is what is and is not considered of economic value.

In both the Soviet Union and China, socialism was imposed in cultures that oriented closely to the configuration of the domination system. The core configuration of this system consists of top-down rankings in the family and state or tribe maintained by physical, psychological, and economic control; the ranking of the male half of humanity over the female half, and with this, the devaluation by both men and women of anything stereotypically considered feminine; and a high degree of culturally accepted abuse and violence—from child- and wife-beating to pogroms, terrorism, and/or chronic warfare.

A close orientation to this configuration can be found in societies that have little in common when looked at through the lenses of conventional social and economic categories such as communist or capitalist, Eastern or Western, secular or religious, and so forth. For example, viewed from the perspective of conventional categories, Hitler's Germany (a technologically advanced, Western, rightist society), the Taliban of Afghanistan and fundamentalist Iran (two Eastern religious societies), and the would-be regime of the rightist-fundamentalist alliance in the United States seem totally different. But all have the same basic dominator configuration.

Neoliberalism, for example, was part of a regression to a domination system. It can best be understood as a means of maintaining top-down control. Although neoliberal rhetoric is about freedom, what this really means is freedom for those in control to do what they wish, free from government regulation. Neoliberal policies were designed to reconsolidate wealth and power in the hands of those on top, and its mantra of *trickle-down economics* conditioned people to accept the *traditional* order where those on bottom have to content themselves with the crumbs dropping from their masters' opulent tables. The neoliberal promotion of *preemptive war* against Iraq also continued the traditional reliance on violence by dominant groups to impose their control. And the neoliberal's alliance with the so-called religious right reinforced still another core component of domination systems: a *traditional* male-headed family where the ranking of one half of humanity over the other half is presented as normal and moral, and children learn early that it's very painful to question orders no matter how unjust.

Moreover, with this ranking of male over female came another distinguishing feature of neoliberalism: its contempt for the *soft* or stereotypically *feminine*, as in their vitriolic attacks on what they called the *nanny state*. Accordingly, a key neoliberal requirement was that government programs designed to care for people, such as healthcare, childcare, and aid to poor families, be defunded both in the United States and through *structural adjustment policies* in the *developing* world. In short, neoliberalism was really dominator economics.

The partnership system has a very different configuration. Its core elements are a democratic and egalitarian structure in both the family and state or tribe; equal partnership between women and men; and a low degree of violence because it's not needed to maintain rigid rankings of domination.

No society is either a pure partnership or domination system. But the degree to which it is affects everything: from its guiding system of values to the construction of all its institutions—from the family, education, and religion to politics, and economics.

Economics and Caring

Nordic nations such as Sweden, Norway, and Finland are the contemporary countries that have moved most closely to the partnership side of the partnership-domination continuum. They have more equality in both the family and the state; a higher status of women (approximately 40 percent of their national legislators are female); and concerted efforts to leave behind traditions of violence (they pioneered the first peace studies and the first laws prohibiting physical discipline of children in families, and have a strong men's movement to disentangle *masculinity* from its equation with domination and violence).

Supported by their more partnership-oriented social configuration, these nations developed economic policies that combine positive elements of socialism and capitalism—but go beyond both to an economics in which caring for people and nature is a top priority. These nations have government-supported childcare, universal healthcare, stipends to help families care for children, elder care with dignity, and generous paid parental leave.

These more caring policies, in turn, made it possible for these nations to move from extreme poverty (famines in the early 20th century) to societies with a generally high standard of living for all. Today these nations not only rank high in the United Nations annual Human Development Reports in measures of quality of life; they are also in the top tiers of the World Economic Forum's annual Global Competitiveness reports.

Nordic countries don't have the huge gaps between haves and have-nots characteristic of dominator-oriented nations. While they're not ideal societies, they have succeeded in providing a generally good living standard for all. They have low poverty and crime rates and high longevity rates. Their children score high on international tests. And studies show that workers in these nations are more satisfied and happier than people in countries like the United States where GNP is higher.

Nordic nations also pioneered environmentally sound industrial approaches such as the Swedish *Natural Step*. Not only that, some of the first experiments in industrial democracy came from Sweden and Norway, as did studies showing that a more participatory structure where workers play a part in deciding such basic matters as how to organize tasks and what hours to work can be extremely effective.

Moreover, Nordic nations have a long history of business cooperatives, jointly owned and democratically controlled enterprises that have
included as one of their guiding principles concern for the community in
which they operate. Their cooperatives have also been heavily involved in
renewable energy projects. For example, many Swedish housing cooperatives are switching to alternative energy sources to help meet Sweden's goal
of oil-independence by 2015.

The Nordic nations' success has sometimes been attributed to their
relatively small and homogeneous populations. But in smaller, even more
homogeneous societies such as some oil-rich Middle-Eastern nations
where absolute conformity to one religious sect and one tribal or royal
head is demanded, we find large gaps between haves and have-nots and
other inequities characteristic of the domination system.

So we have to look at other factors to understand why the Nordic
nations moved out of poverty to develop a prosperous, more caring and
equitable economic system in a relatively short time. Once we do, we
see that what made these nations successful was that moving toward the
partnership configuration made it possible for them to become what they
sometimes call themselves: "caring societies."

The core components of this configuration are mutually supporting
and reinforcing. And one of its core components, in contrast to the
domination system, is equality between the male and female halves of
humanity. So women can, and do, occupy the highest political offices
in the Nordic world. And this higher status of Nordic women has had
important consequences for the values that guide Nordic policies.

In domination-oriented systems, men are socialized to distance themselves from women and anything stereotypically considered feminine. But
in partnership-oriented cultures, men can give more value to caring, caregiving, nonviolence, and other traits and activities deemed inappropriate
for men in dominator societies because they're associated with *inferior*
femininity. So, along with the higher status of Nordic women, many

men and women back more caring policies—policies that give value and visibility to the work of caring for people and nature.

With the ascendancy of neoliberalism and the globalization of unregulated capitalism, over the last decades of the 20th century Nordic nations too began to move somewhat toward more privatization. Nonetheless, they have been able to maintain most of their caring policies and hence their high rankings in international surveys of quality of life—ranging from infant mortality rates (where the US by contrast fell behind every industrialized nation and even poor ones like Andorra and Cuba) to human rights and environmental ratings.

The basic reason is that these nations continue their massive investment of resources in caring for people and nature. Indeed, these nations contribute a larger percentage of their gross domestic product than other developed nations to caring international programs: programs working for fair economic development, environmental protection, and human rights.

Making the Invisible Visible

All this takes us back to where we started: the need to restructure economic systems in ways that go beyond the old capitalism vs. socialism debate. To effectively address our growing economic, social, and environmental problems, we need a new economics. We need a system that leaves behind the dominator elements of capitalism and socialism, preserves their partnership elements, and is governed by economic structures, policies, and practices that give visibility and real value to caring for ourselves, others, and our Mother Earth.

A first step is recognizing that the exclusion of caring and caregiving from mainstream economic theory and practice has caused enormous, and unnecessary, human suffering. Indeed, the systemic devaluation of the activities that contribute the most to human welfare and development lies behind a kind of economic insanity that is reflected in, and perpetuated by, conventional indicators of productivity such as GDP (gross domestic product) and GNP (gross national product).

These measures of *economic health* actually place activities that *harm* life (like selling cigarettes and the health and funeral costs from smoking) on the plus side. Yet they give absolutely no value to the life-sustaining activities of both the household economy and the natural economy. So an old stand of trees is only included in GDP when it's cut down—whereas the fact that we need trees to breathe is ignored. Similarly, the caring and caregiving work performed in households is given no value whatsoever, and economists speak of parents who do not hold outside jobs as *economically inactive*—even though they often work from dawn to late at night.

Some people will say that this household work—without which there would be no workforce—cannot be quantified. But the reality is that it not only can be, but is being quantified. Thanks to the activism of women's organizations worldwide, many nations now have *satellite* accounts that quantify the value of the work of caring for people and keeping healthy home environments that have traditionally been considered *women's work*. For instance, a Swiss government report shows that if the unpaid *caring* household work were included, it would comprise 70 percent of the reported Swiss GDP! Yet none of this information is found in conventional economic treatises—be they capitalist or socialist.

Not only is the work of caregiving given little or no visibility (and hence economic value) in measurements of *productivity* when it's done in the home. The devaluation of this work is further reflected in the fact that in the market economy professions that involve caregiving are paid far less than those that do not.

So in the United States, people think nothing of paying plumbers, the people to whom we entrust our pipes, $50 to $100 per hour. But childcare workers, the people to whom we entrust our children, according to the US Department of Labor are paid an average of $10 an hour, with no benefits. And we demand that plumbers have some training, but not that all childcare workers have training.

This is not logical. It's pathological. But to understand, and change, this distorted system of values—and to effectively address seemingly intractable problems such as poverty and hunger—we again have to look at matters that are only visible once we recognize the configurations of the partnership system and the domination system.

Economic Policy, Poverty, and the Hidden System of Gendered Values

Many people, including politicians, think it's okay to have big government deficits to fund prisons, weapons, and wars—all stereotypically associated with men and *real masculinity*. But when it comes to funding caring for people—for child care, health care, early childhood education and other such expenditures—they say there's not enough money.

If we look back just a few hundred years, we see this devaluation of the *feminine* in stark relief. At that time, Western culture still looked like some of the most repressive societies do today. The norm was an authoritarian structure in both the family and the state. Wars and religious persecutions were chronic. And women and anything associated with them were so devalued that some theologians seriously doubted whether woman has an immortal soul.

There has obviously since then been movement toward the partnership system—albeit against enormous resistance and periodic regressions. But the gendered system of valuations we inherited is still extremely resistant to change—so much so that when men embrace traits considered *soft* or *feminine* they are tarred with derisive terms such as *effeminate* and *sissy*. Another symptom of this devaluation of women and anything associated with them is that discrimination against the female half of humanity is still generally seen as *just a women's issue*—to be addressed after more important problems are solved.

So while politicians often say their goal is ending, or at least decreasing, poverty and hunger, they hardly ever mention a staggering statistic: women represent 70 percent of those in our world who live in absolute poverty, which means starvation or near starvation. Also ignored in conventional discussions of poverty is that globally, women earn an average of two-thirds to three-fourths as much as men for the same work in the market economy and that most of the work women do in families—including child care, health and elder care, housekeeping, cooking, collecting firewood, drawing and carrying water, and subsistence farming—is not remunerated.

This is by no means to say that only women suffer economically from our domination heritage. Men also suffer, and this is particularly true of the men at the bottom of the domination pyramid. Yet women are still, as John Lennon wrote, "the niggers of the world."

Even in the rich United States, woman-headed families are the lowest tier of the economic hierarchy. In addition, according to the US Census Bureau, the poverty rate of women over sixty-five is almost twice that of men over sixty-five.

The fact that worldwide poverty and hunger disproportionately affect women is neither accidental nor inevitable. It is the direct result of political and economic systems that still have a strong dominator stamp. For example, that even in an affluent nation like the United States older women are so much more likely to live in poverty than older men is not only due to wage discrimination in the market economy; it is largely due to the fact that these women are, or were for much of their lives, care-givers—and this work is neither paid nor later rewarded through social security or pensions.

Again, this is not to say that economic inequities based on gender are more important than those based on class, race, or other factors. These inequalities are all inherent in domination systems. But a basic template for the division of humanity into *superiors* and *inferiors* that children in dominator families internalize early on is a male-superior/female-inferior model of our species. And this template can then be applied to ranking race over race, religion over religion, and so forth.

Economics through a New Lens

When societies move toward the partnership side of the partnership-domination continuum (and it's always a matter of degree), women and the *feminine* are not devalued. And this benefits not only women but men and children of both genders.

We have empirical evidence of this—although once again it is still ignored in conventional economic and social analyses.

The study "Women, Men, and the Global Quality of Life" conducted by the Center for Partnership Studies compared statistical measures from 89 nations on the status of women with measures of quality of life such as infant mortality, human rights ratings, and environmental ratings. We found that in significant respects the status of women can be a better predictor of quality of life than Gross Domestic Product (GDP).

Other studies also verify this relationship between the status of women and a society's general quality of life. The World Values Survey is the largest international survey of attitudes and how they correlate with economic development and political structure. For the first time, in 2000 this survey focused attention on attitudes about gender. Based on data from 65 societies representing 80 percent of the world's population, it found a strong relationship between support for gender equality and a society's level of political rights, civil liberties, and quality of life.

There are many reasons for a correlation of the status of women with a higher or lower quality of life for all. One, of course, is that women are half of humanity. But the reasons go much deeper, to the still largely unrecognized and undiscussed dynamics of domination systems. Here are just two examples:

Dominator Male Preference:

In some world regions the ranking of males over females is so ingrained that parents (both mothers and fathers) often not only deny girls access to education and give them less health care but also feed girls less than boys. These practices obviously have extremely adverse consequences for girls and women. But giving less food to girls and women also adversely impacts the development of boys.

It is well known that children of malnourished women are often born with poor health and below-par brain development. So this gender-based nutritional and healthcare discrimination robs *all* children, male or female, of their birthright: their potential for optimal development. This in turn affects children's and later adults' abilities to adapt to new conditions, tolerance of frustration, and propensity to use violence—which in their turn impede solutions to chronic hunger, poverty, and armed conflict, and with this, chances for a more humane, prosperous, and peaceful world for all.

Dominator Intra-household Resource Allocation:

The above is just one consequence of something else left out of conventional economic analyses: the patterns of intra-household resource allocation characteristic of domination systems.

There is empirical evidence across diverse cultures and income groups that women have a higher propensity than men to spend on goods that benefit children and enhance their capacities. How much higher this propensity is was shown by Duncan Thomas in his report "Intra-Household Resource Allocation." He found that in Brazil, $1 in the hands of a Brazilian woman has the same effect on child survival as $18 in the hands of a man. Similarly, Judith Bruce and Cynthia B. Lloyd found that in Guatemala an additional $11.40 per month in a mother's hands would achieve the same weight gain in a young child as an additional $166 earned by the father.

Of course, there are men even in rigidly male-dominated cultures who give primary importance to meeting their families' needs. Typically, however, men in these cultures are socialized to believe it's their prerogative to use their wages for nonfamily purposes, including drinking, smoking, and gambling, and that when women complain, they are nagging and controlling. As Dr. Anugerah Pekerti, chair of World Vision, Indonesia, notes, many fathers seem to have no problem putting their immediate desires above the survival needs of their children.

Yet traditional economic theories, capitalist and socialist, are based on the assumption that the male head of household will expend the resources he controls for the benefit of all family members. Not only that, development aid programs still allocate enormous funds to large-scale projects in which women have little or no say—and from which poor women and children derive few if any benefits. Even microlending or *village loan* programs that largely target women generally provide only minimal amounts—often at exorbitant interest rates. And the bulk of large bank loans go to businesses owned by male elites or to male *heads of household*.

Indeed, it is well known that much of the humanitarian government aid from developed to developing nations winds up in the hands of elites who deposit it in Swiss banks, build mansions, and otherwise line their pockets with it. Even when funds go directly to the poor, these too often end up in the pockets of men who use them for themselves rather than for their families. The effect of this on the general quality of life is not hard to see.

I want to again emphasize that what I'm reporting is not intended to blame men for our world's economic ills. We're dealing with a system in which both women and men are socialized to accept the notion that one half of our species is put on Earth to be served and the other half to serve, and that mothers, but not fathers, must subordinate their needs and desires to those of their families.

This economic double standard, and with it the subordination of the stereotypically feminine to the stereotypically masculine, not only hurts women, it hurts us all. It hurts men in a myriad ways—from the psychological pain of having to disassociate themselves from the *feminine*, including their own mothers, to the economic and political consequences of devaluing and subordinating women and anything associated with them.

Yet in the domination system there is no partnership alternative. There are only two perceived choices: you dominate or you're dominated.

Domination, Our Environment, and Technology

Even our environmental crisis is largely a symptom of the distorted values inherent in domination systems. We're often told that the scientific-industrial revolution that began to gain momentum in the 18th century is to blame for the havoc we're wreaking on our natural life-support systems. But the *conquest of nature* worldview goes back much further.

We've inherited an economics based on the premise that man is entitled to control both woman's and nature's life-sustaining activities. In Genesis 1:28, we read that man is to "subdue" the earth and have "dominion . . . over every living thing that moveth upon the earth.." In Genesis 3:16 we read that man is to rule over woman, who is to be his subordinate.

I want to emphasize that this notion of male control over nature and woman was *not* introduced in the Bible. We already find it millennia earlier. For example, the Babylonian *Enuma Elish* tells us that the war god Marduk created the world by dismembering the body of the Mother Goddess Tiamat. This myth superceded earlier myths about a Great Mother who created nature and humans as part of nature through her life-giving powers with a story where the violence of a male deity brings forth the world. It not only signals the beginning of a period when female deities, along with women and anything associated with them, were subordinated; it also signals a shift to a domination system in which masculinity is equated with domination and conquest—be it of women or of nature.

Domination systems have always despoiled nature. This goes way back to a time of massive climate change when prehistoric herders created scarcities that, in turn, fostered relations based on domination.

Using a large computerized database correlating information on climate change over thousands of years with archaeological data, geographer James DeMeo mapped these changes in the great desert belt he calls Saharasia (extending roughly from North Africa through the Middle East into central Asia). He found that what was once a garden of plenty gradually became a barren, cruel land. But climate change was only part of the story. When the land grew drier, farming became impossible so herding became the primary technology. And, as vegetation became ever sparser, human agency itself became a cause of desertification.

Trees were felled to open up more grazing land. As trees and plants disappeared, there was even less rain, as happens when forests are decimated to our day. As herds overgrazed more pastures, soils became even more barren.

In this ever harsher environment, habits of domination and exploitation became routine. Some groups began to fight others for access to grassland and water, and as men increasingly relied on brute force for a livelihood, women lost status and power. Gradually, raiding and killing spread from deserts to more fertile areas. The nomadic tribes of the wastelands began to encroach on the more fertile areas, first in occasional incursions and later as conquerors who imposed their rule.

As cultural historian Brian Griffiths notes, everything was now geared to conquest and control—of women, *inferior* men, and the land. And this conquest mentality—of nature, women, and other men—continues to our day.

Only at our level of technological development, this ethos of domination threatens not just one region but our entire ecosystem. Already in 2005, the U.N.-sponsored *Millennium Ecosystems Assessment* reported that over the past 50 years human activity has depleted 60 percent of the world's grasslands, forests, farmlands, rivers, and lakes. Emissions from cars and power plants are responsible for higher temperatures that are melting polar ice so fast that glaciers on Greenland are slipping into the ocean twice as fast as they were just five years ago. Polar bears are drowning. And scientists warn that rising seas may engulf coastal cities in just a few decades.

Almost every day another study details the insanity of our present course. But the plunder of nature, now aided by powerful technologies that cause terrible harm in a matter of years, or even months and days, continues unabated.

Yet none of this is inevitable. It can be changed.

Endings and Beginnings

The mix of high technology and an ethos of domination is not sustainable. Therein lies the danger. But the upheavals and dislocations of our time also offer an opportunity for a fundamental social and economic shift.

It's not only that the old economic models—both capitalist and socialist—came out of the industrial era and we're rapidly moving into the postindustrial era. The current economic meltdown and the meltdown of the icecaps are not isolated events: both are symptoms of the domination system reaching its logical end.

We must build economic structures, rules, policies, and practices that support caring for ourselves, others, and nature in *both* the market and nonmarket economic sectors. At the same time, we must accelerate the shift to partnership cultures and structures worldwide so that anything stereotypically considered *soft* or *feminine*—such as caring and caregiving—is no longer devalued.

Market rules—both locally and globally—must be changed to reward caring business practices and penalize uncaring ones. To make these changes we must show that this benefits not only people and nature but business.

Hundreds of studies show the cost-effectiveness of supporting and rewarding caring in the market economy. To give just one example, companies that regularly appear on the *Working Mothers* or Fortune 500 lists of the best companies to work for—that is, companies with good healthcare, childcare, flex time, parental leave, and other caring policies—have a higher return to investors.

On the national policy level, we already saw how in Nordic nations caring policies played a major role in their move from dire poverty to a high quality of life for all. Other examples abound, like the enormous financial benefits from investing in parenting education and assistance (as shown by the Healthy Babies, Healthy Children Canadian program) and investing in high quality early childhood education (as shown by follow up studies of the US Abecedarian Project).

There are many ways of funding this investment in our world's human infrastructure—which should be amortized over a period of years, as is done for investments in material infrastructure, such as machines and buildings. One source is by shifting funding from the heavy investment in weapons and wars characteristic of domination systems. Another is through the savings on the immense costs of *not* investing in caring and caregiving: the huge expenditures of taxpayer money on crime, courts, prisons, lost human potential, and environmental damage. Taxes on financial speculation and other harmful activities, such as making and selling junk food, can also fund investment in caring for people and our natural habitat.

Good care for children will ensure we have the flexible, innovative, and caring people needed for the postindustrial workforce. Both psychology and neuroscience show that whether these capacities develop largely hinges on the quality of care children receive.

Educating and remunerating people for caregiving will help close the *caring gap*—the worldwide lack of care for children, the elderly, and the sick and infirm. And it will eventually lead to a redefinition of *productivity* that gives visibility and value to what really makes us healthy and happy—and in the bargain leads to economic prosperity and ecological sustainability.

Economic systems are human creations. They can be changed. We must build a political movement to pressure policy makers to make these changes—or change the policy-makers. We must see to it that our world's governments make a massive investment in parenting education, paid parental leave, and innovative measures such as tax credits for caregivers and social security credit for the first years of caring for a child (as is already done in Norway).

We can all be leaders in building a social and economic system that really meets human needs—not only our material ones but also our emotional and spiritual ones. The sidebar below describes the six foundations needed for a truly new economic system. If we join together, we can build these foundations—and help create a future where all children can realize their great potentials for consciousness, empathy, caring, and creativity: the capacities that make us fully human.

Become a Certified Caring Economy Leader

The online Caring Economy Leadership Program prepares you to join a growing international chorus of voices speaking out for a saner, more practical economic system—one that acknowledges that the work of caring for people and the planet is the essential foundation of economic success.

"I thought it was a perfect training program."
Micki, Pennsylvania

About the Program

The Caring Economy Leadership Training program is a seminar-style, interactive online course. Participants engage deeply with the principles of Caring Economics, build meaningful connections with other grassroots leaders from around the world, acquire or expand valuable presentation and facilitation skills, and increase their confidence in speaking about the vital economic role of care and care giving.

After completing the program and earning the Certificate, program graduates create ongoing opportunities to share Caring Economics with others through presentations, study groups, teaching and writing, and they find ways to integrate the principles of Caring Economics into their work and their activism.

Changing the Conversation All Around the World

All Certified Caring Economy Conversation Leaders complete a practicum experience by leading a conversation about Caring Economics in their community or organization. The practicum gives students a supported opportunity to personalize their approach to the material and get feedback so that they leave the program feeling confident and fully prepared to continue their work as a Caring Economy Conversation Leader.

The Caring Economy Leadership Program Includes:

- Professionally facilitated online lecture and discussion sessions, including a special session devoted to live Q&A with Dr. Riane Eisler.

- Access to a scripted slide presentation that can be customized for local audiences

- A toolkit of facilitation guides and step-by-step activities to build audience engagement

- A supported practicum experience through which students have an opportunity to present Caring Economy messages in their own voices

- Opportunities to join the growing international community of Certified Conversation Leaders, with ongoing access to resources and invitations to special gatherings and events.

- Dedicated online resource center, The Conversation Leader Community Center (CLIC!) blog.

Choose from Two Formats

The Caring Economy Leadership Program is offered in a 9-week, seven session weekday format and a 5-week, 3 session weekend format. See the schedule and the information packet for details.

For more information, please go to **www.caringeconomy.org**

The New Age of Women's Creativity

Neither birth nor sex forms a limit to genius.
   Charlotte Brontë

Man cannot fulfill his destiny alone, he cannot redeem his race unaided.... The world has never yet seen a truly great and virtuous nation, because in the degradation of women the very foundations of life are poisoned at their source.
   Lucretia Mott

If the first woman God ever made was strong enough to turn the world upside down all alone, these women together ought to be able to turn it back, and get it right side up again! And now they is asking to do it, the men better let them.
   Sojourner Truth

We are told that "the hand that rocks the cradle rules the world." I have lived in this world for over fifty years, but find no evidence of rulership in the act of cradle-rocking. If it had been recorded that "the hand that rocks the cradle" bears the burdens of the world, the connection between truth and poetry would have been self-evident.
   Rebecca Latimer Felton

In a time lacking in truth and certainty and filled with anguish and despair, no woman should be shamefaced in attempting to give back to the world, through her work, a portion of its lost heart.
   Louise Bogan

The full and complete development of the world and the cause of peace require the maximum participation of women as well as men in all fields.

United Nations Declaration on Elimination of Discrimination Against Women

Women have always been the guardians of wisdom and humanity which makes them natural, but usually secret, rulers. The time has come for them to rule openly, but together with and not against men.

Charlotte Wolff

Love is our synthesis.... Only from the heart centre can stream, in reality, those lines of energy which link and bind together.

Djwhal Khul

The heart that breaks open can contain the whole universe.

Joanna Macy

THE ROLE OF BIOREGIONAL CURRENCIES IN REGIONAL REGENERATION

Bernard Lietaer, MEN, MBA

This essay will focus on complementary currencies as a necessary ingredient for the success of regional regeneration, particularly via the creation of tighter human networks.

We will start by looking at the bigger picture that explains why such regional regeneration has become so important today. Next, we will provide two case studies which explain the role of currency in this process, giving both a negative example and a positive one. We will conclude by giving a conceptual framework explaining the findings from the case studies.

The Big Picture

There is a general consensus that we are swiftly moving from the Industrial Age into a Post-Industrial Age. The historical precedent for a process of this scale is the momentous shift from the Agrarian to Industrial societies, which took place in Japan at the Meiji Restoration. Such shifts are not painless: look at what happened to the farmers when the agrarian age was ending; or to the landed gentry that saw their values, power and traditions fade into irrelevancy. Similarly, the over-hyped Dawn of the Information

Age or Knowledge Age has as its underbelly the End of the Industrial Age. It is just a question of perspective.

We have heard a lot—too much actually—about the positive aspects of the Information Age, but there is definitely no consensus on how to reduce the pain of the transition out of the old development model. The one certainty is that such a transition will imply a rapid and unpredictable change. In other words, we have entered *The Age of Uncertainty.*[1]

As long as the assumption that we were living in an environment that is both predictable and controllable was valid, it made sense to centralize information and leave the decisions to *experts*. The most coherent management structure in such circumstances is the traditional command and control hierarchical structure, which is now almost ubiquitous. This structure dates actually from the Roman legions, more than two millennia ago. By now, it has become so habitual that we may not even think that other ways of organizing ourselves are available and could be more effective. However, if breakdowns and crises continue to spread to more and more domains (such as government, medical care, environment, jobs, money, and the like), if the transition toward an information economy becomes indeed an Age of Uncertainty, then the time is ripe to reconsider the old assumptions. Under such circumstances, holding on the old expert driven hierarchical solutions through command and control structures will predictably kill the needed innovations.

Old Environment (Mature Industrial Age)	New Environment (Post-Industrial Age)
Predictability and Control Assumed	Structural Changes Assumed
Intelligence and Information Centralized	Intelligence and Information Distributed
Expert driven solutions	Many agents experimenting new patterns
Command and Control Structures	Complex Adaptive Structures

If this analysis of our on-going transition is valid, it should be understandable why universal solutions applicable across entire nations to solve issues like unemployment, social care, education, health and many others, are starting to fail all over the industrial world.

That is why the questions addressed in this essay on regional regeneration and network creation are so relevant today. The core thesis of this chapter is that *regional regeneration requires regional currencies* to be successful, the way plants need water. It is a necessary condition—although not a sufficient one—to obtain the desirable results.

Rather than start from theory, we will begin by using two real-life case studies. First a negative example: how regional sustainability has been destroyed by the purposeful introduction of a monopoly of a centralizing national currency. Next, a positive example will show how a regional currency has successfully strengthened a regional economy.

A Negative Example: How to destroy regional sustainability

Britain colonized the Gold Coast (today the coast of Ghana) during the 19th century. When in 1896 this colony was expanded towards the interior as the protectorate of Sierra Leone, it was faced with an interesting problem. At the time this hinterland was inhabited by hundreds of perfectly sustainable communities, each within its own traditional region. The Africans lived in a cashless society and earned no wages. They did trade amongst each other; however such trade occurred within closed circuits established by tradition among the different tribes.

But what is the point of having a colony if the people there don't need any of your goods? The question was how to break up those centuries-old regional patterns to create a demand for the goods the Britain was eager to export to their colony?

The solution was not to start a big advertising or marketing campaign. It wasn't even to try to prohibit the old exchange patterns or use military coercion to create new ones. It was a lot cheaper, simpler and more elegant than all that.

The British simply introduced a centralized *national currency* and in 1898 instituted a very modest *hut tax* (3 shillings per year) that was payable only in that currency. The official excuse for this tax was to pay for the protection provided to the tribes. That this was a transparent excuse is obvious by the fact that whites (who really needed the protection) remained tax-exempt until 1921.

But *presto!* Within a few years, all the traditional regional systems collapsed. Why?

Every *hut*—every extended family unit in the country—needed to find a way to earn some of this new currency to pay their hut tax. That could only be done by trading outside of the traditional framework in the new *national* system. That was sufficient to break up the sustainable regional patterns.

The lesson should be clear: trying to encourage local or regional development while simultaneously keeping a monopoly of a national currency is like treating an alcoholic with a prescription for gin.

It is also surprising that, while 19th century colonial administrators knew perfectly well how to destroy regional sustainability by imposing a national currency, our collective money blind spot is now so universal that even the policy makers, who talk about the desirability of more regional autonomy, completely overlook the monetary implications of their statements.

A Positive Example[2]

Our second example, operating now for nearly 40 years, comes from a modern city environment in Brazil. In 1971, Jaime Lerner became mayor of Curitiba, the capital of the southeastern state of Paraná, Brazil. He was an architect by profession. Quite typically for the region, the urban population had mushroomed from 120,000 people in 1942 to over a million when Jaime became mayor. By 1997, the population had reached 2.3 million. Again, quite typically, the majority of these people lived in *favelas*, the shanty towns made out of cardboard and corrugated metal.

One of Jaime Lerner's big headaches was garbage. The town garbage collection trucks could not get into the favelas because there were no streets wide enough for them. As a consequence, garbage just piled up, rodents got into it, and all kinds of diseases broke out. A mountain-sized mess.

Because Curitiba didn't have the money to apply *normal* solutions, such as bulldozing the area and building streets, Lerner's team invented another way. Large metallic bins were placed on the streets at the edge of the favelas. The bins had big labels on them which said: glass, paper, plastics, biodegradable material, and so on. Anyone who brought down a garbage bag full of presorted garbage was given a bus token. A school-based garbage collection program also supplied the poorer students with notebooks. Soon the neighborhoods were picked clean by tens of thousands of kids, who learned quickly to distinguish between different types of plastic. The parents used the tokens to take the bus downtown, where the jobs are.

What Jaime Lerner did, from my perspective, is invent Curitiba money. His bus tokens are a form of local complementary currency. His program, "Garbage which is Not Garbage," might as well have been baptized, "Garbage which is Your Money." Today, seventy percent of all Curitiba households participate in this process. The sixty-two poorer neighborhoods alone exchanged 11,000 tons of garbage for nearly a million bus tokens and 1,200 tons of food. In the past three years, more than 100 schools have traded 200 tons of garbage for 1.9 million notebooks. The paper recycling component alone saves the equivalent of 1,200 trees each day.

What began as a garbage and public health problem became a way to solve public transportation and unemployment difficulties in a uniquely innovative way. The secret is not that this city or population has something unique, but that an integrated systems approach used *complementary currencies* to tackle the problems at hand.

The impact of these complementary currency systems is identifiable in conventional economic terms. The average Curitibano makes about 3.3 times the country's minimum salary, but his real income total is at least 30% higher than that, about 5 times the minimum salary. This 30% difference in income is derived directly from non-traditional monetary forms, such as the food for garbage program. Curitiba has by far the most developed social programs in Brazil, and one of the country's most vibrant cultural and educational programs; yet its tax rate is no higher than that of the rest of the country.

Even at the macroeconomic level there are clear indications that something unusual is going on in Curitiba. The Domestic Product of Curitiba increased between 1975 and 1995 by around 75% over that of the entire state of Paraná and 48% more than Brazil as a whole. Such difference in growth rate has continued in the recent past. Between 1993 and 1995, Curitiba's Domestic Product grew 41% faster than the state of Paraná and 70% faster than Brazil's.[3]

Curitiba is a practical case study, with 40 years of experience showing that using *both* the traditional national currency and well-designed local complementary currencies is beneficial to everybody, including people who are focused exclusively on the traditional economy denominated in national currencies. It enabled one Third World city to join First World living standards in one generation's time. In 1992, Curitiba was awarded the title of "the most ecological city in the world" by the United Nations.

Note that Lerner's team did not start off with the idea to create a complementary currency. *What happened instead is that they used an* integrated systems *analysis for all the major issues at hand, and spontaneously ended up creating a complementary currency to solve them.* Jaime Lerner was elected mayor of Curitiba three times by a landslide, then Governor of the State of Paraná twice.

Relevant Lessons

The Ghana case study shows that when a centralizing currency is given a monopoly as the medium of exchange, particularly via a legally enforced tax obligation, it will produce a powerful countercurrent to any attempt at regional autonomy. The Curitiba case study reveals that a dual currency approach—the conventional national currency combined with a local or regional one—helps substantially in creating a balance between the regional and the broader economic systems. The main lesson we take from both case studies can be summarized as follows: a regional currency is a *necessary but not a sufficient* condition for a sustainable and vibrant regional development to occur. We obviously do not claim that dual currency systems are a panacea to solve all problems—economic, social, cultural, environmental, or otherwise. But the point should be clear that dual currencies *can* make a big difference.

Other Historical Precedents

The idea of introducing regional currencies to foster regional development may sound revolutionary to many people. But in fact, it is a very old one that happens to have fallen out of fashion only over the past two centuries. Recent research[4] has revealed that—contrary to a widespread prejudice—the history of regional currencies has not only been long, but also one mostly of success. The gradual generalization of the gold standard during the 19th century and the concomitant imposition of national currency monopolies suppressed these smaller scale regional systems.

The "Money Blind Spot"

Our national currency system is considered to be *value neutral*—that is, it is not supposed to affect the kind of transactions that are performed, or the relationships among the people using it. This hypothesis has been embedded into economic theory since the days of Adam Smith, and has remained by and large unchallenged until today. Indeed, it doesn't matter whether one uses Euros, dollars or Yen in one's transactions: they are all currencies of an identical nature, created as bank-debt bearing interest. More important still, economists are in agreement that bank-debt currencies derive their value from scarcity relative to their usefulness.[5] In other words, for modern money to function, scarcity has to be artificially and systematically maintained to avoid inflation.

The hypothesis of value neutrality is simply not valid when one compares behaviors or relationships among users of currencies that are created by rules different from those underlying today's conventional money system. There seems to be a general blind spot on this issue, even though several studies have already proven it with facts. For instance, significantly different behaviors have been detected in commercial exchanges using barter currencies or loyalty currencies as opposed to conventional money.[6] Even stronger are the differences in relationships when people use social purpose local currencies instead of national money. For instance, Japanese elderly using the services paid in an elderly care currency *Fureai Kippu*[7] (caring relationships tickets) as opposed to professionals paid in Yen tend to prefer services provided by people paid in the complementary currency *because the relationships are different*. Similarly, studies of German Local Exchange Systems (LETS)[8] systems reveal that paying *friends* for services rendered with LETS units is significantly more acceptable than paying them with national currency.

Here we will focus on the difference that the use of national *vs.* regional currencies makes in terms of regional autonomy and regeneration.

Defining our Terminology

To better explain the role of regional currencies, we should start by defining our terms.

While economic theory always defines money in terms of what it *does* (its functions as a standard of value, medium of exchange, store of value), it never defines what it actually *is*. We define *money as an agreement* within a community to use something as a medium of exchange. The community can be the national one (as is the case with conventional national currencies), a global one (as is the case with the dollar since the Bretton Woods agreement in 1945), a local one (as is the case for Curitiba's bus tokens), or a regional one.

Complementary currencies are agreements within a community to accept something other than legal tender as a means of payment. Their role is to link unmet needs with otherwise unused resources. There has recently been an explosion of the number of such systems all over the world, as illustrated in Figure 1.

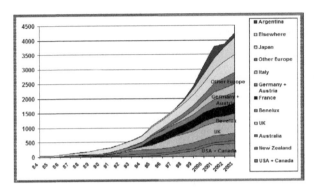

Figure 1: Number of complementary currency systems in a dozen countries (1984-2004)

Full details are available elsewhere about the variety of the purposes and technicalities of these systems,[9] and about the psychological and social implications of such currencies.[10]

We will define a *region* as a geographical area with which people tend to identify themselves, because of history or other reasons. In this sense, the physical size of a region is less important than the potential density of human interactions, their *pride of belonging*.

A *bioregion* is created by the natural organization of biological life on the basis of geographical features such as watersheds, climate, and natural physical boundaries (such as rivers, mountains, valleys, forests). This concept has been supported over the past decades by a substantial body of literature.

A *metropolitan bioregion* integrates two key systems—a bioregion and a city—that should be of interest to integral planners.[11] Jane Jacobs[12] has argued convincingly that the city region is the basic unit of human economic activity, as it is the unit within which natural resources and the human divisions of labor combine to address a full range of human needs.

From the perspective of planners, it makes sense to view their effective integration as a primary goal for planning a sustainable world. Often, the bioregion and the city region are overlapping entities anyway.

The Metropolitan Bioregion as Planning Unit for Regeneration

The proposal here is to use a *metropolitan bioregion as the ideal unit for designing regional regeneration* strategies, and to design a complementary bioregional currency specifically for such units. Specifically, a *bioregional currency would be a complementary currency that aims at bringing together unmet needs with unused resources, those that are produced in the region both by humans and by nature.*

In practice, this would mean systems that are designed to operate on a scale larger than the purely local one, as tends to be the case for LETS, Time Dollars, Fureai Kippu or other smaller scale systems—those typically included in Figure 1. Local systems do not tend to scale up beyond a thousand people. For example, one of the largest LETS worldwide—the Blue Mountains LETS near Sydney, Australia—counts about 1,000 active members. At the other end of the spectrum, as on a national level, millions or perhaps hundreds of millions of people are typically involved. A *regional currency system* should be able to operate on a scale or at a level between these two extremes: serving 10,000 up to an order of magnitude of one million people for example. Over forty of such systems are in operation in Germany under the name of *regiogeld*.

All regional economies are currently trying to produce for international trade, and with our proposal they would still want to do so. Everyone wants to be part of the globalizing economy. It is true now, as it was in the time of Adam Smith that being a net exporter is a strategy for achieving faster economic growth. However, it is also true that becoming a net exporter is an extremely competitive undertaking. This prescription ignores the logical requirement that a positive balance of trade by one country or area requires a trade deficit in some other place, and thus is an inherently unstable arrangement.

¦¦ A community that imports more than it exports will tend to have a liquidity problem, especially if it is also sending its savings to financial centers not investing in the community that is the source of the savings/capital. This problem is particularly acute in rural communities and inner city poverty zones, or during periods of recession or unemployment in a region. Most income is rapidly spent on imported commodities and goods. Jane Jacobs suggests that tying all of the city regions in a country to a national macroeconomic policy is like connecting the respiratory systems of all of the spectators and players at a tennis tournament to one central nervous system. The result would require all players and spectators, whether resting, sitting, or actively playing, to function at one average level of respiratory activity.

Conceptual Framework

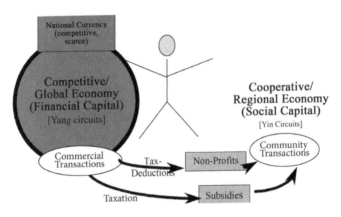

Figure 2: Global Economy and Regional Economy under a Monopoly of National Currency

Figure 2 depicts the flow of currency in the case of a monopoly of a central national currency. On one side is the global competitive economy, the one where commercial transactions are facilitated through the national currency, often in a relatively impersonal manner. It is also the space where financial capital is allocated and created. In traditional Chinese philosophical terms we could call it the space where *Yang* circuits are active.

On the other side is the space where most of the *Yin* activities are expressed. It is the space where the exchanges tend to be more personal, with people one knows. It is where cooperation and the social sector—education, health care, elderly care, and the like—build up social capital. Finally, it is the space where the resurgence of the regional economy through tighter human networks would blossom with the biggest impact.

The social sector by nature needs to be financially supported by the rest of society. When a monopoly of the national currency is compulsory, and the regional economy isn't a net exporter to the competitive economy, the only way money becomes available to the regional/cooperative economy is through government subsidies (paid by taxes) and transfers via non-profit organizations (funded through tax deductions). Taxes have never been popular. The net result is that the Yin space is always starved of the medium of exchange. This is particularly a problem for regional economies where the social sector is almost entirely based in regional economies.

As a result, the community transactions in the economy are always suffering from insufficient liquidity to actualize all of the potential transactions that could meet human needs with available resources. Thus the regional economy suffers from chronic underutilization of its productive capacity. Complementary regional currencies can be designed to assure adequate liquidity in the regional economy. They can also be designed to make important contributions to social services and environmental sustainability. Finally, today's cheap decentralized computing also makes such parallel payment approaches very cost-effective.

A number of groups are already addressing the problem of scarcity in medium of exchange by agreeing to use a complementary currency created for specific purposes. What complementary currency systems do is foster the regional economy with its own cooperative currency, created in sufficiency. This idea is graphically presented in Figure 3.

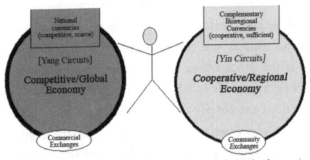

· Complementary Currencies are *complementary* to (not replacing) national currencies
· Complementary Currencies create ADDITIONAL Wealth, Work, and a safety net
below official system

Figure 3: Global Economy and Regional Economy when National and Complementary Currencies are both Operational

In short, conventional money is still needed in both circuits, but a scarcity of the national currency will have less negative consequences when it is complemented with a bioregional currency.

Conclusion

We have analyzed, in light of the transition to a post-industrial society, why it has become critically important to regenerate regional economies and the human networks that support them. Our thesis is that in order to achieve that aim, regional currencies will be needed. The ideal unit for planning such systems is the metropolitan bioregion, a natural unit that incorporates a city and its ecological hinterland. Furthermore, we have explored the importance of liquidity in assuring the health of regional economies.

By focusing on metropolitan bioregions, together with the possibilities for designing complementary currency systems, we've seen new horizons opening up for solving the socio-economic and ecological problems brought in a globalizing economy.

Whom Shall We Trust to Create Our Money?

The study of money, above all other fields in economics, is the one in which complexity is used to disguise truth or to evade truth, not to reveal it. The process by which banks create money is so simple the mind is repelled.

John Kenneth Galbraith, 1975

History records that the money changers had used every form of abuse, intrigue, deceit, and violent means possible to maintain their control over governments by controlling money and its issuance.

James Madison

Men rise from one ambition to another; first they seek to secure themselves against attack, and then they attack others....

The fear to lose stirs the same passions in men as the desire to gain, as men do not believe themselves sure of what they already possess except by acquiring still more; and, moreover, these new acquisitions are so many means of strength and power for abuse.

Niccolò Machiavelli

Neoliberalism is the defining political economic paradigm of our time—it refers to the politics and processes whereby a relative handful of private interests are permitted to control as much as possible of social life in order to maximize their personal profit.... These parties and the policies they enact represent the immediate interests of extremely wealthy investors and less than one thousand large corporations.... At their most eloquent, proponents of neoliberalism sound as if they were doing poor people, the environment, and everybody else a tremendous service as they enact policies on behalf of the wealthy few.

Robert W. McChesney

If Congress has the right under the Constitution to issue paper money, it was given them to use themselves, not to be delegated to individuals or corporations.

Andrew Jackson

The Government should create, issue, and circulate all the currency and credits needed to satisfy the spending power of the Government and the buying power of consumers. By the adaptation of this principle, the taxpayers will be saved immense sums of interest. Money will cease to be a master and become the servant of humanity.

Abraham Lincoln

Issue of currency should be lodged with the government and be protected from domination by Wall Street. We are opposed to... provisions [which] would place our currency and credit system in private hands.

Theodore Roosevelt

The real truth of the matter is, as you and I know, that a financial element in the large centers has owned the government ever since the days of Andrew Jackson.

Franklin D. Roosevelt, 1933

When a government is dependent upon bankers for money, they and not the leaders of the government control the situation, since the hand that gives is above the hand that takes.... Money has no motherland; financiers are without patriotism and without decency; their sole object is gain.

Napoleon Bonaparte, 1815

The bank hath benefit of interest on all monies which it creates out of nothing.

William Paterson, founder of the Bank Of England in 1694

Money is a new form of slavery, and distinguishable from the old simply by the fact that it is impersonal—that there is no human relation between master and slave.

Leo Tolstoy

8

THE POSSIBILITY OF A PLURALIST COMMONWEALTH AND A COMMUNITY-SUSTAINING ECONOMY

If you don't like capitalism and you don't like socialism… what do you want?

Gar Alperovitz, PhD, and Steve Dubb, PhD

It is increasingly obvious that the United States faces systemic problems. When protestors occupy Wall Street and Ben Bernacke, the Chairman of the Federal Reserve, not only responds to the protestors, but actually casts the actions of the protestors in a favorable light, it is clear these are not ordinary times. Testifying to the Joint Economic Committee of Congress, Bernanke observed that the protestors "blame, with some justification, the problems in the financial sector for getting us into this mess, and they're dissatisfied with the policy response here in Washington. And at some level, I can't blame them."[1]

Income and wealth disparities have become severe and corrosive of democratic possibilities. The economy is in tatters. Unemployment, poverty, and ecological decay deepen day by day. Corporate power now dominates decision-making through lobbying, uncontrolled political contributions, and political advertising. The planet itself is threatened by global warming. The lives of millions are compromised by economic and social pain. Our communities are in decay.

Is there any way forward?

For the most part, serious scholars and activists have addressed the possibility of progressive change in capitalist systems from one of two perspectives: The *reform* tradition assumes that corporate institutions remain central to the design and structure of the system and that *politics* in support of various *policies* (for example, taxation, spending, incentives, regulation) will contain, modify and control the inherent dynamic of a corporate dominated system. Liberalism in the United States and social democracy in many countries are representative of this tradition. The *revolutionary* tradition assumes that change can come about only if the major corporate institutions are largely eliminated or transcended, usually but not always by violence—often precipitated by a crisis collapse of the system, leading to one or another form of revolution.

But what happens if a system neither *reforms* nor collapses in *crisis?*

This is essentially where the United States finds itself today. Put slightly differently, we believe the United States is entering a potentially decades-long period characterized by a situational logic of this kind. In a context of *neither reform nor crisis collapse* very interesting strategic possibilities may sometimes be viable. Such possibilities are best understood as neither *reforms* (policies to modify and control, but not transcend corporate institutions) nor *revolution* (the overthrowing of corporate institutions), but rather a longer term process that is best described as an *evolutionary recon-struction*—that is, systemic institutional transformation of the political economy that unfolds over time.

Like reform, evolutionary reconstruction involves step-by-step nonviolent change. But like revolution, evolutionary reconstruction changes the basic institutions of ownership of the economy, so that the broad public, rather than a narrow band of individuals (the "one percent"), increasingly owns more and more of the nation's productive assets.

• We suggest that such processes of evolutionary reconstruction are becoming observable in many parts of the current American system, and that they are likely to become of continuing—and potentially system-altering—force over time.

One area where this logic can be seen at work is in the financial industry. At the height of the financial crisis in early 2009, for example, some kind of nationalization of the banks seemed possible. It was a moment, President Obama told banking CEOs, when his administration was "the only thing between you and the pitchforks."[2] The President chose to opt for a soft bailout engineered by Treasury Secretary Timothy Geithner and White House Economic Adviser Lawrence Summers; but that was not the only choice available: Franklin Roosevelt attacked the "economic royalists"[3] and built and mobilized his political base. Obama entered office with an already organized base and largely ignored it.

When the next financial crisis occurs—and in the opinion of many experts, it will, perhaps soon—a different political resolution with more systemic changing consequences may well be possible. (If not the next crisis, the one after that, or the one beyond…) One option has already been put on the table. In 2010, thirty-three Senators voted to break up large Wall Street investment banks that were *too big to fail*. Such a policy would not only reduce financial vulnerability; it would alter the structure of institutional power.

• Nor is an effort to break up banks, even if successful, likely to be the end of the process. The modern history of the financial industry—to say nothing of anti-trust strategies in general—suggests that the big banks, even if broken up, will ultimately regroup and re-concentrate as *the big fish eat the little fish* and restore their domination of the system. So what can be done when *breaking them up* fails?

The potentially explosive power of public anger at financial institutions was evidenced in May 2010 when the Senate voted by a stunning

96-0 margin to audit the Federal Reserve's lending (a provision included ultimately in the Dodd-Frank legislation—something that had never been done before.[4,5] Traditional reforms have aimed at improved regulation, higher reserve requirements, and the channeling of credit to key sectors. But future crises may bring into play a spectrum of sophisticated proposals for more radical change offered by figures on both the right and the left. For instance, a Limited Purpose Banking strategy put forward by conservative economist Lawrence Kolticoff would impose 100% reserve requirements on banks.[6] Since banks typically provide loans in amounts many times their reserves, this would transform them into modest institutions with little or no capacity to finance speculation. It would also nationalize the creation of all new money as Federal authorities, rather than bankers, directly control system-wide financial flows.

On the left, the economist Fred Moseley has proposed that for banks deemed too big to fail "permanent nationalization with bonds-to-stocks swaps for bondholders is the most equitable solution…." Nationally owned banks, he argues, would provide a basis for "a more stable and public-oriented banking system in the future."[7] Most striking is the argument of Willem Buiter, the Chief Economist of Citigroup no less, that if the public underwrites the costs of bailouts, "banks should be in public ownership…."[8] In fact, had the taxpayer funds used to bail out major financial institutions in 2007-2010 been provided on condition that voting stock be issued in return for the investment, one or more major banks would, in fact, have come essentially public banks.[9] Nor is this so far from current political tradition as many think. Unknown to most, there have been a large number of small and medium-sized public banking institutions for some time now. They have financed small businesses, renewable energy, co-ops, housing, infrastructure and other specifically targeted areas. There are also 7,500 community-based credit unions. Further precedents for public banking range from Small Business Administration loans to the activities of the US-dominated World Bank. In fact, the federal government already operates 140 banks and quasi-banks that provide loans and loan guarantees for an extraordinary range of domestic and international economic activities. Through its various farm, housing, electricity, cooperative and other loans, the Department of Agriculture alone operates the equivalent of the seventh largest bank in America.[10] And just recently, under pressure from American business, Congress re-authorized the Export-Import Bank to support US trading interests.[11]

The economic crisis has also produced wide-spread interest in the Bank of North Dakota,[12] a highly successful state-owned bank founded in 1919 when the state was governed by legislators belonging to the left-populist Nonpartisan League. Between 1996 and 2008, the bank returned $340 million in profits to the state.[13] The Bank enjoys broad support in the business community, as well as among progressive activists. Legislative proposals to establish banks patterned in whole or in part on the North Dakota model have been put forward by activists and legislators in Oregon, Massachusetts, Illinois, Maryland, Washington, Minnesota, Florida, Vermont, Idaho, Hawaii, Louisiana, and Virginia. Campaigns to create similar institutions have been launched in Maine and California. In Oregon, with strong support from a coalition of farmers, small business owners, and community bankers, and backed by State Treasurer Ted Wheeler, a variation on the theme—"a virtual state bank"[14] (one that has no storefronts but channels state-backed capital to support other banks) may be formed in the near future. How far the various strategies may develop is likely to depend on the intensity of future financial crises, the degree of social and economic pain and political anger in general, and the capacity of a new politics to focus citizen anger in support of major institutional reconstruction and democratization.

That paradoxically a long era of social and economic austerity and failing reform might open the way to more populist or radical *evolutionary reconstructive* institutional change—including various forms of public ownership—is also suggested by emerging developments in health care. Here the next stage of change is already underway. At first, it is likely to be harmful, characterized by Republican efforts to cut back the mostly unrealized benefits of the Affordable Care Act, passed in 2010. The first stages, however, are not likely to be the last. Polls show overwhelming distrust of and deep hostility toward insurance companies. We can also expect growing public anger to be fueled by media accounts of stories like that of Gambino Olvera, an uninsured paraplegic, who was dumped on skid row in nothing more than a soiled hospital gown by Hollywood Presbyterian Hospital in 2007.[15]

Cost pressures are also building up—and, critically, in ways that will continue to undermine US corporations facing global competitors, forcing them to seek new solutions. The federal Center for Medicare and Medicaid Services projects health care costs to rise from the 2010 level of 17.5 percent of GDP to 19.6 percent in 2019.[16] It has long been clear that the central question is to what extent, and at what pace, cost pressures ultimately force development of some form of single-payer system—the only serious way to deal with the underlying problem.

A new national solution is ultimately likely to come about either in response to a burst of pain-driven public outrage, or more slowly through a state by state build up to a national system. Massachusetts, of course, already has a near universal plan, with 99.8 percent of children covered and 98.1 percent of adults.[17] In Hawaii, health coverage (provided mostly by non-profit insurers) reaches 91.8 percent of adults in large part because of a 1970s law mandating low cost insurance for anyone working twenty hours a week.[18] In Vermont, Governor Peter Shumlin signed legislation in May 2011 creating Green Mountain Care, a broad effort that would ultimately allow state residents to move into a publicly funded insurance pool—in essence a form of single-payer insurance. Universal coverage, dependent on a federal waiver, would begin in 2017 and possibly as early as 2014.[19] In Connecticut, legislation approved in June 2011 created a SustiNet Health Care Cabinet directed to produce a business plan for a non-profit public health insurance program by 2012 with the goal of offering such a plan beginning in 2014.[20] In all, nearly 20 states will soon consider bills to create one or another form of universal health care.

One can also observe a developing institution-changing dynamic in the central neighborhoods of some of the nation's larger cities, places that have consistently suffered high levels of unemployment and underemployment, with poverty most commonly above 25 percent. In such neighborhoods democratizing development has also gone forward, again paradoxically, precisely because traditional policies—in this case involving large expenditures for jobs, housing and other necessities—have been politically impossible. *Social enterprises* that undertake businesses in order to support specific social missions now increasingly comprise what is sometimes called a *fourth sector* (different from the government, business, and non-profit sectors). Roughly 4,500 not-for-profit community development corporations are largely devoted to housing development. There are now also more than 10,000 businesses owned in whole or part by their employees; nearly three million more individuals are involved in these enterprises than are members of private sector unions. Another 130 million Americans are members of various urban, agricultural, and credit union cooperatives. In many cities, important new *land trust* developments are underway using an institutional form of nonprofit or municipal ownership that develops and maintains low- and moderate-income housing.[21]

Although the financially stressed popular press covers very little of this, the various institutional efforts have also begun to develop innovative strategies that suggest broader possibilities for change. In Cleveland, Ohio, an integrated group of worker-owned companies has developed, supported in part by the purchasing power of large hospitals and universities.[22] The cooperatives include a solar installation and weatherization company, an industrial scale (and ecologically advanced) laundry, and soon a greenhouse capable of producing over three million heads of lettuce a year. The Cleveland effort, which is partly modeled on the 85,000-person Mondragón cooperative network, based in the Basque region of Spain, is on track to create new businesses, year by year, as time goes on. However, its goal is not simply worker ownership, but the democratization of wealth and community building in general in the low-income

Greater University Circle area of what was once a thriving industrial city. Linked by a community-serving non-profit corporation and a revolving fund, the companies cannot be sold outside the network; they also return ten percent of profits to help develop additional worker-owned firms in the area.

A critical element of the strategy, moreover, points to what is essentially a quasi-public sector planning model: Hospitals and universities in the area currently spend $3 billion on goods and services a year—none, until recently, from the immediately surrounding neighborhood. The *Cleveland model* is supported in part by decisions of these substantially publicly financed institutions to allocate part of their procurement to the worker-co-ops in support of a larger community-building agenda. The taxpayer funds that support programs of this kind do double duty by helping, too, to support the broader community through the new institutional arrangements. The same, of course, is true for a range of municipal, state and other federal policies available to local businesses, including employee-owned firms.

Numerous other cities are now exploring efforts of this kind (including Atlanta, Pittsburgh, Amarillo, Texas, and the metropolitan Washington, D.C. area.) Related institutional work is now underway, too, through the leadership of the United Steelworks, a union that has put forward new proposals for a co-op-union model of ownership.[23]

Another innovative enterprise is Market Creek Plaza in San Diego. A project of the Jacobs Center for Neighborhood Innovation, Market Creek Plaza is a mixed use commercial-retail-residential development, anchored by a Food 4 Less supermarket. The project was conceived, planned, and developed by teams of community members working with the Jacobs Center. Together they assembled a diverse package of public and private funding for the $23 million Phase I project (ultimately, the total value of the project, which involves master planning and redevelopment of a total of 52 acres of land, is estimated to reach $700 million in public and private investment).[24]

Market Creek Plaza is also a green project, and aims to expand to become a transit-oriented village with 800 units of affordable housing and extensive facilities for nonprofit organizations. The project has restored 1,400 linear feet of wetlands, while generating 200 permanent jobs (70 percent filled by local residents), provided 415 residents with a 40-per-cent ownership stake in the project, and generated $42 million in economic activity (in 2008).[25]

Yet another arena of institutional growth involves municipal development. By maintaining direct ownership of areas surrounding transit station exits, public agencies in Washington, D.C., Atlanta and other cities earn millions capturing the increased land values their transit investments create. The town of Riverview, Michigan has been a national leader in trapping methane from its landfills and using it to fuel electricity generation, thereby providing both revenues and jobs. There are roughly 500 similar projects nationwide.[26] Many cities have established municipally owned hotels. There are also nearly 2,000 publicly owned utilities that provide power (and, increasingly, broadband services) to more than 45 million Americans, in the process generating $50 billion in annual revenue. Significant public institutions are also common at the state level. CalPERS, California's public pension authority helps finance local community development needs. In Alaska, state oil revenues provide each citizen with dividends from public investment strategies as a matter of right; in Alabama, public pension investing has long focused on state economic development (including employee owned firms).*

* **AU NOTE:** For further information on various community building efforts, see www.community-wealth.org. See also Democracy Collaborative of the University of Maryland, Building Wealth: The New Asset-Based Approach to Solving Social and Economic Problems, Washington, DC: The Aspen Institute, 2005.

Although such local and state ownership is surprisingly widespread, it can also be vulnerable to challenge. The fiscal crisis—and conservative resistance to raising taxes—has led some mayors and governors to sell off public assets. In Indiana, Governor Mitch Daniels sold the Indiana Toll Road to Spanish and Australian investors.[27] In Chicago, recently retired Mayor Richard Daley privatized parking meters and toll collection on the Chicago Skyway, and even proposed selling off recycling collection, equipment maintenance, and the annual *Taste of Chicago* festival.[28]

How far continuing financial and political pressure may lead other officials to attempt to secure revenues by selling off public assets is an open question. On the other hand, public resistance to such strategies, although less widely publicized, has been surprisingly strong in many areas. Toll road sales have been held up in Pennsylvania[29] and New Jersey[30], and newly elected Chicago Mayor Rahm Emanuel recently rejected an attempt to privatize Midway Airport as previously attempted by Daley.[31] An effort to transfer city-owned parking garages to private ownership in Los Angeles also failed when residents and business leaders realized parking rates would spike even if the deal went through.[32]

At the heart of the paradoxical strategies of development in these varied and increasingly widespread illustrations is one or another form of democratized ownership—a form at the national, state, municipal and neighborhood level that stands in contrast to traditional ideas that only corporations or private businesses can own and manage productive wealth.

Nor should it be forgotten that at the height of the recent financial and economic crisis two of the nation's largest manufacturing corporations—General Motors and Chrysler—were nationalized because the alternative was all but certain to be the collapse of the heart of the US manufacturing economy in general.

How far might evolutionary reconstructive developments of these various kinds go if ongoing difficulties continue to create ever deepening pain and traditional policies, both liberal and conservative, fail to deal with growing social and economic pain?

One thing is certain: traditional liberalism, dependent on expensive federal policies and strong labor unions, is in a moribund state in the

United States. The government no longer has much capacity to use progressive taxation to achieve equity goals or to regulate corporations effectively. Congressional deadlocks on such matters are the rule, not the exception. At the same time, ongoing economic stagnation or mild upturns followed by further decay—and *real* unemployment rates in the 15-16 percent range—appear more likely than a return to booming economic times.

Our contention is that, in fact, a different kind of progressive change is emerging—one that involves an extended, slow and difficult transformation of institutional structures and power. Such efforts, over time, are also likely to offer possibilities for the bolstering of progressive political relationships. Liberal activists and policy-makers since the time of the New Deal and the Great Depression have implicitly assumed they were providing one or another form of *countervailing power* against large corporations. With the decay of this approach, evolutionary reconstructive efforts aim either to weaken or displace corporate power. Strategies like anti-trust or efforts to *break up* big banks aim to weaken corporations by reducing their size. Public banking, municipal utilities and single-payer health plans attempt slowly to displace privately owned companies. At the same time, community-based enterprises offer local public officials alternatives to paying large tax-incentive bribes to big corporations.

To be sure, a several-decade-long developmental trajectory of *evolutionary reconstruction* may fail to alter fundamental institutional relationships and political power balances, or result in only modest changes, as have most kinds of top-down national reforms. The era of stalemate and decay might simply continue and worsen. Like ancient Rome, the United States could simply decline, falling into the status of a nation fundamentally unable to address its social ills.

The alternative possibility—that a painful and sustained era of stalemate and decay may allow for the development and ultimate politicization of a coherent new long-term progressive strategic direction—is not to be dismissed out of hand, however. Such a direction would build upon the remaining energies of traditional liberal reform, animated over time by new populist anger and movements aimed at confronting corporate power, the extreme concentration of income, failing public services, the ecological crisis, and military adventurism. And it would explicitly advocate the slow construction of new institutions run by people committed to developing an expansively democratic polity—an effort that could give political voice to the new constituencies emerging alongside the new developments, adding a new, potentially powerful and growing element in support of longer term progressive change.**

** **AU NOTE:** Paradoxically, evolutionary reconstructive processes of institution- *NB* shifting change over an extended period of time may be more viable in the United States than in many European nations—in part because of the nation's traditions of decentralization, in part precisely because American liberalism's reform capacity has historically been weaker than most social democratic political formations in Europe. Moreover, the decline of American labor unions from 34.7 percent of the labor force in the 1950s to 11.8 percent now and only 6.9 percent in the private sector continues to further weaken traditional progressive reform capacities.

New organizations like the Business Alliance for Local Living Economies *!!* (BALLE) and the American Sustainable Business Council (ASBC) have also *NB* been quietly developing momentum in recent years. BALLE, which has more than 22,000 small business members, works to promote sustainable local community development. ASBC (which includes BALLE as a member) is an advocacy and lobbying effort that involves more than 150,000 business professionals and thirty separate business organizations committed to sustainability. Leading White House figures and such Cabinet level officials as Labor Secretary Hilda Solis have welcomed the organization as a counter *!!* to the US Chamber of Commerce. Jeffrey Hollender, Chair of ASBC's Business Leadership Council and former CEO of Seventh Generation, has denounced the Chamber for "fighting democracy and destroying America's economic future" because of its opposition to climate change legislation and its support for the Citizens United decision.[33]

At the heart of the spectrum of emerging institutional change is the traditional radical principle that the ownership of capital should be subject to democratic control. In a nation where one percent of the population owns nearly as much investment wealth as the bottom 99% (49.7 percent of total), this principle is likely to be particularly appealing to the young—the people who will shape the next political era.[34] In 2009, even as Republicans assaulted President Obama and his liberal allies as immoral *socialist*, a Rasmussen poll reported that Americans under thirty were "essentially evenly divided" as to whether they preferred *capitalism* or *socialism*. The finding has been confirmed in additional polls. A December 2011 Pew survey, for example, found those aged 18 to 29 have a more favorable reaction to the term *socialism* then *capitalism* by a margin of 49 to 43 percent. A 2000 Pew Research Center poll also found a majority of Americans now having an unfavorable view of corporations—down from nearly three quarters holding favorable views only twelve years before.[35]

Even if many of the youth who prefer socialism to capitalism may well be unsure what *socialism* is, they are clearly open to something new, whatever it may be called. A non-statist, community-building, institution-changing, democratizing strategy could well capture their imagination and channel their desire to heal the world. It is surely a positive direction to pursue, no matter what. And plausibly it could open the way to an era of true progressive renewal, even one day perhaps step-by-step systemic change or the kind of unexpected explosive movement-building power evidence in the Arab Spring and, historically in our own Civil Rights, feminists and other great movements.

Themes of Emerging Systemic Design

A long painful era of social and economic decay, on the one hand, and of the slow build up, community by community, state by state of democratizing strategies, on the other, may be understood also as the preliminary historical developmental work needed to clarify new principles for larger scale application. As in the decades prior to the New Deal, state and local experimentation in the *laboratories of democracy* may suggest new democratizing approaches for larger scale system-defining institutions when the appropriate political moment occurs.

It is possible to begin to clarify the parameters of a systemic model (1) to which the various emerging trajectories of the institution-building and democratization point—and (2) which are suggested by the logic of longer-term challenges being created by issues of political stalemate, of scale, and ecological, resources and climate change. Different in its basic structures both from corporate capitalism and state socialism, the model might be called *A Pluralist Commonwealth* (to underscore its plural forms of democratized ownership) of *A Community Sustaining System* to underscore its emphasis on economically and democratically healthy local communities, anchored through wealth-democratizing strategies as a matter of principle.

Four critical axioms underlie the democratic theory of a model that builds on the evolving forms and on structural principles appropriate also to the larger emerging challenges: (1) democratization of wealth; (2) community, both locally and in general, as a guiding theme; (3) decentralization in general; (4) and substantial but not complete forms of democratic planning in support of community, and to achieve longer-term economic, democracy-building and ecological goals.

Democratization of Wealth

A beginning point is the simple observation that traditional *after-the-fact* redistributive measures depend upon power relations that no longer hold. As noted, particularly important has been the decline of the labor union institutional base of traditional progressive politics. Hence, either another way forward is possible, or the power that attends high levels of income and wealth is likely to continue to produce growing inequity of income and wealth, on the one hand, and political power, on the other—and thereby also to subvert genuine democratic processes.

The various institutions briefly highlighted above—from co-ops to land trusts, and including municipal enterprise of state investing, as well as national financial, health, and manufacturing forms all challenge the dominant ideologies which hold that private corporate enterprise offers the only possible way forward. They also help open new ways of conceptualizing practical approaches to meaningful larger scale democratization. The steady illumination of this principle has important political implications both locally and nationally, introducing new conceptions into American political dialogue in ways appropriate to American culture.

New wealth-building forms may also contribute directly to building progressive political power either, as noted, through the *displacement* principle or by offering local officials alternative strategies, or both. Historically, cooperative and other federations also helped establish institutional and organizational support for explicit political efforts in support of specific policies. Critically, worker-owned firms, co-ops, land trusts, municipal enterprises and the like help stabilize local community economies. Unlike major corporations, which commonly come and go (often after extracting large subsidies), such institutions tend to be anchored locally by virtue of their democratic ownership structure.

Community

A systemic model that hopes to alter larger patterns of distribution and power must also nurture a culture that is supportive of broad and inclusive goals, and in particular, must contribute to the reconstruction of principles of *community*. In economic terms, building community means introducing and emphasizing practical forms of community ownership in systemic design, vision, and theory. In the Cleveland effort discussed above, the central institution is a community-wide, neighborhood-encompassing nonprofit corporation. The board of the nonprofit institution includes representatives both of the worker cooperatives and other key community institutions. Worker co-ops are linked to this (and to a revolving fund at the center), and though independently owned and managed, they cannot be sold without permission from the founding community-wide institution.

Furthermore, it is only because of the larger community-benefiting legitimating principle that serious political and moral claims on broader public support can be put forward with integrity, and with force. It is because the linked co-ops have a larger community-building purpose that major hospitals, universities and other community-serving institutions are also involved—and why public or public-supported funds are appropriately shifted to their support when possible. Individual co-ops, worker-owned firms, small businesses and the like, though indispensable, inevitably represent distinct interests different from that of the community as a whole. Moreover the people who comprise the workforce at any one time do not comprise the entire community. The *community as a whole* includes older people, stay-at-home spouses, children, and the infirm.

Put another way, as opposed to some theories that simply emphasize worker-ownership of specific enterprises, the model is based on a broader theoretical and cultural concept—namely, that the interests of the workers—and particularly workers in any particular sector—are not inherently and institutionally the same as those of the overall community understood in terms of its necessarily broader and more encompassing concerns. This is not to suggest that freestanding, worker-owned cooperatives are unimportant or to be left out of the comprehensive model. It is simply to suggest that any genuine effort to emphasize equality must come to terms with the fact that large order systemic models based entirely—rather than partly—on worker ownership, as urged by some theories, are likely to develop power relationships of a particular kind. The workers who might control the garbage collection enterprise, for instance, are obviously inherently on a different footing from the workers who might control the oil industry in a model structured along pure worker ownership lines. Furthermore, worker-owned businesses operating in a challenging market environment can easily be overwhelmed by competitive forces that undermine larger social and ecological goals. Though to a degree regulations and after-the-fact efforts aimed at controlling the inherent dynamics of such models can modify and refine outcomes, they are unlikely to be able to alter the underlying conflict of institutional interest and power involved.

Decentralization

To emphasize the importance of local communities—and within that, of institutions of democratized ownership both of encompassing and of independent and diverse forms—is implicitly to emphasize a third systemic design principle—namely, decentralization in general. This raises an additional challenging question: Can there be meaningful democracy in a very large system without far more rigorous decentralization than is commonly assumed in the United States?

It is a commonplace that Washington is now *broken*, that decision-making at the center is stalemated, in decay. Part of this is clearly constitutional (for example, the "checks and balance" system, voting procedures in the Senate, the over-representation of small states, etc.). But part of the problem has to do with scale—and in two quite distinct ways. First, we rarely confront the fact that the United States is a very, very large geographic polity—one difficult to manage in general, or to manage through meaningful democratic participation in particular: Germany could easily be tucked into Montana; France into Arizona and New Mexico.[36] In the words of George F. Kennan, compared with most nations it is a "monster" country.[37]

Furthermore, it is very large in population—currently more than 310 million, likely to reach 500 million shortly after mid-century and, in the *high estimate* of the US Census Bureau, could reach or approach over a billion by 2100.[38] Decentralization in these circumstances is nearly inevitable, and if the continental nation is too large and most states too small to deal with economic matters, what remains is the intermediate scale we call the region—a unit of organization much discussed in serious theoretical work by conservatives and liberals and radicals at various points in modern history—and a unit of scale, we suggest, that is likely to become of increasing importance as time (and population growth) go on. The question is almost certainly how to regionalize, not whether to do so—what powers to maintain at the center and what powers to relegate to various smaller scale units. The principle of subsidiarity—keeping decision-making at the lowest feasible level, and only elevating to higher levels when absolutely necessary—is implicit as a guiding principle of the emerging model. Making it explicit, we also suggest, is likely to become both inevitable and strategically critical.[39]

Clearly we are discussing long-term change, not abrupt shifts in direction. Inherent in any long developmental effort of the kind suggested by *evolutionary reconstructive* processes is a profound need to clarify large order matters of principle. At each stage very serious questions need to be asked of specific projects—whether genuine democracy can be maintained without altering current patterns of wealth ownership, without nurturing a culture of community, and without dealing with the problem of scale, particularly as population and the economy grow in our continent spanning system.

Planning

A fourth principle involves the importance of democratic planning— and of two kinds (and including variations and contributions from the market). In the Cleveland effort the principle of community-wide economic benefit and stability is partly affirmed by the inclusive structure of the model. It is also affirmed, however, by the carefully structured relationship to institutions that can help stabilize the local *market*—in this case, the so-called *anchor institutions* (non-profit hospitals and universities) that rarely leave the community. As noted, the arrangement sketched above—in which such (significantly publicly supported) institutions agree to purchase some part of their needs from new businesses that are owned by the employees and are part of the larger integrated community-wide effort—is, in fact, a planning system. It is one that alters relationships between firms and the community, on the one hand, and the market on the other, and approximates a design in which community is a central goal (but with worker-ownership as a subsidiary feature)—and in which substantial support is provided through a partially planned market. Note carefully: partially planned, not totally planned. There are no subsidies involved, and outside competitors may challenge local firms. In principle, however, since there are much broader community benefits (including rebuilding the local tax base, and a better local economic environment for independent small businesses, co-ops, and worker-owned firms), the principle of support for the larger community-building effort is seen as both socially and economically important.

Two further related points of principle: One is that substantial local economic stability is clearly necessary if community is a priority and—critically—if democratic decision-making is also a priority (and to be meaningful in local communities): First, because without stability, the local population is unstable, tossed hither and yon by uncontrolled economic forces that undermine any serious interest in the long term health of the community. Second, because to the extent local budgets are put under severe stress by these processes, local community decision-making (as political scientist Paul Pierson in particular has shown) is so financially constrained as to make a mockery of democratic process.[40]

Even more important to the larger systemic model is the judgment that an authentic experience of local democratic practice is also absolutely essential for there to be genuine national democratic practice (as theorists from Alexis de Tocqueville and John Stewart Mill to Benjamin Barber, Jane Mansbridge, and Stephen Elkin have argued.)[41] To the degree this central judgment is accepted, some form of explicit public planning to achieve the local economic stability required to allow for genuine local democratic processes becomes absolutely essential as well.

In this context, too, experiments in participatory budgeting, stemming from innovations in Porto Alegre in Brazil, offer a good deal of promise. The basic idea is that citizens meet in popular assemblies throughout the city to deliberate about how the city budget should be spent. Most of these assemblies are organized around geographical regions of the city;

a few are organized around themes with a citywide scope—like public transportation or culture. Attempts have been made to adopt elements of participatory budgeting in the United States, notably in Chicago. These efforts have definite limits since they are restricted to municipal budget decisions. Nonetheless, to the extent that the practice of participatory budgeting can be extended over time to municipal, state, regional and national economic planning and other questions, it could provide an important mechanism for increasing meaningful democracy.

Elsewhere we have suggested ways to think about larger scale system-wide planning approaches, little different in principle from that exhibited on smaller scale in Cleveland, by considering the nation's longer term mass transit and high-speed rail needs.[42] The United States has very little capacity to build equipment for any of this. (Though there is one small firm in Portland, Oregon, in the main we assemble parts, most of which are produced by foreign companies.) When the next crisis generates future problems (perhaps again in the auto industry) a future systemic model might well use public contracts needed to build mass transit and high speed rail in ways that also help support quasi-public national and community-based firms—both to produce what is needed and simultaneously to help stabilize local communities.

It is again important to note that taxpayer money and commuter fares will inevitably finance the effort. The approach—which might appropriately involve joint public-worker owned firms—could clearly be applied in connection with other industries as well; and, again, some carefully structured forms of competition might be encouraged to keep the model on its toes.

A related point of principle has to do with community stability and global warming. It is not widely realized that community stability is required to help deal with climate change issues as well—and again for two quite distinct reasons. One is simply that it is impossible to do serious local *sustainability planning* that reduces a community's carbon footprint if such planning is disrupted and destabilized by economic turmoil. Stability is especially important in achieving high-density housing and in transpor-

! tation planning. Stability is also important because it is very carbon costly, as well as capital costly, to continue our current policy of literally *throwing away cities.* Unplanned corporate decision-making commonly results in the elimination of jobs in one community, leaving behind empty houses, half empty schools, roads, hospitals, public buildings and the like—only to have to build them again in the new location to which the jobs have been moved. The process is wasteful of capital and human resources in the extreme, but also extremely wasteful in terms of the carbon content both of the structures discarded—and then of replacements built anew in a different location.

It follows, quite simply, that any serious approach to achieving ecological sustainability in the nation's communities—one that can allow for the reduction of the carbon footprint of cities—requires a system of planning sufficiently robust to substantially stabilize communities.

Democratization of Wealth (Again) at Larger Scale

A systemic model aimed at dealing with economic issues, ecological challenges and local community stability must inevitably also come to terms with corporate power and corporate dynamics—especially in the era of global warming and resource limits. Publicly listed, large-scale corporations are subject to Wall Street's first commandment: Grow or die! "[S]tockholders in the speculation economy want their profits now," observes Laurence Mitchell, author of *The Speculation Economy,* "and they do not much care how they get them."[43] Indeed, if a corporate executive does not show steadily increasing quarterly earnings, the grim quarterly returns reaper that haunts the stock market will cut him down sooner or later.

Growing carbon emissions come with the territory of ever-expanding growth—both as an economic matter and above all as a political matter, where opposition to anything that adds costs is part and parcel of the basic corporate dynamic. And climate change in general and global warming in particular are the central challenges of the 21st century, challenges that go well beyond any we have previously faced.

Moreover, to the degree that businesses (including worker-owned businesses) are subjected to intense market competition, to that very extent most must also attempt to steadily expand sales, profits, and growth. If they do not they are likely to be severely punished by the markets, or, alternatively, competitors will find ways to achieve gains as they expand, often to the detriment of a less aggressive firm.

The destructive *grow or die* imperative inherent in the current market- !! driven system cannot be wished or regulated away. In addition to the √ over-riding issue of global warming, countless studies have documented growing energy, mineral, water, arable land and other limits to unending growthlimits corporations are desperately trying to avoid through one or another technological fix that is often equally or more environmentally destructive—such as fracking, tar sands extraction, deep water drilling. Yet the trends continue: The United States, with less than 5% of global population, consumes 22% of the world's oil, 13% of world coal, and 21% of world natural gas.[44] In the brief period 1940-1976, Americans used up as large a share of the earth's mineral resources as did everyone in all previous history.[45]

At some point, a society like that of the United States, which already !! produces the equivalent of over $190,000 for every family of four, must ask when enough is enough. As Juliet Schor has argued, one important step *NB* is to shift the economy to encourage less consumption and more leisure time.[46] A number of policy measures could help facilitate this shift, such ! as reforming unemployment insurance policy to encourage work sharing, changing government hiring practices to model shorter working hours, and changing labor policies to discourage excessive overtime. In addition to improving work-life balance for families, such a shift can also facilitate ! lower impact forms of consumption: taking the bike instead of the car or cooking at home instead of buying fast food are two obvious examples.

While a focus on restoring balance on a personal level is important, it is also necessary to confront the systemic dynamics that promote a continued focus on growth. As former Presidential adviser James Gustav

Speth has bluntly observed: "For the most part we have worked within this current system of political economy, but working within the system will not succeed in the end when what is needed is transformative change in the system itself."[47]

As a matter of cold logic, if some of the most important corporations have a massively disruptive and costly impact on the economy in general and the environment in particular—and if experience suggests that regulation and anti-trust laws in important areas are likely to be largely subverted by these corporations—a public takeover becomes the only logical answer. This general argument was, in fact, put forward most forcefully not by liberals, but by the founders of the Chicago School of economics. Conservative Nobel Laureate George Stigler repeatedly observed that regulatory strategies were "designed and operated primarily for [the corporation's] benefit."[48] Henry C. Simons, Milton Friedman's teacher and one of the most important Chicago School thinkers, was even more forceful. "Turned loose with inordinate powers, corporations have vastly over-organized most industries," Simons held. The state "should face the necessity of actually taking over, owning, and managing directly… industries in which it is impossible to maintain effectively competitive conditions."[49]

Recent research on public and quasi-public forms of enterprise, contrary to conventional wisdom, also suggests new possibilities in this area. For example, between 2004 and 2008, 117 state-owned companies from Brazil, Russia, India, and China appeared for the first time on the Forbes 2000 global list of the world's largest companies. In 2009, three of the top five global companies by market value were Chinese state-owned firms: ICBC (Industrial and Commercial Bank of China), China Mobile, and Petro China.[50]

Nor, research on both past and emerging developments suggests, is public enterprise necessarily inefficient.[51] Public enterprise in Great Britain, for example, allegedly under-performed, yet the numbers do not bear this out. Between 1950 and 1985, annual productivity growth in English public sector mining, utilities, transportation, and communications companies consistently exceeded private sector productivity growth in the same industries in the United States.[52] In the modern era, as Francisco Flores-Macias and Aldo Musacchio document in a recent Harvard International Review article, state-owned enterprises in many areas are, or can be, as efficient as their private counterparts.[53]

Implicit in the above argument are also two judgments about the role of ideas (as well as ideology) in certain contexts: We have noted, first, the practical introduction into American culture of projects, models, and public efforts involving the democratization of wealth at various levels. In a nation with little experience with such ideas, the various forms may also be thought of as positive ways of challenging in everyday life what Antonio Gramsci termed the dominant hegemonic ideology. The introduction of such themes in local experience may also be understood as the necessary precondition of larger scale applications of the same principles at the appropriate moment.

At a very different level is the question of ideas in general—and when they may have meaningful impact. Rarely do important ideas matter in politics. What usually matters is the momentum of entrenched power. But not always. Sometimes—when the old ideas no longer explain the world, when it is obvious that something is wrong—then new ideas often matter, and matter a very great deal. The judgment implicit in the above argument is that now may well be such a time. Now, and continuing through the emerging era of stagnation, stale-mate and decay.

As the global and domestic economic, political and climate change crisis both increase pain and force people to ask ever more penetrating questions, there is a need for—and hunger for—new understanding, new clarity, and a new way forward that is intelligible and intelligent. Accordingly, not only may the new *evolutionary reconstructive* models begin to suggest practical ways forward, they also suggest ideas about what might become of strategic political importance, hence offer hope of building longer term political common ground among serious activists and intellectuals.

Similarly, for many decades the only choices for many have seemed state socialism, on the one hand, or corporate capitalism, on the other—with one or another form of social democratic or liberal reform as perhaps a moderating form. When traditional systems either falter and fail, or appear in decline, ideas concerning the development of coherent new systemic designs also may become of far greater importance. They begin to offer specific answers to specific questions concerning whether a new system (or any system) may offer hope of genuine democracy, equality, community, and ecological sustainability.

A minimal goal of the above proposals, accordingly, is that they may offer hand-holds on processes of potentially important new forms of change (and therefore strategy), on the one hand, and on possibilities for systemic design, on the other—hand-holds that, in turn, may permit further refinement and ongoing development that may contribute to longer term change.

The Time of the Great Awakening

The age of human blindness is rapidly passing away. The distinction between truth and falsehood, between compassion and greed, between good and evil, is being brought rapidly into focus in human consciousness. Once we have begun to see clearly, a planetary transformation will begin to take place the likes of which none of us today can imagine. Global media and social networking will lead to the rapid spread of new ideas. Awareness of and sensitivity to greed, selfishness, corruption, propaganda, deception, exploitation, and overt and covert forms of violence will lead to mass movements for global change on many fronts. Humanity will be forced to choose between a past that has benefited only a privileged few and a future which cares for and benefits every human being on earth, as well as Mother Nature. On which path do we wish to journey into our future?

The conflicts we are witnessing today—social, political, religious, and economic—between conservatives and progressive, between reactionaries and visionaries, is about this *choice of destiny*, which humanity is now struggling to decide for itself. The opportunity exists at this particular time for humanity to make the greatest evolutionary leap forward since our species first appeared on Earth. The door of opportunity that is open at this time for *choosing* will eventually close, and the choice we will have made will decide our planetary future for thousands of years to come. This is indeed the Time of the Great Awakening. Let each of us do all in our power each day to help create a better world. Let no opportunity pass unused.

Finley Eversole

I rejoice to live in such a splendidly disturbing time!

Helen Keller

Every one of us was born into this time because we have a mission.

John Perkins

A Prophesy: The Day of Reckoning

The ways of the occultist and the spiritualist and the scientists are rapidly converging, though the latter may not know it, or prefer not to acknowledge the fact.

Indeed, by their own long and painstaking methods have scientists discovered many truths long years ago proclaimed by initiates of the Arcane Science, but at that time repudiated as false and fanciful.

Yet whereas human beings can lie and be deluded, not so instrument; and the time is not far hence when instruments of such great sensitiveness will be devised, that Nature will be compelled to lay bare yet more of her secrets before the eyes of even the most skeptical.

And by means of these instruments will the experts be enabled to differentiate between the diverse rates of vibration in the ether, and come to perceive how they are being utilized for good or evil ends.

And lo, when the hour shall strike, an instrument will be devised so finely attuned and of such surpassing delicacy that the unseen will become the seen, and the unheard the heard.

And certain strata of the inner worlds will be revealed, and the denizens of those worlds—the evil together with the good.

And those who dwell in the outer world yet use the forces of the inner worlds will also be revealed.

Then will the Day of Reckoning be at hand; for, as in a mirror will mine enemies be reflected, singly or assemble together, intent for ever on bending the will of men to their own iniquitous ends.

And thus, suddenly, that which for generation after generation has been veiled in darkness shall be brought to light.

And the tidings thereof will be noised abroad in all the chronicles, and man will rise up in his wrath and overthrow his enemies and mine enemies with the concentrated force of his righteous indignation.

Yea, like a mighty bombardment will he direct his thought-power ???
against his age-long oppressors, having in the interim acquired
knowledge of the incalculable potency of Thought.

So will at long last that great brotherhood of oppressors be
destroyed, and the abuse of the power of thought recoil on each
of its progenitors, as also on the organization for which they have
sacrificed even their very souls.

Cyril Scott, *The Vision of the Nazarene*, 1955

Three things cannot hide for long: the Moon, the Sun and the Truth.
Siddhartha

THE GROWING GREEN ECONOMY[1, 2]

Hazel Henderson, DSc (Hon), FRSA

A climate prosperity strategy is the *win-win* upon which all countries meeting at Rio+20, June 2012, agreed. The wrangling between the North's industrial countries, whose many decades of burning fossil fuels has caused the climate warming, versus the needs of the newly developing countries of the South now can be bypassed. As private investors have shown, shifting from the Fossil Fuel Age to the information-rich, green economies of the Solar Age is the greatest opportunity for all countries and all humanity. Stock market newsletters, still below Wall Street's radar, cover all of the cleaner, greener companies and stocks and see this historic transition to the global green economy as a $45 trillion new market. Billionaire venture capitalist John Doerr says, "We are talking about nothing less than the re-industrialization of the whole planet." New investments continue to pour in to grow what the UN agencies, United Nations Environmental Programme (UNEP), United Nations Development Programme (UNDP) and International Labor Organization (ILO) call the Green Economy Initiative. The UN General Assembly in June 2009 and its Expert Committee on the Financial Crisis, chaired by Joseph Stiglitz, endorsed this Global Green New Deal as the best approach to overcoming the global financial crisis and creating millions of new jobs.

The *Climate Solutions 2* computer model prepared by Climate Risk Pty of Australia and Britain (www.climaterisk.net) provides the roadmap on investing $1 trillion every year from 2010 until 2020 in energy efficiency (the earliest, biggest payoff), wind, solar, geothermal, ocean and hydropower. As economies of scale are reached in each of these sectors, they will become cheaper than coal and oil and are already cheaper than nuclear power, all of which create uncounted social costs and are heavily subsidized by taxpayers in most countries.

By 2020, this $10 trillion ramp-up of the new sustainability sectors of the Solar Age can prevent further global temperature from rising beyond 2° Celsius which scientists say can avert runaway climate chaos. Paybacks of up to $30 trillion by 2020 make laddered maturity climate bonds suitable for pension funds. Such bonds are designed by many experts, including the global Network for Sustainable Financial Markets Climate Bonds Initiative in association with the Carbon Disclosure Project and the Climate Prosperity Alliance.

There is No Shortage of Money

All the evidence now shows that there is no shortage of money to finance the global green economy. The only shortage is time, and we have all the technology needed for this transition- Re-deploying just 10% of institutional, pension and endowment funds, which total some $120 trillion, away from fossilized sectors, hedge funds, oil and commodities, derivatives and speculation on interest-rates can add trillions to the $4 trillion already privately invested since 2007, as tracked by the Green Transition Scoreboard®. Cutting wasteful subsidies to fossil fuels and nuclear power, as reported by the International Institute for Sustainable Development, would release additional trillions (www.globalsubsidies.org). McKinsey & Company's July 2009 Report on energy efficiency shows that investments of $520 billion can yield $1.2 trillion by 2020, reducing US energy demand by 23%.

The financial crisis of 2008-09 presents the best opportunity in over a century to simultaneously reform money systems and create additional mediums of exchange and financing mechanisms to accelerate the shift from the fossil-fuel/nuclear-Industrial Era to the greener information-rich Solar Age. Today's convergence of global warming, financial crisis and the growing green economy signify a new stage in human awareness and understanding of our place in Nature and are fueling the needed paradigm shift to the Solar Age.[3]

Today, all of the proposals for reform of central banking, the history of money and alternative currencies, together with suppressed contemporary work on local currencies, barter and electronic trading systems, as well as ecology-based finance and economics, such as Ethical Biomimicry Finance™ and the global TEEB (The Economics of Eco systems and Biodiversity) study, are coming to the fore. Such outside-the-box approaches are now essential (see Additional Resources). All these proposals for fundamental reform are still being pushed aside by incumbent money authorities and private-sector financial players. Demands for reform of financial systems include fairer representation of developing countries and more transparency at the International Monetary Fund, World Bank and World Trade Organization. The G-20 inclusion of China, India, Brazil and other developing countries was necessary but not sufficient. We now need the G-193, that is, all UN member countries.

Even these long-overdue reforms were over-shadowed by most monetary authorities' usual chorus of inside-the-box remedies: lowering interest rates, *injecting capital* into their banking systems, bailing out other companies deemed *too big to fail* and indiscriminate stimulating for faster GDP-growth. Perverse subsidies to fossil fuel and nuclear energy were slated for phase out by G-20 countries but are still stifling the growth of the green economy. All these shopworn policies are rooted in the laissez-faire Anglo-American, Chicago School economics typified by the Washington Consensus which has become the dominant global economic paradigm.

The new opportunity presented by the spectacular failure of this economic paradigm is empowered by the relative decline of the USA and the rise of China, India, Brazil and the other G-20 countries. In addition, the world economy has the countervailing weight of the European Union despite problems of Greece, Ireland, Spain, Italy and Portugal's debts— still less serious than the US, which is still the world's largest debtor. The euro, now representing 25% of global reserve currencies, is the world's competing reserve currency to the US dollar. Though still the highest reserve currency due to its historical role as a *safe haven*, the US dollar has fallen since 2008 as global investors in US sovereign bonds grasp the true fundamentals in the US economy and the extent of the corruption on Wall Street and levels of government gridlock and capture by special interests.

Changing the Economics Paradigm

Until the 2008 financial crisis, the prevailing economic/monetary paradigm and controlling incumbent financial, political and academic interests have dominated all discussions and drowned out alternative paradigms and proposals for reform and innovation. This economic paradigm is based on money and central banking and the global money circuits they create and control. All other valuable assets from human skills and knowledge to ecological productivity and assets are *off the balance sheets* in most corporations, financial firms, and central banks. This is changing due to the innovative initiatives of the United Nations Environment Protection Programme Finance Initiative (UNEP-FI), the UN Principles of Responsible Investing and the movement for socially responsible investing, as well as non-profit civic groups, including the Club of Rome, the Rocky Mountain Institute, the Carbon Disclosure Project, the new economics foundation, Focus on the Global South and others.

Obsolete economic textbooks still govern in academia and business schools whose graduates sought quick bucks as *financial engineers* on Wall Street. Luckily for humanity, this money paradigm has blown up. The money circuits were too narrow in *bandwidth* to contain the explosion of new knowledge and innovation in today's ecologically aware, information-rich societies. As money circuits blow out, we can see their inadequate design, and we can now read the decades of critiques and reform proposals with new eyes (see Additional Resources).

!!! Just as the gold standard broke down due to its inadequate *bandwidth* to carry all the increased innovation, information flows and transactions required by the growth of industrialism, so too, today's money circuits can no longer contain the transition from the fossil-fuel era to the Solar Age. This is why since the late 1990s we have seen the explosion of transactions and commerce moving to the internet (see Fig. 1: Evolution of Money).

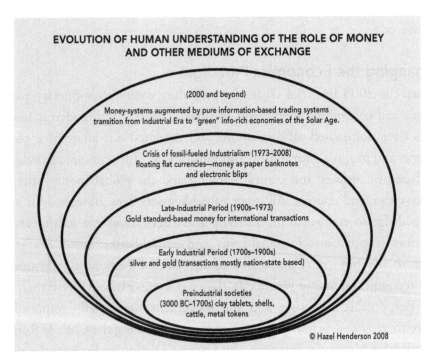

EVOLUTION OF HUMAN UNDERSTANDING OF THE ROLE OF MONEY AND OTHER MEDIUMS OF EXCHANGE

(2000 and beyond)
Money-systems augmented by pure information-based trading systems transition from Industrial Era to "green" info-rich economies of the Solar Age.

Crisis of fossil-fueled Industrialism (1973–2008)
floating flat currencies—money as paper banknotes and electronic blips

Late-Industrial Period (1900s–1973)
Gold standard-based money for international transactions

Early Industrial Period (1700s–1900s)
silver and gold (transactions mostly nation-state based)

Preindustrial societies
(3000 BC–1700s) clay tablets, shells, cattle, metal tokens

© Hazel Henderson 2008

Figure 1: Evolution of Money

NB Alan Greenspan was half-right in thinking about the New Economy, but he could not extricate himself from his obsolete economics and central banking toolbox. This is the same error that Ben Bernanke, Henry Paulson and the Bush $700 billion bailout made in 2008. They and Obama's economists, like Timothy Geithner, Ben Bernanke and new Treasury Secretary Jack Lew, think the only option is to expand the money circuits by cutting interest rates and printing more fiat money to provide to Wall Street banks. Today's notional volume of derivatives is over $1.2 quadrillion[4] while global GDP is only $63 trillion.[5] Many economists still call for stable money by returning to the gold standard. This would make matters worse. Clearly monetary policy is part of the problem—not the solution.[6]

Today, real-world thinking focuses on Main Street where real people create real products and services. Wall Street and other financial sectors have metastasized and become parasitic on the real economy. Reality-focused politicians, including US President Barack Obama, have gone beyond the bankers' money illusion and seen that fiscal policy must now be mobilized, as in the $787 billion stimulus, to invest in creating the new infrastructure, for example, smart electric grids, preventive public health care and revamping education to grow the green economy. The blindness of bankers, media and the public to the soundness of such productive investments in our human future are also caused by statistical errors, for example, categorizing investments in education and preventive health care as *consumption* in GDP and national accounts. Furthermore, GDP does not even include an asset account where all public investments can be recorded and amortized over their useful life—to offset the public debt these investments incurred.[7]

The mantras from the old economics paradigm are typified by the cover story in *The Economist*, November 22, 2008, which claims that "All You Need is Cash" and the ubiquitous cry, "Where is all the money coming from to fund all this new spending in infrastructure, education and health care and the green economy?" Even economists are now calling for massive additional stimulus in spite of rising deficits as the only option left in the old tool kit. The paradox is that money is not scarce! Money is not a real commodity; as we know, it is a brilliant and useful construct of the human mind, information. Money is a numeraire, a tracking and scoring system for production and transactions by real people interacting with each other and ecosystems. Money is nothing more than a particular measuring device, like slide rules, abacuses, centimeters, kilometers or inches. If properly overseen and managed, money is an excellent means of exchange and a store of value.[8]

But today, money-creation is distorted and out of control. Central bankers are printing money in clear sight on TV, while Wall Street's derivatives, collateralized debt obligations (CDOs), CDSs (credit default swaps) and the securitization of mortgages (MBSs, CMOs), car loans, credit-card debt, student loans, and so forth, are unofficial forms of money creation by investment banks. They are now disappearing in the meltdown and have been called the USA's *shadow banking system* which grew after 1999 with the repeal of the Glass-Steagall Act and other deregulation. Both political parties enabled the spree of deregulation that began with Ronald Reagan and accelerated under George W. Bush. President Obama's first Treasury Secretary, Timothy Geithner was too close to Wall Street to push for the reforms, as I suggested in my "Changing the Game of Finance," October 2009.[6]

Today, government-issued money, coins and banknotes, as required by the US Constitution, represents less than 10% of the US and UK money supply. The other 90% is created by banks as loans—out of thin air.[7] Sensible reforms of this fractional reserve banking system have been ignored for decades and are now summarized in a bill in the US Congress as the Monetary Reform Act (www.monetary.org). The current monetary system based on debt[8] has turned the USA into the world's largest debtor. China has resisted the Washington Consensus paradigm and focuses on equity not debt, and is now the world's largest creditor, along with Japan and OPEC. The campaign in the USA by the Peterson Institute and its leaders, the former head of the US General Accounting Office, David Walker, and Peter Peterson, founder of the private equity firm Blackstone, is reactionary, with a special-interest fear-mongering focus on cutting social spending while ignoring bloated military budgets and tax cuts for the wealthy, as well as the wasted and misdirected funds in the Department of Homeland Security and other agencies.

Unfortunately, US President Obama has too many special-interest, *///* tainted economic advisers. He needs to ignore further advice from Robert Rubin ("Mr. Leverage," as the former Goldman-Sachs chief was known, who presided over the demise of Citibank and its billions of toxic "assets"); Larry Summers, former Treasury Secretary, should also return to advising hedge funds. Summers, together with Rubin, blocked lawyer Brooksley E. *///* Born, head of the Commodity Futures Trading Commission, from regulating credit default swaps. She testified before Congress in the late 1990s that they could blow up the global financial system. Summers, Rubin and Alan Greenspan severely criticized Born, and she resigned. Timothy Geithner should have been replaced sooner as Treasury Secretary. While Ben Bernanke is no longer Chair of the Federal Reserve, I expect the obsolete economism will continue to hamper reforms.

The Real Economy

So how can the world's academic, political, governmental and civic society *//./* forces who share an ecological understanding of how economies function, embedded as they are within societies and ecosystems, gain the upper hand? These new movements worldwide are about human survival and *//* do not seek power or control for its own sake, as do those self-described *masters of the universe* in London, Wall Street and other financial centers. They seek to foster the new paradigm and expose the errors in financial and economic models, such as Herman Scheer has done in Germany. The Bank of Sweden Prize in economics lobbied on to the Nobel committee in the 1960s was to trump opposition and elevate the discipline and profession of economics as a *science*. Economists are still trying to use this phony 'Nobel' prize to justify why central bankers should be free of political oversight—even in democratic societies. The truth that economics was never a science is now revealed.

Ecologically literate, socially responsible companies, venture investors
NB and business schools (see *Ethical Markets: Growing the Green Economy,*
2006) must now join forces with civic society, labor unions, politicians
and bureaucrats—to reform money circuits and expand pure-information
based trading systems, such as crowdfunding, e-Bay, Craigslist, Freecycle,
Time Banking, LETS systems, cell phones, radio and new electronic
socially responsible trading systems for growing the green economy. Ethical
NB Markets Media's goal is to reform markets and grow the green economy
globally. We are a new *green Bloomberg* to accelerate the rollout of this
green economy with the research of our Green Transition Scoreboard®
which will regularly update the total private investments in the green
sectors, so far estimated at $4 trillion since 2007.

!!! The evolution of human understanding of money and mediums of
exchange is the essential basis for completing the great transition from
the fossil fuel era to the Solar Age (see Figure 1). Incumbent players in
the money circuits need not fear that money will no longer be valuable.
!! Indeed, shifting some of the transactional burden from overloaded money
circuits will actually restore and retain the value of today's money. Just as
gold is still valuable while no longer backing the world's paper currencies, money will still be valuable when created in more transparent and
ecological ways in support of real economies and not for speculative gain.
A new kind of economy based on information-sharing and cooperation
is growing with the internet, as documented in *Wikinomics*, 2008; *The
Wealth of Networks*, 2007; *The Future of Knowledge*, 2003, and earlier
studies of gift economies (see Additional Resources).

Meanwhile, pure information-based transaction systems will bypass
Wall Street and provide the needed *bandwidth*, interfacing with honest
money. Such alternative trading systems will bring investors together with
companies providing all the needed new infrastructure and production
facilities to bring wind, solar, geothermal and ocean technologies to scale.
For example, one of our Advisory Board members, Dr. Shann Turnbull,
building on the work of the late Robert Swann and our colleagues at

the New Economics Institute (formerly the Schumacher Society, USA), *NB* proposes a simple shift to finance renewable energy: a unit of value based on kilowatt hours of renewably generated electricity. This is similar to the energy-based currency proposed in the 1930s by the Technocrat movement (see Additional Resources). The essence of Turnbull's proposal would have governments issue interest-free loans directly to construct the new smart grid and renewable energy facilities in *KWH dollars*, to be repaid from the revenues of their electricity sales. Turnbull shows that if usual interest rates of 8% are removed, then wind-generated electricity is cheaper than coal, even without accounting for coal's external costs. Germany's Renewable Energy Act for feed-in tariffs spearheaded by Herman Scheer, Ernst U. von Weizsacker and others employs similar tools. These, as well as Berkeley, California's solar rooftop program, now copied in many states, the Schumacher Society's *Berkshares* currency as well as Edgar Cahn's time banking, are the true financial innovations needed for our green future.

Special interest-free loans from governments would be far more efficient in reducing greenhouse gas (GHG) emissions and growing the green economy than either carbon taxes or cap-and-trade programs (both of which raise prices). Direct interest-free loans actually reduce prices instead. These kinds of loans are also proposed for rebuilding public infrastructure, retro-fitting public buildings for energy efficiency savings, in the Sovereignty plan of Kenneth Bohnsack, now incorporated into the Monetary Reform Act of 2008. Ellen Brown, JD, author of *Web of Debt* and *The Public Banking Solution*, founded the Public Banking Institute to support the establishment and demonstrate the success of state-chartered banks such as the Bank of North Dakota in the USA and those foolishly disbanded in Canada and Australia.

Local barter-clubs, like Freecycle.com, Craigslist and LETS, and scrip currencies are proliferating—as they always do when central bankers and the International Monetary Fund fail or apply the wrong remedies and make matters worse. Some of the most successful complementary currencies are Switzerland's WIR and the Schumacher Society's Berkshares, with equivalent to $2 million in circulation and accepted by banks and businesses in Massachusetts. Similar complementary currencies are matching needs and resources and clearing local markets in Britain, Canada, Australia, Argentina, Brazil and other countries.

People-to-people lending, crowdfunding and microfinance projects are booming in many countries. Women's World Banking, Basic Realignment and Closure Commission (BRAC) and the Grameen Bank in Bangladesh, now emulated in many countries, FINCA and ACCION in Latin America, as well as the newer online versions, including Microplace, Kiva, as well as lenders Prosper.com in the USA and Zopa.com in Britain. Credit unions, operated in Europe and North America for a century, are becoming more proactive. They are filling new local needs, reaching out to poorer people and adding microfinance and lending to small businesses.

Associations of small local banks and businesses are wielding more political clout, as are credit unions. In the USA, they are demanding equal treatment in the government's Troubled Asset Relief Program (TARP), Term Asset-Backed Securities Relief Faculty (TALF), and other bailout funds currently showered on the big banks whose reckless lending triggered the financial mess. Venture capital and venture philanthropy firms, including the Rudolf Steiner Foundation, Acumen and the foundations of EBay founders Pierre Omidyar and Jeffrey Skoll, are investing in social enterprises which meet social needs while making modest profits. Such social capital is now creating a new hybrid sector in many economies.

The Business Alliance for Local Living Economics (BALLE) is such a network in North America, as well as the New Voice of Business, Green America, the Social Enterprise Alliance, the Fourth Sector Network and the Business-NGO Working Group. Entrex.net focuses on helping small businesses with their Private Company Index (PCI) which outperforms most stock indexes. Britain's new economics foundation (nef) has been generating both local initiatives, such as the Transition Towns movement, as well as its Green New Deal and alternative indicators to correct GDP, measuring wellbeing and ecological sustainability. The nef's proposal to save Britain's 11,500 postal offices by adding local banking functions is backed by trade unions, small businesses, public interest groups and pensioners.

Time banking, a brainchild of Edgar Cahn in the USA (see www. ethicalmarkets.com and www.ethicalmarkets.tv), is now helping local people connect and share services in Japan, Europe and other countries. Neighbors contact each other via a local *time banking* to provide meals and help for shut-ins, babysit each other's children, watch over property, mow lawns and share appliances. Car-sharing has now spawned many new companies such as Zip Car in the USA (bought by Avis for $500 million) and others in Canada and Europe where people can make ride arrangements rapidly on cell phones and tablets.

China is host to many such local initiatives, linking small businesses on networks, including Baidu.com, Alibaba.com, as well as Qifang.com which provides affordable loans to China's 25 million students. Circle Pleasure, a private company selling prepaid consumer cards, has formed a joint venture with Qifang for people-to-people banking, the first private company to receive a banking license from China's Central Bank. In many countries in Africa, cell phone banking has taken off. Cell phones are the basis for the *phone ladies* in Indian and Bangladeshi villages, who rent out use of their cell phones to other villages. Rural farmers and fishers can consult prices being offered in nearby towns and markets on their cell phones to make sure they take their goods to the best places to sell them.

Other Steps to Reform Finance

These are but a few of hundreds of examples of how reforming finance can resolve today's financial turmoil while at the same time growing the green economy. Other needed reforms to global finance which have been suppressed include taxing transactions in the $3 trillion daily currency exchange markets (90% of which is speculation). Currency exchange taxes were taken off the table at such forums as the UN Summit on New Finance for Development in Monterrey, Mexico, in 2002, as well as the

UN Social Summit in Copenhagen in 1995 where they were advocated in the report of the Global Commission to Fund the UN, which I co-edited with Harlan Cleveland and Inge Kaul—*The UN: Policy and Financing Alternatives*, Elsevier Scientific, UK 1995, 1996. Happily, financial transaction taxes are now on the agenda in many G-20 countries as the most effective way of curbing speculation while repaying taxpayers and diverting money back to the real economies of Main Street.

One proposal for levying a less than 1% tax on currency exchange is the Foreign Exchange Transaction Reporting System (FXTRS). This system operates like an electronic version of Wall Street's venerable *uptick rule*, enacted in 1934 but repealed during the Bush II administration. Today's Wall Street traders themselves are calling for its re-instatement to curb naked short-selling. The FXTRS computerized *uptick rule* gradually raises the basic tax whenever a bear raid starts attacking a weak currency. Such bear raids are rarely to *discipline* a country's policies, as traders claim, but rather to make quick profits. In the transparent FXTRS system, traders selling falling currencies begin to see that the rising tax is cascading into the country's currency stabilization fund and cutting into their gains. Seeing no further profit, traders can voluntarily exit the market and search for some other currency or arbitrage opportunity. The funds collected from such currency exchange taxes would raise hundreds of billions of dollars, which could, in turn, be directed to health, education, infrastructure and other public goods. (See www.HazelHenderson.com click on FXTRS.)

Since today's money allocation is now revealed as steered toward the political priorities of incumbent special interests, we can confront these interests, such as the military-industrial sectors, directly. Another proposal is for the United Nations Security Insurance Agency (UNSIA) to reduce the over $1 trillion countries spend annually on military hardware. Militarism is ever-less useful in resolving today's conflicts in Iraq, Afghanistan and other guerilla insurgencies. This UNSIA proposal, backed by four Nobel laureates, would allow countries which wish to follow Costa Rica's lead in 1947 and abolish their armed forces. Instead, countries could buy the insurance of a peacekeeping force from the UN Security Council (expanded and veto-less). Their premiums would be determined by insurance industry risk assessors contracted to see that the country had no WMD or secret weapons and did not teach militarism and xenophobia. Countries, say those in Central America, which decided to all buy UNSIA insurance would all get lower premiums. The premiums would fund a standing, properly trained UN peace-keeping force and complimentary contingents of NGO peace-making conflict-resolution groups. The UNSIA proposal is taught in many university programs and was debated in the UN Security Council in 1996 (see UNSIA at www.hazelhenderson.com). The green economy diverts wasteful weapons toward energy efficiency, public transport and smart grids.

These proposals and other fundamental reforms and innovations were pooh-poohed by the International Monetary Fund, World Bank, the US Treasury at the UN Social Summit in 1995 and by US Ambassador to the United Nations John Negroponte during the PrepComs for the Monterrey Summit in 2002. While many reforms need global cooperation and standards, many others can be enacted at national, state and local levels. Meanwhile many new initiatives to defend the global commons include the Global Marshall Plan, the Global Innovation Commons, the Global Green New Deal and many open source groups.

The need today is for all the constituencies supporting green economies to join forces with the weak ministries, Environment, Education, and Health and Welfare, to put political pressure on the strong ministries, Finance, Central Banks, Commerce, Business and Trade and force them to adopt the new ecological/information/commons paradigm. This will require the help of mass media whose mainstream editors will also need re-education beyond the obsolete economics/money box. The power of these strong ministries is still guarding the dying money/finance/fossil fuel order. I saw their influence as one of the co-organizers of the Beyond GDP Conference in the EU Parliament, November 2007. I tried my best to call for correction of errors of GDP in continuing to *externalize* the social and environmental costs of money-dominated economic growth. I was over-ridden by statisticians and academics who are still invested in the obsolete economics box. Even the survey by GlobeScan, London, in ten countries, funded by my company Ethical Markets Media in 2007 (and again in 2010 and 2013), which found huge majorities favoring inclusion of indicators of health, education and environment in national accounts, was down-played (www.GlobeScan.com). Ever since the UN Earth Summit in 1992 and its Agenda 21 signed by over 170 countries calling for the correction of GNP/GDP, the United Nations System of National Accounts (UNSNA), politicians, academics and statisticians have preferred to obtain endless grants to research *satellite* accounts, rather than confront the strong ministries dominating national policies.

This long-standing denial of the changes wrought by globalization of finance and technology has prevented needed reform and innovation since the de-regulation in the 1980s which led to all the recent financial crises. I have been covering these issues in my books, editorials and in mass media through my company, Ethical Markets Media, LLC. I joined forces with the socially responsible investing movement in 1982 as a member of the Advisory Council of the Calvert Group. Today, this movement's success has spawned the UN Global Compact, the UN Principles of Responsible Investing ($32 trillion), the CERES Principles ($11 trillion), the Equator Principles, the Carbon Disclosure Project ($78 trillion) and other efforts. Gradually, formerly externalized costs are being forced back and internalized on company balance sheets and cost/benefit analyses. Traditional discount rates are being reduced and avoided costs are no longer ignored. Triple bottom line (ESG) accounting is gaining favor over the defunct *efficient markets* models: Modern Portfolio Theory (MPT), Capital Asset Pricing Models (CAPM), Black-Scholes Options Pricing Models and the most systematically pernicious, Value At Risk (VAR) which contributed to the underestimation of risk which led to the financial meltdown of 2008-2009.

The old financial sector is gradually waking up to the green economy as confidence in Wall Street, and even in the monetary authorities, collapses.

Why have the companies in wind, solar, geothermal and alternative *NB* energy been hammered—losing as much as 50% of their value along with other DOW and S&P, Wilshire indexes, along with other companies? For three reasons: (1) These small renewable energy companies are often traded over-the-counter and prey to algorithmic short-selling, often naked shorting which can destroy their capital structure. Naked shorting *!!* which has been illegal since 1934 in the USA flourished during the past decade of deregulation, where even the *uptick rule* was abolished. (2) The second reason renewable companies have been hard hit is that obsolete asset allocation models are all still based on the industrial categories of the fossil-fueled sectors (see my "Updating Fossilized Asset-Allocation Classes—The Next Big Thing: The Sustainability Sector"). This obscures *!!* the emerging green economy from traders' screens, so that they do not see this emerging *sustainability sector*. (3) These small companies are in their rapid growth phase and needed dependable sources of working capital and credit, so they are more vulnerable to credit squeezes and market uncertainty. New electronic trading platforms are vitally needed, so that these green companies can list their shares in an honest, secure market where they can find the bridge loans and new, patient, socially-responsible investors. Private investors' networks help, including the Social Venture Network, Investors Circle, Slow Money, Entrex and green brokers such as *N B* Centerpoint Investment Strategies and others.

The Green Economy Initiative and the Green Economy Coalition, of *!!!* which Ethical Markets is a member, are fitting follow-ups to UNEP-FI, a key social innovation that has educated a new generation of investors and asset managers about ecological and social valuation models. Now, we must pull together all the constituencies and seize the opportunity of the financial crisis to harness mainstream media and politics in completing the build out of the new green economy worldwide. A truly efficient financial *NB* services sector should be less than 10% of a country's GDP. Those in Britain and the USA grew to 25% of GDP, metastasizing with their *finan-*

cial engineers preying on the real economy. Now students are looking for jobs as real engineers, teachers, doctors and entrepreneurs.

In a very real sense, we humans don't have a financial crisis but *a crisis of perception*. We are beginning to see our world differently than mainstream media portrays. We see our choices with new eyes. We know that money is not real wealth. We learn as we watch central bankers printing money on TV. Real wealth is generated by productive people using the Earth's resources wisely. Money is a great invention. When it is managed properly, locally, nationally, globally or electronically, it is a useful medium of exchange. Hoarding money is no longer a reliable store of value. We are all rediscovering the many stores of value in our own communities. We find wealth beyond money. We can change our values for the new times we live in and restore the love economies to their central role in our lives.

Disclosures

For full disclosure, I am a private investor across the full range of green and renewable energy companies, some publicly traded, such as Suntech (China) and Cree (US), Nevada Geothermal (US), Ormat (Israel and US), Natcore (US), Waterfurnace, Nevada Power (US) and privately held companies Envision Solar, Grainpro, Equal Exchange, Green Garmento (all US).

The Prophesy of the Eagle and the Condor

A prophecy originated in the Amazon over 2000 years ago and traveled up into the Andes, then across the Isthmus, influencing the legends of the Maya, Aztec, Hopi, and many North American tribes. In summary, the legend says that during ancient times human societies were divided into two groups. The Condor People represented 'the path of the heart,' adhering to the ideals of the deep feminine, opting for lifestyles that create peaceful, sustainable environments favorable to giving birth, raising families, and passing knowledge about the natural world to their children. The Eagle People followed 'the path of the mind,' advocating values we associate with masculine traits, creating societies that developed technologies for conquering other tribes and dominating nature.

According to this prophecy, the two paths would converge during the Fourth Pachacuti ('Pachacuti' is a Quechua/Inca word designating a 500-year period) that would begin in about 1500 by our calendar. There would be wars, terrible violence, and the Eagle would drive the Condor to the brink of extinction. Of course, we know that is exactly what happened after Columbus' voyage. The prophecy was realized; the industrial cultures of the world practically destroyed the indigenous ones. Then, according to the prophecy, 500 years later, starting around 2000, a new Pachacuti would begin, the fifth. It is said to be a time when the Condor and Eagle would have the opportunity to reunite. This is not a given, for it is we who must make it happen, but the opportunity exists for the Eagle and the Condor—mind and heart—to soar together in the same sky, dancing, mating, and restoring balance. And now it is happening. We're seeing it in so many parts of the world: the Condor people sharing their wisdom and the Eagle people trying to learn from them and beginning to repair the damage we have wrought. The old dream was based on exploring and conquering nature and people; the new is about cooperation, compassion and being sustainable.

‼ The prophecy is really about human evolution. We have arrived at the time to elevate ourselves and human cultures to a new level of consciousness where heart and mind are truly integrated.

‼ The current economic crisis and so much turmoil around the planet are no flukes. They are happening to shake us awake.

John Perkins

10

TERRA: A CURRENCY TO STABILIZE THE GLOBAL ECONOMY

Bernard Lietaer, MEN, MBA

O ur world today is faced with global systemic issues such as the lack of an international standard of value, currency instability and the uncertainties of the business cycle. While such concerns may at first seem like boring economic or financial problems of little concern to the average person, they are in fact key issues. Their continued lack of resolution significantly impacts our world: a lack of investments in developing nations, the ongoing conflict between the short-term financial demands of shareholders and long term sustainability, the many currency crises and associated suffering that has affected no less than 87 nations over the course of these last twenty five years. All these concerns are related to the unresolved systemic issues cited above.

These key global issues require a response of sufficient scope and magnitude if they are to be redressed in an effective manner. Furthermore, such a response, if it is to succeed, must acknowledge the requirements and concerns of the most influential decision makers of our world today—the multi-nationals and take carefully into consideration, as well, the realities of our present-day geopolitical climate and monetary system.

This essay will examine The Terra Trade Reference Currency (Terra TRC, hereafter referred to in shorthand as Terra)—a supra-national complementary currency initiative, intended to work in parallel with the current international monetary system to provide an effective mechanism by which to redress such important global issues.

The Terra is poised to create more stability and predictability in the financial and business sectors by providing a stable international currency for planning, global contracting and payment purposes worldwide. This will be the first time since the gold-standard days that a robust, inflation-resistant standard of value will be available globally. It is designed to counteract the booms and busts of the business cycle and stabilize the global economy. Most importantly, it will resolve the conflict between short-term financial interests and long-term sustainability and does not require any new legislation or international agreements to become operational.

It should be understood that the Terra Initiative is presented here not merely as a hypothetical presentation, but as a viable monetary initiative for immediate application in international trade. Its design and potential have been carefully scrutinized by some of the most respected authorities in the world today. Gernot Nerb, a recognized international expert on the business cycle, head of the research department of the Institute for Economic Research in Germany, and creator of the business sentiment index (which enables forecasting of business cycles), offers this opinion: "The Terra mechanism would provide an automatic counter-cyclical stimulus to the world economy, thereby dampening the depth of recessions as well as reduce the risk of inflationary booms. Such a tool could be particularly useful in a period of a simultaneous recession of the three major world economies as we are currently engaged in."

While a privately-issued, complementary trade reference currency may perhaps seem an unconventional methodology, such an approach is now considered inevitable by some of the most respected icons of finance and banking, including two former Chairmen of the Federal Reserve Board. Alan Greenspan has stated: "I foresee new private currency markets in the 21st century." His predecessor Paul Volcker went on record in 2000, saying: "The ultimate logic of economic globalization is a stable and common unit of account and an internationally accepted means of payment in other words, a common world currency."

This new Trade Reference Currency (TRC), the unit of account being the Terra, would provide a safety net in support of the conventional money system while mobilizing the vast energies of global corporations towards a sustainable future for all. This is most effectively accomplished not by regulation/legislative imperatives or moral indignation, but rather by providing a strong financial incentive in the right direction.

This chapter will briefly review some of the more important monetary-related issues facing the world today (Systemic Monetary Issues). We will then examine the features of a complementary currency proposal, The Terra Trade Reference Currency Initiative (the Terra Mechanism), specifically designed to address the systemic monetary issues cited. The general and specific benefits and advantages of the Terra will be covered last (Benefits of the Terra).

Systemic Monetary Issues

The world today is facing some key economic and financial concerns, which persist despite the efforts aimed at ameliorating them. These concerns are:

- Growing unemployment pressures worldwide;
- A possible world recession, which now threatens simultaneously the world's three major world economies;
- A lack of hard currencies and decreasing investments in Less Developed Countries (LDCs);
- Conflict between short-term financial interests and long-term sustainability.

These economic and financial concerns are directly related to and are being amplified by the monetary system.

Monetary Instability

!! Over $4 trillion is traded per day in foreign exchange markets, a figure that is 100-fold the trading volume of all of the world's stock exchanges combined.

!! Nearly 96% of these transactions are purely speculative; they do not relate to the real economy; they do not reflect global movements or exchanges of actual goods and services.[1] Functioning mostly as a speculative market, current national currencies can be undermined not only by tangible economic news, but also by mere rumor or changes in perception as well. This unstable monetary situation has resulted in the many foreign exchange crises that have affected no less than 87 different countries over the past 25 years, such as Mexico, South-East Asia, Russia and Argentina.

!! This growing instability of our current monetary system has been brought about by changes to our monetary system that have cumulated over the past three decades.

Monetary Changes

The instability of our international monetary system over the course of the last several decades has been fueled principally by three major changes to our money and banking systems:

1. **Structural Shift**. On August 15, 1971, President Nixon unilaterally disconnected the dollar from gold, inaugurating an era without an international standard of value; currency values would now be determined predominantly by market forces. Thus began floating exchanges—a monetary arrangement in which currency values could fluctuate significantly at any point in time. Since this decision, the world's monetary system has not had any reliable international standard of value or a unit of measure (like the yard for distance, degrees Fahrenheit for temperature or Watt for electricity).

2. **Financial Deregulation**. In the 1980s, the Thatcher and Reagan administrations embarked simultaneously on a massive financial deregulation program. This was followed by the Baker Plan which imposed

similar deregulations in 16 key developing countries. This reform package enabled many more new players to participate in currency trading.

3. **Technological Shift.** The computerization of foreign exchange trading created the first ever 24-hour, fully integrated, global market. (This shift to electronic money has been described as one of only two exceptional innovations over the 5,000-year course of money's history, the other occurring when the printing of paper began to supplement the minting of coins).[2]

With floating exchanges, financial deregulation and a 24/7 global financial market, it is now possible for a currency to lose much or even most of its value in a matter of hours. As John Maynard Keynes noted: "Speculators may do no harm as bubbles on a steady stream of enterprise. But the position is serious when enterprise becomes the bubble on a whirlpool of speculation. When the capital development of a country becomes a by-product of the activities of a casino, the job is likely to be ill-done."[3]

Economic & Financial Consequences
The shifts mentioned above have resulted in the following consequences to both national and global economies.

Lack of an International Value Standard
The current volatility of our money system has resulted in significantly increased commercial risks with regard to the use of foreign currencies. Currency risks are now typically larger than political risks (for example, the possibility that a foreign government nationalizes the investment), or even market risks (such as the possibility that clients do not want the product). In a US Fortune 500 survey, all corporate participants reported foreign exchange risks as one of the most important risks of doing business internationally today.[4]

The three principal measures used to counteract such currency risks derivatives, lost opportunities and countertrade each present significant shortcomings, as described below.

- **Derivatives**. In a survey of US Fortune 500 corporations, 85% reported the need to use derivative hedging strategies to try to control foreign exchange risks. Aside from associated risks, derivatives are expensive. It should be noted that those firms most engaged in such hedging were also the largest and most sophisticated.[5]
- **Lost Opportunities**. Another countermeasure currently employed is abstention. Many foreign investments end up not being made at all because the currency risk cannot be covered or its coverage is too expensive. These lost opportunity costs are detrimental not only to the corporations involved but to society at large, especially to those Less Developed Countries where investments have dropped over the past decades.
- **Countertrade**. Countertrade International corporate barter is in operation in an estimated 200 countries worldwide, with a volume that now ranges from $800 billion to $1.2 trillion per year.[6] This represents 10% to 15% of all international trade. Fortune (US) reports that two out of three major global corporations now perform such transactions routinely, with specialized departments dedicated to the execution of these deals. Though expensive, countertrade does make it safer to get paid in something that has a known worth and use, rather than accept a currency that may have dropped significantly in value from the time a deal was made. Some barter deals also occur because the countries involved simply don't have access to hard currency financing (for example, Pepsi Cola dealing with Russia through payments in Stolichnaya Vodka or even in the form of 17 submarines and 3 military surface ships!)[7]

The Terra initiative will introduce a reference currency that is fully backed by a dozen or so of the most important commodities and services in the global market, thereby providing, for the first time since the gold-standard days, an international standard of value that is inflation-resistant.

Boom & Bust Amplification

The money-creation process by the banking system tends to amplify the fluctuations of the business cycle. The banking system simultaneously tends to either making credit available or restricting it. Specifically, when business is good in a particular market, banks tend to be more generous in terms of credit availability, thereby pushing the good times into a potentially inflationary boom period. Conversely, as soon as the business horizon looks less promising, banks logically tend to reduce credit availability, thereby contributing to the deterioration of a minor business dip into a full-blown recession.

Notwithstanding the attempts by Central Banks to reduce such fluctuations by giving interest rate signals, the current process of creating money through bank-debt remains, in practice, a significant boom/bust-amplification mechanism. Net result: the collective actions of the banking system tend to exacerbate the business cycle in both boom and bust directions.

The Terra, in contrast, is specifically designed to act as an automatic cycle-stabilization mechanism.

Institutional Deadlock

A master of understatement such as Paul Volcker has gone on record to express his concern about the growth of "a constituency in favor of instability." What he is referring to is an influential group of special interests who are opposed to reforming the global monetary system (taking steps to make the system more stable) because the current instability is a source of substantial profits for this group.

Indeed, a whole industry has evolved around creating, selling and trading a full range of sophisticated hedging instruments that provide protection against currency fluctuations. In some cases, the trading of such instruments has become the most important profit center, not just for major banks, but also for the treasury departments of major corporations.

Political Inaction

Finally, for national governments to engage in significant currency reforms would be virtually unprecedented. [Note what happened to Abraham Lincoln's efforts as told in the introduction to this volume.] While the reasons for such prevailing postures are varied and often complex, the end result is nevertheless the same—a customary lack of initiatives until a major crisis or a world war forces change.

Added to this is today's geopolitical environment in which the United States has emerged as the world's sole superpower, and the US dollar as the world's pre-eminent currency. This reality confers upon this nation a commanding voice in international monetary policymaking but reduces the likelihood of any significant governmental monetary initiative being taken. As John B. Connally, US Secretary of the Treasury under Nixon remarked: "The dollar may be our currency, but it is your problem." This benign neglect approach makes a cooperative governmental initiative by the United States unlikely. And any attempt at reform without the United States would be futile.

Therefore, any monetary initiatives that are to be taken preventatively must be initiated by the private sector.

The Terra initiative takes vested interests and geo-political reality into account.

The Terra Mechanism

The Terra is a complementary, privately issued, demurrage-charged, Trade Reference Currency that is backed by an inflation-resistant, standardized basket of the dozen most important commodities and services in the global market.

The Terra Characteristics

Complementary Currency. The Terra is designed as a complementary currency operating in parallel with national currencies. Therefore, everything that exists today as monetary and financial products or practices continues to exist. The Terra mechanism is only one additional option available for those international economic actors who voluntarily choose to use it.

Private Issue. The Terra will be issued as an <u>inventory receipt</u> by the Terra Alliance, a private, non-governmental initiative with an organizational structure that is open to all newcomers meeting certain pre-established criteria (organizationally similar to that of the Visa credit card system). Such inventory receipts are issued for the value of the commodities sold to the Terra Alliance by producers of those commodities that are components of the Terra Basket. As a private initiative this does not require governmental negotiations or international agreements. From a legal and taxation viewpoint the Terra is simply a standardization of countertrade. And legislation for countertrade exists already in practically all nations around the world.

Trade Reference Currency. The Terra is backed by a standardized basket of the most important commodities as well as some standardizable services traded in the global market. Though conceptually similar to a fully backed gold standard, Terra backing would consist not of one single commodity, but a dozen of the main international commodities, including gold. Since it is fully backed by a physical inventory of commodities, it would be a secure, very robust, and stable mechanism for international contractual and payment purposes.

Demurrage-Charged. The Terra is a demurrage-charged currency. A demurrage charge acts like a parking fee, incurring a cost over time to its holder. The cost for holding onto the Terra currency is estimated at 3.5%-4% per annum and corresponds to the costs incurred for storing the physical commodities included in the Terra basket. This demurrage charge insures the currency's use mainly as a planning, contractual and trading device: it would not be hoarded but tend always to remain in circulation. It would thereby strongly activate commercial exchanges and investments wherever it circulates. In short, the Terra purposely fulfills only two of the three traditional monetary functions. It is designed to serve only as unit of account and medium of exchange, and not as a store of value.

¶ *Inflation-Resistant.* The Terra is designed as an inflation-resistant currency by its very composition. Inflation is always defined as "the changes in value of a standardized basket of goods and services." By selecting the appropriate ingredients to be placed in the basket, the Terra can be protected against inflation. For example, the composition of 100 Terras could include 1 barrel of oil, 5 bushels of wheat, 10 pounds of copper, 3 pounds of tin plus, 1/10th ounce of gold, 1 Carbon Emissions Right, etc.

Practical Operations of the Terra

The following scenario and accompanying diagram walks through the key elements that are involved in the Terra mechanism from the creation of Terras to their final cash-in. The numbers listed in parenthesis in the description below corresponds to the steps illustrated in the following diagram.

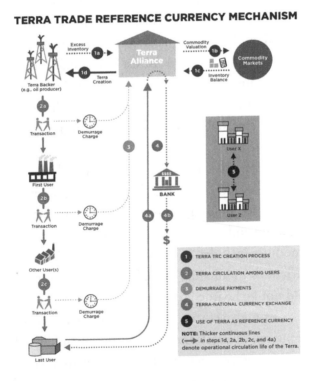

TERRA TRADE REFERENCE CURRENCY MECHANISM

(1) **The Terra Creation Process**

(1a) *Excess Inventory Sale.* The process whereby the Terra Trade Reference Currency is created begins with the sale of some excess commodity inventory to the Terra Alliance by one of its backer/members (say, 1 million barrels of crude oil by an oil producer).[8]

(1b) *Commodity Valuation in Terras.* The value of this sale of oil to the Terra Alliance (for example, how many Terras the one million barrels of oil will be worth) is calculated at market prices. This is accomplished by determining the commodity prices at the time of the sale for both the inventory in question (in this case oil) and the sum of each of the commodities in the Terra basket using a pre-agreed-upon procedure.[9]

The formula used to calculate the commodity valuation in Terras is:

Commodity value per unit X number of units =
Terras based on Terra Unit Value

Let us assume in our example that the commodity price for a barrel of oil at the time of the sale is $20. The commodity prices for each of the items in the Terra Basket at the time of the sale (copper, grains, lead, one unit of Carbon emissions rights, etc., including oil,) totals $200. Assume that one million barrels of oil are sold. Therefore, 100,000 Terras are created:

$20 per barrel of crude oil X one million barrels =
100,000 Terras valued at $200 each

(1c) *Inventory Balance.* The Terra Alliance rebalances its portfolio to take into account the inclusion of the 1 million barrels of oil. This may be accomplished through future market transactions or through spot transactions.[10]

(1d) *Terra Creation.* The Terra Alliance credits the oil producers' account with 100,000 Terras. (Note that all Terra currency movements in the diagram are denoted by the thicker continuous arrowed lines).

(2) Terra Circulation among Users.

Once the Terra is created, it enters into and may remain in circulation for a period determined entirely by users.[11] For example:

(2a) *First User*: The oil producer may decide to pay one of its suppliers (say, a German engineering company for the construction of an off-shore rig). It may pay partially or completely in Terras for this project.[12]

(2b) *Other User(s)*: The German engineering firm decides in turn to purchase specialty steels from a Korean steel mill and may decide to pay partially or completely in Terras. The Korean steel mill may then use the Terras to pay a mining company in Australia, etc.

(2c) *Last User*: Each Terra remains in circulation for as brief or long a time as its various users continue to use this currency, creating from one to an infinite number of transactions and without any particular date of expiration. The process comes to an end only when a particular user determines to cash in the Terras, becoming in effect the last user.

(3) Demurrage

Throughout the circulation life of each Terra, from its creation to its final cash-in, a demurrage fee of 3.5 to 4% per year is in effect. Demurrage is a time-related charge on money, acting much like a rental fee. Anybody holding the Terra would be charged a demurrage fee proportionate to the time held. At 3.5% to 4%, the cost of holding the Terra for a few days or even a few months is still low when compared to today's normal international transactions costs. Because the Terra exists only in electronic form, it is easy to know exactly how much time has elapsed between its acquisition by one user and its transfer to another.

The demurrage charge serves two key functions: as an incentive to circulation and to cover Terra operational costs:

- Terra Circulation Incentive. The demurrage charge is designed as an incentive to keep the Terras circulating in a timely fashion among users. The Terra demurrage charge increases the longer it is held, as calculated below. In this way, the demurrage charge insures the Terras' usage as a mechanism of exchange and not as a mechanism of storage

- Terra Operational Cost Coverage. Terra demurrage charges are calculated to cover the costs of the entire operation of the Terra mechanism (storage costs of the basket, administrative overhead, transaction costs in the futures markets).

The demurrage fees for a particular Terra transaction may be calculated by the following formula:

$$\text{(Terra Operation Costs/time unit)} \times \text{(Terra holding period)} \times \text{(Terras on account)} = \text{Demurrage Charge}$$

Let us assume the Terra operation costs are evaluated at 3.65% per year or 0.01% per day. Let us further assume the German engineering firm (First User in our diagram) received all 100,000 Terras from the oil producer and has kept these on account for a period of 10 days, prior to paying the Korean steel mill in transaction 2b in our diagram. The demurrage charge (represented by the dotted blue line) in Transaction 2b would be calculated as follows:

$$0.01\%/\text{per day} \times 10 \text{ days} \times 100,000 \text{ Terras} = 100 \text{ Terras}$$

(4) Terra Cash-In

The circulation (and existence) of a particular Terra comes to an end when one entity (designated Last User in our diagram) decides to cash in part or all of its Terras (for example, to pay its taxes and/or payroll and requires national currency to do so).

A transaction fee equal to 2% of the amount of the Terras cashed in is then charged. This transaction fee serves two purposes:

- Terra Circulation Incentive. The transaction fee is designed as an incentive to keep the Terras in circulation and not cash in Terras too readily, thus continuing the beneficial effects of the circulating Terras. In effect, the 2% transaction fee requires any entity in possession of Terras to make the following consideration: "Cashing in the Terras now will cost me the same as paying the demurrage fee for more than six months (assuming a demurrage of 3.65% per year). It is likely I will be able to pay someone at least partially in Terras over the next six months. After all, most suppliers would rather be paid earlier than later...."

- Cash-In Operational Costs. When the last user decides to cash in its Terras, the Terra Alliance sells the necessary volume of commodities from its basket to the commodity markets to obtain the necessary funds in conventional currency.

The Terras are then handed into the Terra Alliance (4a) and converted either to national currency or a volume of Terra commodities (as determined by the last user) in the amount equal to the value of the Terras cashed in, minus the transaction fee. The cash-in may take place directly with the Terra Alliance itself or by means of an intermediary bank like any foreign exchange transaction today. (4b)

(5) Reference Currency

Once the Terra mechanism is operational and the advantages of using an inflation-resistant international standard is known, there is nothing to impede two entities (user X and user Z in the diagram), who may have no direct involvement in the Terra mechanism, to denominate contracts in Terras, even if the final settlement takes place in the corresponding value in conventional currency. The Terra, in this instance, functions purely as a Trade Reference Currency, a reliable standard of value. This is similar to the gold standard days when two parties agreed on contracts denominated in gold, even if neither party owned gold or had any involvement in gold mining or processing. The only significant difference is that the Terra is backed not by a single commodity such as gold, but by the dozen or so commodities and services which make up the Terra basket, making it an even more stable reference than existed with the gold standard.

Benefits of the Terra

The Terra Initiative addresses each of the major economic and financial concerns mentioned earlier and offers both general benefits and specific benefits to particular interest groups. General and specific benefits will be examined next, followed by an analysis differentiating the Terra from all other proposals and initiatives aimed at redressing present monetary concerns.

General Benefits of the Terra

The Terra mechanism, by virtue of its demurrage charge and being inflationary-resistant, endows this trading instrument with three unique economic advantages. These are:

- It provides a robust international standard of value.
- It counteracts the boom/bust fluctuations of the business cycle, thereby improving the overall stability and predictability of the world's economic system.
- It realigns financial interests with long-term concerns.

Robust International Standard of Value

The Terra would provide a robust international standard of value, something which has been missing for decades. Since it is fully backed by a physical inventory of not one, but a dozen or so of the world's most important commodities, including gold, the Terra would serve a very robust and credible payment unit offsetting volatility and currency risks.

This robust standard of value benefits commerce as follows:

- By lowering costs by reducing the need for expensive hedging countermeasures.
- By enabling greater opportunities, including investments in developing countries by providing stable alternative mechanisms with which to conduct commerce.
- By offering a dependable, cost-effective reference mechanism for global trade.

Cycle-stabilization

The Terra automatically tends to counteract the fluctuations of the business cycle, thereby improving the overall stability and predictability of the world's economic system.

When the business cycle is weakening, corporations customarily have an excess of inventory and a need for credit. The excess inventories can now be sold to the TRC Alliance, who would place these inventories into storage. The TRC Alliance would pay for these inventories in Terras, thus providing corporations with a means of payment (typically, less readily available in this part of a business cycle). These corporations would immediately spend the Terras to pay their suppliers so as to avoid the demurrage charges a holding cost which accumulates over time. Suppliers, in turn, would have a similar incentive to pass on the demurrage-charged Terras as a medium of payment. The spread of this currency with its built-in incentive to trade would automatically activate the economy at this point in the cycle.

On the other hand, when the business cycle is in a boom period, demand for goods and services goes up and both suppliers and corporations have an increased need for inventory. The Terras would now be cashed in with the TRC Alliance for a 2% transaction fee and the now-needed inventories would be taken out of storage and delivered to the respective commodity markets to obtain the conventional currency required. This would also reduce the amount of Terras in circulation when the business cycle is at its maximum, counteracting an inflationary boom phase.

None of this is theory. There is now quantitative proof that the availability of a complementary currency designed for business use spontaneously tends to stabilize the business cycle and overall economy. Detailed analysis of the WIR system, a complementary currency program that originated in Switzerland in 1934 and is used today by 70,000 Swiss businesses, provides the relevant evidence (see insert).

Complementary Currencies, the WIR & Economic Stabilization

The impact of commercial exchanges facilitated by computer networks without the use of conventional money is a hotly debated topic of late. A few prominent economists have speculated that computer-networked barter might eventually replace our money as well as its centralized protector central banking. Such questions have recently been asked by leading macroeconomists such as Mervyn King,[13] Deputy Governor of the Bank of England, and Benjamin Friedman of Harvard.[14]

"Friedman's view that central banking may be seriously challenged was a lead topic at a recent World Bank conference on the 'Future of Monetary Policy and Banking' (World Bank, 2000).[15] His warnings have even sparked a pair of skeptical reviews in the Economist Magazine of London.[16] But no one, until now, has looked at the direct evidence on this issue the large-scale barter networks, in existence for decades."[17]

A quantitative study on the direct evidence on this issue was conducted by Dr. James P. Stodder, Professor at the well-respected Lally School of Management & Technology at Rensselaer University. It is based on the high quality data from the Swiss WIR system.[18] His conclusion: "The WIR system is counter-cyclical, rising and falling against, rather than with, the business cycle... because... credit advanced by the WIR is highly counter-cyclical, correlated against GDP."[19] This contributes measurably to the stability of the Swiss economy, because WIR credits automatically expand when the economy turns down, that is, when credit in conventional Swiss Francs dries up.[20] Furthermore, the WIR system also stabilizes employment. "Growth in the number of WIR participants has tracked Swiss Unemployment very closely, consistently maintaining a rate of about one-tenth the increase in the number of unemployed." This means that when the conventional Swiss Franc economy slows, job losses are avoided partly by having more people getting involved in the WIR economy.

Professor Tobias Studer from the Center of Economic Studies of Basel University, Switzerland, considers the Stodder study a breakthrough because: "For the first time, an independent American researcher has arrived at a surprising conclusion: far from representing a factor of disturbance for national monetary policy, the credits created by WIR constitute a support of the National Bank (Swiss Central Bank) in pursuit of its monetary policy objectives."[21]

In case one might think such effects are valid only for Switzerland, Prof. Stodder also evaluated the effects of commercial barter by members of the International Reciprocal Trade Association (IRTA) on the US economy.[22] Though the data here covers only 21 years (instead of WIR's 50 plus), exactly the same type of impact occurs. But with IRTA exchanges proportionally smaller in the US economy than the WIR for the Swiss economy, the overall effect is also proportionally less powerful.

In summary, the Terra-denominated exchanges would stabilize the business cycle by providing additional monetary liquidity to counterbalance the pattern observed in the money-creation process of conventional national currencies.

Realignment of Financial Interests with Long-term Concerns

The demurrage feature of the Terra would provide a systematic financial motivation to realign financial interests with long-term concerns. This is in direct contrast with what happens today with conventional national currencies. The discounted cash flow of conventional national currencies with positive interest rates systematically emphasizes the immediate future at the expense of the long-term. The same discounted cash flow with a demurrage charged currency produces the exact opposite effects. The use of the Terra for planning and contractual purposes will therefore reduce the conflict that currently prevails between the stockholder's financial priorities and the long-term priorities of humanity as a whole.

Specific Group Benefits

Virtually everyone stands to benefit from the Terra. A partial list of the specific advantages applying to humanity at-large, multinational corporations, the banking sector and financial services, Less Developed Countries and developed nations are outlined here.

Humanity as a Whole

- As long as business is focused on short-term profits, chances are minimal that any long-term sustainability will be achievable. Inevitably, it is humanity as a whole that ends up paying for failures in sustainable development. By contrast, the introduction of the Terra with its demurrage functionality makes long-term thinking profitable, and therefore, long-term sustainability much more likely.
- The typical booms/bust of the business cycle will automatically decrease, creating a more dependable economic environment which will translate into more reliable job employment opportunities and less job instability.

Multinational Corporations

The Terra offers corporations the following advantages:

- Makes it possible to convert inventories of illiquid assets, such as major raw materials, into usable Terras. This is a significant advantage, given that inventories are otherwise a cost item to businesses. Over time, such storage costs can become substantial.
- Provides working capital at a lower cost than with conventional national currencies, as the Terra demurrage fees only kick in for a particular user if the Terras are not spent.
- Makes available to businesses a robust international standard of value with a consistent value in real terms for international contracts. No party would lose out because of monetary instability or currency fluctuations.

- Lowers the cost of doing business by reducing the need for expensive currency hedging counter-measures and providing a dependable, low-cost insurance against uncertainties deriving from international currency markets.
- Offers a dependable, more cost-effective reference mechanism than conventional corporate barter.
- Develops new markets and provides greater opportunities for the conduct of global commerce, including investing in developing countries, by providing a stable international currency. Currency instability has limited the creation of new markets because entire continents remain too poor to participate in the global marketplace.
- Saves money and vital resources. Corporations, as a result of the boom and bust business cycle phenomenon, are often over-equipped and over-staffed or under-equipped and looking for qualified staff. The costs of training people are considerable, especially if one must fire them afterwards. Expenses incurred in plant and equipment over-investments or under-investments are also considerable.
- And, it is well known that political instabilities often occur during, and result from, economic downturns. Such instability does not contribute to a healthy climate for businesses either. The Terra counteracts such downturns.

Benefits to Financial Services and the Banking Sector

There are three main advantages of the Terra mechanism for the banking system:

- It introduces standardization in countertrade, thus making the countertrade mechanism bankable. Currently, the banking system has no role at all in the fast-growing countertrade field (countertrade grows at a rate of 15% per year[23], three times faster than trade facilitated in conventional currencies). Banks will be able to provide traditional foreign exchange services utilizing the Terras, which can then be converted into any and all other national currencies. They can, as well, provide their customers services such as Terra account management, as they do today with any foreign exchange.

• The counter-cyclical impact of the Terra mechanism will stabilize the value of banking loan portfolios. There have been numerous major banking-related crises around the world over the past two decades brought on by the inability of borrowers to repay their loans, even as the collateral upon which the loans were based depreciates. These conditions are aggravated by the boom/bust cycle and currency fluctuations. Therefore, as the Terra mechanism helps to stabilize economic cycles, the number and severity of crises in bank portfolios would also be reduced.

• Finally, the task of central banks would also be made a bit easier with the Terra mechanism in play. Not only would there be fewer banking crises to manage, but their routine job of trying to counteract the business cycle would also be eased as already demonstrated in practice by the Swiss WIR.

Less Developed Countries (LDCs)

Currently, as a direct result of currency instability, less developed countries suffer from a lack of investments. Moreover, the degradation of terms of trade with developed nations and the scarcity of hard currencies create debt traps resulting in their inability to repay foreign loans.

This is illustrated by the comment on his country's debt made after the G8 summit in Okinawa in 2000 by President Obasanjo of Nigeria: "All that we had borrowed up to 1985 or 1986 was around $5 billion. So far we have paid back about $16 billion. Yet we are being told that we still owe about $28 billion. That $28 billion came about because of the foreign creditors' interest rates. If you ask me what is the worst thing in the world, I will say it is compound interest." When President Obasanjo spoke out, [11] the developing world was spending $13 on debt repayment for every one dollar it received in foreign aid and grants.

!} The Terra mechanism helps to address these problems and offers two distinct and important benefits to Less Developed Countries.

- A stable international currency enables greater opportunities by which to conduct commerce and make investments in developing countries. As noted earlier, because of the instability created by floating exchanges, there has been a decrease in investments in Less Developed Countries of around 33%.
- LDCs that produce commodities raw materials such as copper that are components in the basket of the Terra would be in a position similar to other producer members of the TRC Alliance. By virtue of the fact that the Terra is a commodity-backed currency, LDCs would find themselves in a situation similar to that of gold-producing countries during the gold standard days: The gold they extracted was instantly convertible into internationally currency.

Developed Countries

As stated earlier, the developed world has faced recurring economic downturns since the 1930s. At that time, only a World War got us out that economic stranglehold. A better way is available. If the Terra were implemented now on a sufficient scale, it would help re-launch the world economy by injecting international liquidity that would reactivate the global economy.

- By helping Less Developed Countries, new markets are created.
- By stabilizing the business cycle, greater job stability and opportunities would become available as well.

Differences with Earlier Proposals

The Terra is a commodity-basket currency. For more than a century there have been several proposals for commodity-basket currencies by a series of well-known economists. The main reason they have not been implemented is due not to a technical fault of the concept, but rather because they were aiming at replacing the conventional money system. Such replacement would have put in jeopardy powerful vested interests. This is not the case with the Terra proposal.

On the contrary, the win-win strategy underlying the Terra mechanism includes the financial sector as well. Anything that exists under the current monetary modus operandi would remain in operation after the introduction of the Terra, as it is a complementary currency designed to operate in parallel with the existing system.

Finally, as earlier stated, the political context for an international monetary treaty has not been available. The Terra avoids this pitfall by relying on private initiative. From a legal or tax standpoint, it would fit within the existing official framework of countertrade and would not require any formal governmental agreements to make it operational.

The other conceptual difference, and perhaps the most important one between the Terra proposal and all previous proposals, is the introduction of the demurrage concept. The fact that the storage costs of the basket would be covered by the bearer of the Terra resolves the inherent problem that previous commodity proposals were facing, namely: Who will pay for it all?

The Terra mechanism is a win-win approach for all participants in the global game, and that is why it can succeed where other proposals for monetary innovations in the past have failed.

Glossary of Terms

Baker Plan. A plan by former US Treasury Secretary James Baker under which 16 principal middle-income debtor countries would undertake growth-oriented structural reforms, to be supported by increased financing from the World Bank and continued lending from commercial banks.

Barter. The direct exchange of goods or services un-mediated by any type of currency.

Booms and Busts. A recurrent cycle of growth, bust, recession, and recovery in the economic activity of a capitalist country. There have been 47 major asset boom/bust cycles since 1637, the last two being the Japanese real-estate bubble, and the US high-tech stock market bubble that crashed respectively in 1990 and 2000. For an explanation of the mechanism behind boom/bust cycles and their relationship to money systems, see B. Lietaer, *Mysterium Geld* (Munich: Riemann Verlag, 2000), Chapter 5.

Bretton Woods Agreement. The major world powers met in 1944 in Bretton Woods, New Hampshire, to organize an international monetary system that would alleviate foreign-exchange problems created by WW II. The result was the Bretton Woods Agreement, the first global monetary constitution. The World Bank and International Monetary Fund (IMF) were established there. The participating nations, agreed to tie the values of their currencies to the value of the US dollar.

Business Cycle. A term used in economics to designate cyclical changes in the economy. Ever since the Industrial Revolution, the level of business activity in industrialized countries has veered from high to low and back up again. The timing of a cycle is not predictable, but its phases seem to be. Many economists cite four phases: prosperity, liquidation, recession or depression, and recovery; using the terms originally developed by the American economist Wesley Mitchell.

Capital. In its narrow financial sense, capital is a sum of money from which an income can be derived. The two most traditional means for such income is interest (in the case of loans) and dividends (in the case of stocks). In broader terms, capital is a resource that enhances life, of which several types can be distinguished: financial capital, physical capital (for example, plants, equipment), intellectual capital (for example, patents, copyrights), social capital (for example, relationships) and natural capital (Mother Nature).

Central Bank. A financial institution whose function is to regulate a state's monetary activities. It is responsible for the issue of bills and for controlling the flow of currency. In the US, the Federal Reserve plays that role.

Clearing House. A central collection place where institutions and individuals exchange checks, drafts and currencies. Participants maintain an account with the Clearing House against which credits or debits are posted.

Commodity-Backed Currency. A currency whose value is guaranteed by the physical availability of the commodity that backs the currency. The owner of a backed currency can normally ask for delivery of the physical good or service in exchange for the currency. Backed currency is typically issued by whoever owns the product or service accepted as backing (for example, the 19th century gold standard backed by gold).

Complementary Currency. An agreement within a community to create its own currency to link unmet needs with unused resources. These currencies do not replace but rather supplement (complement) the national monetary system and provide greater functionality to money.

Countertrade. Barter at the corporate, multinational level.

Currency. Synonymous with money, but emphasizing the medium of exchange function of money.

Currency Crisis. A dramatic and sudden change of value of a country's currency relative to other currencies, typically accompanied by a swift increase of the flow of capital in or out of the country.

Demurrage Charge. A time-related charge on money. It acts in a manner similar to a rental fee, which increases the longer it is held onto. For example, a 5% annual demurrage charge on $100 incurs a $5 fee, leaving a remainder of $95. The demurrage feature wields two profound effects, namely: It promotes a currency's circulation as a trading device; and it encourages long-term thinking.

Deregulation. Dismantling of legal and governmental restrictions on the operation of certain businesses. When governments want to encourage competition and make economies more productive, they often deregulate, removing restrictions on companies' behavior. After deregulation, companies (for example, airlines, telephone service providers) may make their own decisions on prices and markets, regardless of the effect on consumers.

Derivatives. A financial instrument that enables the segmentation of different types of risk. The main derivatives types are futures (contracted in a regulated exchange), forwards (contracted in the unregulated "over the counter" market) and options. Exotic derivatives are complex combinations of simpler derivatives (for example, forwards and options).

Development Banks. Multilateral banks that lend money toward or invest in the economic development of countries. The World Bank (officially called the International Bank for Reconstruction and Development) and regional banks such as the European Bank for Reconstruction and Development (EBRD), and the Asian Development Bank (ADB) are such institutions.

Discounted Cash Flow. Calculates the value of a future cash flow in terms of an equivalent value today. For instance, $100 a year from now is equivalent to $90.91 today if one uses a discount rate of 10% (conversely, a one-year, risk-free investment of $90.91 at a rate of 10% will yield $100). The three factors that make up the discount rate are: the interest rate of the currency used, the cost of capital, and an adjustment for the risk of the investment.

Dollar-Gold Equivalence Standard. A guarantee of the convertibility of US dollars into gold on demand. This was established at the fixed rate of $35 per ounce by the Bretton Woods Agreement (1944), but abandoned by the Nixon administration (1971).

Economic Development. The promotion of more intensive and more advanced economic activity through education, improved tools and techniques, increased financing, better transportation facilities, and creation of new businesses.

Emerging Markets. Nations whose economies are transitioning or have recently transitioned from heavy state control to economic policies that are more market-oriented.

Euro. The European supra-national monetary unit, implemented on January 1, 2002. It officially replaced the national currencies of twelve member states of the European Union, namely: Belgium, Germany, Greece, Spain, France, Ireland, Italy, Luxembourg, The Netherlands, Austria, Portugal and Finland.

Exchange Rates. The value of currencies worldwide is provided by exchange rates that determine what each currency is worth in terms of other currencies. Just like any other commodity, a currency is now worth whatever people will pay for it. A Norwegian krone, for example, is worth a given amount of euros, dollars or yen.

Fiat Money. Money that is created by the power of an authority. Fiat Lux ("Let light be") were the first words that God pronounced, according to Genesis. Fiat money is money created out of nothing ("ex nihilo") by the power of the word of an authority and is not backed by goods or services. All national currencies today are fiat currencies.

Financial Deregulation. The reduction of government's role in controlling financial markets; relying on market forces to function without governmental intervention.

Fixed Exchange Rate. Rate fixed by an authority at which one currency can be exchanged against another.

Floating Exchanges. The flexible exchange rate system in which the exchange rate is determined by the market forces of supply and demand without governmental intervention.

Globalization. Integration of the world's culture, economy, and infrastructure, driven by the lowering of political barriers to transnational trade and investment, and by the rapid proliferation of communication and information technologies. The term is often used in reference to the substantial impact of free-market forces on local, regional and national economies.

Gold Standard. In economics, the monetary system wherein all forms of legal tender may be converted on demand into fixed quantities of fine gold, as defined by law; having three principal aims: to facilitate the settlement of international commercial and financial transactions; to establish stability in foreign exchange rates; to maintain domestic monetary stability.

Gross Domestic Product (GDP). The total value of all goods and services produced within a country in a year, minus the net income from investments in other countries.

Gross National Product (GNP). The total annual flow of goods and services in monetary value in the economy of a nation. The GNP is normally measured by totaling all personal spending, government spending, and investment spending by a nation's industry. GNP can also be figured by the earnings and cost approach of accounting, in which all forms of wages and income (for example, corporate profits, net interest returns, rent, indirect business taxes, unincorporated income) are added together.

Hedge Funds. Only remotely related to the practice of hedging, hedge funds borrow money to make speculative investments, usually in areas from which more conservative investors shy away.

Human Wealth. The assets and capital inherent in the spirit, creative genius and unbounded potential of the ever-evolving human species.

Inflation. Depreciation over time of the value of a currency in terms of a reference basket of goods and services. An excess of fiat money supply will tend to create inflation.

Interest. Time-related income for the owner of a currency, or time-related cost for the borrower of a currency. Interest is one of the ingredients in the Discounted Cash Flow calculations.

International Monetary Fund (IMF). International organization, established at the Bretton Woods Conference in 1944, which aims to promote international monetary cooperation, currency stabilization and expansion of international trade. Based in Washington, D.C., with 183 member nations, the United States is the only country with veto power. Web site: www.imf.org

Legal Tender. A currency that is recognized as acceptable payment for all debts, public and private. A debt can be declared void if repayment in legal tender is refused.

Money. Synonymous with currency or means of payment. Our working definition is "an agreement within a community to use something as a medium of exchange."

Multinational Corporation. A large company that operates or has investments in several different countries.

Payment system. Procedure and infrastructure by which the transfer of a currency is executed from one entity (or person) to another.

Scarce. In insufficient quantity. For all national currencies, bank-debt money keeps value only by its scarcity compared to its usefulness. The polarity of scarcity is not over-abundance, but sufficiency. For instance, in a mutual credit system there is always sufficiency of money as participants create it among themselves as a debit and credit at the moment of a transaction.

Stock. A fraction of ownership in a business. Stock markets are the regulated exchanges for stocks of companies listed in a particular exchange.

Terra Trade Reference Currency™ (Terra TRC™). A new, privately issued, complementary currency designed to systematically stabilize the effects on the business cycle and re-align financial interests with long-term sustainability. This internet-based trade reference currency will be fully backed by a dozen or so of the most important commodities and services in international trade, thereby providing, for the first time since the gold-standard days, an international standard of value that is inflation-resistant. Its unit of account is the Terra. It has a built-in circulation incentive via its demurrage feature. As a complementary currency, it will work in parallel with national currencies. Web site: www.terratrc.org.

World Bank (WB). A specialized United Nations agency, established at the Bretton Woods Conference in 1944. The chief objectives of the bank, as stated in its articles of agreement, are "to assist in the reconstruction and development of territories of members by facilitating the investment of capital for productive purposes [and] to promote private foreign investment by means of guarantees or participation in loans [and] to supplement private investment by providing, on suitable conditions, finance for productive purposes out of its own capital." Web site: www.worldbank.org

World Trade Organization (WTO). An international body that promotes and enforces the provisions of trade laws and regulations; established in 1994 to replace the General Agreement on Tariffs and Trade (GATT). Web site: www.wto.org

APPENDICES

APPENDIX A:
ABRAHAM LINCOLN'S
MONETARY POLICY

National Economy and the
Banking System of the United States

Michael Rowbotham has remarked that Lincoln's "monetary policy *!!* is one of the world's great political declarations; a masterpiece of succinct advocacy and irrefutable justice."

The Lincoln monetary policy, reproduced below in its entirety, would have profoundly altered the American economic landscape forever afterwards. Unfortunately, Lincoln was assassinated, and his plans to establish a national bank, introduce legislation to revoke the National Bank Law and, in all probably, establish a permanent national currency based on his earlier experience with the issue of his Greenbacks never came to fruition. The bankers well understood that if the United States created its own debt-free currency and demonstrated that it could prosper under such a system, it would be only a matter of time until such a policy spread throughout the world and the bankers would be out of business. Lincoln's monetary ideas continued to be subjects of debate and discussion well into the Great Depression of the 1930s and are enjoying a revival in the Internet age.

Lincoln's Monetary Policy

Money is the creature of law, and the creation of the original issue of money should be maintained as the exclusive monopoly of national government. Money possesses no value to the state other than that given to it by circulation. Capital has its proper place and is entitled to every protection. The wages of men should be recognized in the structure of and in the social order as more important than the wages of money [interest on money].

No duty is more imperative for the government than the duty it owes the people to furnish them with a sound and uniform currency, and of regulating the circulation of the medium of exchange so that labour will be protected from a vicious currency [private bank-created, interest-bearing debt], and commerce will be facilitated by cheap and safe exchanges.

The available supply of gold and silver being wholly inadequate to permit the issuance of coins of intrinsic value or paper currency convertible into coin in the volume required to serve the needs of the People, some other basis for the issue of currency must be developed, and some means other than that of convertibility into coin must be developed to prevent undue fluctuation in the value of paper currency or any other substitute for money of intrinsic value that may come into use.

The monetary needs of increasing numbers of people advancing towards higher standards of living can and should be met by the government. Such needs can be met by the issue of national currency and credit through the operation of a national banking system. The circulation of a medium of exchange issued and backed by the government can be properly regulated and redundancy of issue avoided by withdrawing from circulation such amounts as may be necessary by taxation, re-deposit and otherwise. Government has the power to regulate the currency and credit of the nation.

Government should stand behind its currency and credit and the bank deposits of the nation. No individual should suffer a loss of money through depreciation or inflated currency or Bank bankruptcy.

Government, possessing the power to create and issue currency and credit as money and enjoying the right to withdraw both currency and credit from circulation by taxation and otherwise, need not and should not borrow capital at interest [from the private banking system or their affiliates] as a means of financing government work and public enterprise. The government should create, issue and circulate all the currency and credit needed to satisfy the spending power of the government and the buying power of consumers. The privilege of creating and issuing money is not only the supreme prerogative of government, but it is the government's greatest creative opportunity.

By the adoption of these principles, the long-felt want for a uniform medium will be satisfied. The taxpayers will be saved immense sums of interest, discounts, and exchanges. The financing of all public enterprises, the maintenance of stable government and ordered progress, and the conduct of the Treasury will become matters of practical administration. The people can and will be furnished with a currency as safe as their own government. Money will cease to be the master and become the servant of humanity. Democracy will rise superior to the money power.

The above is an abstract of Lincoln's monetary policy from Mayor McGeer's *Conquest of Poverty* and *has been certified as correct* by the Legislative Reference Service of the Library of Congress at the instance of Hon. Kent Keller, Member of the House of Representatives. See 76th Congress, 1st Session, Jan 3Aug 5, 1939, Senate Documents #10304, Vol. 3, Senate Document 23, "National Economy and the Banking System of the United States" by Robert L. Owen, former Chairman of the Committee on Banking and Currency of the United States Senate, presented by Mr. Logan on January 24, 1939, page 91.

APPENDIX B:
OCCUPY WALL STREET MANIFESTO

This article presents the full-text of *Occupy Wall Street Movement's* admirably bold and clear declaration, published on the internet on September 30, 2011. Also read:

- Guide to the Occupy Wall Street Movement
- Endorsements, Support for Occupy Wall Street Movement

Declaration and Manifesto of Occupy Wall Street Movement

"As we gather together in solidarity to express a feeling of mass injustice, we must not lose sight of what brought us together. We write so that all people who feel wronged by the corporate forces of the world can know that we are your allies.

"As one people, united, we acknowledge the reality: that the future of the human race requires the cooperation of its members; that our system must protect our rights, and upon corruption of that system, it is up to the individuals to protect their own rights, and those of their neighbors; that a democratic government derives its just power from the people, but corporations do not seek consent to extract wealth from the people and the Earth; and that no true democracy is attainable when the process is determined by economic power.

"We come to you at a time when corporations, which place profit over people, self-interest over justice, and oppression over equality, run our governments. We have peaceably assembled here, as is our right, to let these facts be known.

- They have taken our houses through an illegal foreclosure process, despite not having the original mortgage.
- They have taken bailouts from taxpayers with impunity, and continue to give Executives exorbitant bonuses.
- They have perpetuated inequality and discrimination in the workplace based on age, the color of one's skin, sex, gender identity and sexual orientation.
- They have poisoned the food supply through negligence, and undermined the farming system through monopolization.
- They have profited off of the torture, confinement, and cruel treatment of countless animals, and actively hide these practices.
- They have continuously sought to strip employees of the right to negotiate for better pay and safer working conditions.
- They have held students hostage with tens of thousands of dollars of debt on education, which is itself a human right.
- They have consistently outsourced labor and used that outsourcing as leverage to cut workers' healthcare and pay.
- They have influenced the courts to achieve the same rights as people, with none of the culpability or responsibility.
- They have spent millions of dollars on legal teams that look for ways to get them out of contracts in regards to health insurance.
- They have sold our privacy as a commodity.
- They have used the military and police force to prevent freedom of the press. They have deliberately declined to recall faulty products endangering lives in pursuit of profit.
- They determine economic policy, despite the catastrophic failures their policies have produced and continue to produce.

- They have donated large sums of money to politicians, who are responsible for regulating them.
- They continue to block alternate forms of energy to keep us dependent on oil.
- They continue to block generic forms of medicine that could save people's lives or provide relief in order to protect investments that have already turned a substantial profit.
- They have purposely covered up oil spills, accidents, faulty book-keeping, and inactive ingredients in pursuit of profit.
- They purposefully keep people misinformed and fearful through their control of the media.
- They have accepted private contracts to murder prisoners even when presented with serious doubts about their guilt.
- They have perpetuated colonialism at home and abroad. They have participated in the torture and murder of innocent civilians overseas.
- They continue to create weapons of mass destruction in order to receive government contracts.*
- "To the people of the world, 'We, the New York City General Assembly occupying Wall Street in Liberty Square, urge you to assert your power.
- "Exercise your right to peaceably assemble; occupy public space; create a process to address the problems we face, and generate solutions accessible to everyone.
- "To all communities that take action and form groups in the spirit of direct democracy, we offer support, documentation, and all of the resources at our disposal.
- "Join us and make your voices heard!"

*NOTE—These grievances are not all-inclusive.

Source—NYC General Assembly, Official Website of
#OccupyWallStreet

APPENDIX C:
THE ROARING TWENTIES ARE BACK

William A. Collins, MBA

Not much left
Worth fighting for;
The rich already
Won the war.

Many of us who have reached Social Security age had a pretty good run. We lived through those heady days that followed the Great Depression and World War II, a delightful—though brief—moment in US history when the rich were losing the class war. The middle class gained the high ground and nearly everyone had a shot at a decent income and reasonable retirement. There was plenty of work, and we even started caring for the poor.

No longer. The class war's over and the rich won. The US economy is reverting to the bad old days of a century ago.

Wealth and income for the most privileged among us are booming once again, and they're paying a smaller share in taxes. CEO pay has become obscene, production jobs have been sent abroad or lost to automation, pensions are rarely guaranteed, health care is unaffordable, student debt and home mortgages are often unpayable, and median family income is sinking like a stone. One visible sign of the war's aftermath is that segregation—including by class—is on the rise.

The rich are securing hot spots to live in and fencing them off. Manhattan (following London, Paris, and Dubai) is alive with projects for the ultra-rich—who of course only live there part-time, as they have so many other homes to frequent. This upper-crust housing boom has distorted the market to the point where many builders have lost interest in constructing middle class dwellings.

Education follows suit. The wealthy pick posh suburbs to raise their kids. Schools there are automatically segregated, well-funded, and suitable to train our next generation of rulers. Either that, or Junior gets sent to private school, also a healthy growing industry.

The Great Recession made this disparity of wealth and income notably worse by depressing tax revenue. Given that the Pentagon budget is supposedly sacrosanct, those required budget cuts must come from elsewhere.

Where exactly? Too often, the cuts are made to programs that provide for the most vulnerable Americans. Food stamps and housing benefits are on the chopping block. Meanwhile, the middle class plays musical chairs for an ever-shrinking number of decent jobs.

This stagnation can't keep pace with our growing population, and the leftover workers are stuck with jobs that don't pay a living wage, if they can find work at all.

Could Congress cure all this? Maybe if it tried. It could, for example, raise the minimum wage, levy higher taxes on the wealthy and corporations, root out military pork, universalize health care, cap outrageous CEO pay, block trade deals that encourage the export of American jobs, and keep us out of new wars.

But don't count on our lawmakers to do any of those sensible things. The Roaring Twenties are back—seven years early.

This article was published at NationofChange at: http://www.nationofchange.org/roaring-twenties-are-back-1374413397. Reprinted here by permission of the author.

APPENDIX D:
THE EXTREME CULT OF CAPITALISM

Paul Buckheit, PhD

A 'cult,' according to Merriam-Webster, can be defined as "Great devotion to a person, idea, object, movement, or work (and) a usually small group of people characterized by such devotion."

Capitalism has been defined by adherents and detractors: Milton Friedman said, "The problem of social organization is how to set up an arrangement under which greed will do the least harm, capitalism is that kind of a system." John Maynard Keynes said, "Capitalism is the astounding belief that the most wickedest of men will do the most wickedest of things for the greatest good of everyone."

Perhaps it's best to turn to someone who actually practiced the art: "Capitalism is the legitimate racket of the ruling class," Al Capone said.

Capitalism is a cult. It is devoted to the ideals of privatization over the common good, profit over social needs, and control by a small group of people who defy the public's will. The tenets of the cult lead to extremes rather than to compromise. Examples are not hard to find.

1. Extremes of Income

By sitting on their growing investments, the five richest Americans made almost $7 billion each in one year. That's $3,500,000.00 per hour. The minimum wage for tipped workers is $2.13 per hour.

Our unregulated capitalist financial system allows a few well-positioned individuals to divert billions of dollars from the needs of society. If the 400 richest Americans lumped together their investment profits from last year, the total would pay in-state tuition and fees for EVERY college student in the US.

2. Extremes of Wealth

The combined net worth of the world's 250 richest individuals is more than the total annual living expenses of almost half the world—three billion people.

Within our own borders, the disparity is no less shocking. For every one dollar of assets owned by a single black or Hispanic woman, a member of the Forbes 400 has over $40 million. That's equivalent to a can of soup versus a mansion, a yacht, and a private jet. Most of the Forbes 400 wealth has accrued from nonproductive capital gains. It's little wonder that with the exception of Russia, Ukraine, and Lebanon, the US has the highest degree of wealth inequality in the world.

3. Extremes of Debt

Until the 1970s, US households had virtually no debt. Now the total is $13 trillion, which averages out to $100,000 per American family.

Debt appears to be the only recourse for 21 to 35 year olds, who have lost, on average, 68 percent of their median net worth since 1984, leaving each of them about $4,000.

4. Extremes of Health Care

A butler in black vest and tie passed the atrium waterfall and entered the $2,400 suite, where the linens were provided by the high-end bedding designer Frette of Italy and the bathroom glimmered with polished marble. Inside a senior financial executive awaited his 'concierge' doctor for private treatment.

He was waiting in the penthouse suite of the New York Presbyterian Hospital.

On the streets outside were some of the 26,000 Americans who will die this year because they are without health care. In 2010, 50 million Americans had no health insurance coverage.

5. Extremes of Justice

William James Rummel stole $80 with a credit card, then passed a bad check for $24, then refused to return $120 for a repair job gone badly. He got life in prison. Christopher Williams is facing over 80 years in prison for selling medical marijuana in Montana, a state that allows medical marijuana. Patricia Spottedcrow got 12 years for a $31 marijuana sale and has seen her children only twice in the past two years. Numerous elderly Americans are in prison for life for non-violent marijuana offenses.

Banking giant HSBC, whose mission statement urges employees "to act with courageous integrity" in all they do, was described by a US Senate report as having "exposed the US financial system to 'a wide array of money laundering, drug trafficking, and terrorist financing'" in their dealings with Mexico's Sinaloa cartel, which is considered the deadliest drug gang in the world.

HSBC received a fine equivalent to four weeks' profits. The bank's CEO said, "We are profoundly sorry."

In the words of Bertrand Russell, "Advocates of capitalism are very apt to appeal to the sacred principles of liberty, which are embodied in one maxim: The fortunate must not be restrained in the exercise of tyranny over the unfortunate." Accurate to the extreme.

This article was first published by NationofChange at: http://www.nationofchange. org/extremist-cult-capitalism-1358779216, and is reproduced here by permission of the author.

APPENDIX E:
HOW THE "JOB CREATORS" REALLY SPEND THEIR MONEY

Paul Buckheit, PhD

In his *The Gospel of Wealth*, Andrew Carnegie argued that average Americans should welcome the concentration of wealth in the hands of a few, because the "superior wisdom, experience, and ability" of the rich would ensure benefits for all of us. More recently, Edward Conard, the author of *Unintended Consequences: Why Everything You've Been Told About the Economy Is Wrong*, said: "As a society, we're not offering our talented few large enough rewards. We're underpaying our 'risk takers.'"

Does wealthy America have a point, that giving them all the money will ensure it's disbursed properly, and that it will create jobs and stimulate small business investment while ultimately benefiting society? Big business CEOs certainly think so, claiming in a letter to Treasury Secretary Timothy Geithner that an increase in the capital gains tax would reduce investment "when we need capital formation here in America to create jobs and expand our economy."

They don't cite evidence for their claims, because the evidence proves them wrong. Here are the facts:

1. The Very Rich Don't Like Making Risky Investments

Marketwatch estimates that over 90% of the assets owned by millionaires are held in a combination of low-risk investments (bonds and cash), the stock market, and real estate. According to economist Richard Wolff, about half of the assets of the richest 1% are held in unincorporated business equity (personal business accounts). *The Wall Street Journal* notes that over three-quarters of individuals worth over $20 million are invested in hedge funds.

Angel investing (capital provided by affluent individuals for business start-ups) accounted for less than 1% of the investable assets of high net worth individuals in North America in 2011.

The Mendelsohn Affluent Survey confirmed that the very rich spend less than two percent of their money on new business startups. The last thing most of them want, apparently, is the risky business of hiring people for new innovation.

2. The Very Rich Don't Like Taking on Risky Jobs

CEOs, upper management, and financial professionals made up about 60 percent of the richest 1% of Americans in 2005. Only 3 percent were entrepreneurs. A recent study found that less than 1 percent of all entrepreneurs came from very rich or very poor backgrounds.

In fact, the very rich may not care about US jobs in any form. Surveys reveal that 60 percent of investors worth $25 million or more are investing up to a third of their total assets overseas. Back home, the extra wealth created by the Bush tax cuts led to the "worst track record" for jobs in recorded history. The true American job creator, as venture capitalist Nick Hanauer would agree, is the middle-class consumer.

3. The Very Rich Corporations Don't Like Spending On America

How do corporations spend their money? To a good extent, they don't. According to Moody's, cash holdings for US non-financial firms rose 3 percent to $1.24 trillion in 2011. The corporate cash-to-assets ratio nearly tripled between 1980 and 2010. It has been estimated that the corporate stash of cash reserves held in America could employ 3.5 million more people for five years at an annual salary of $40,000.

The top holders of cash, including Apple and Google and Intel and Coca Cola and Chevron, are spending their money on stock buybacks (which increase stock option prices), dividends to investors, and subsidiary acquisitions. According to Bloomberg, share repurchasing is at one of its highest levels in 25 years.

Apple claims to have added 500,000 jobs to the economy, but that includes app-building tech enthusiasts and FedEx drivers delivering iPhones. The company actually has 47,000 US employees, about one-tenth of General Motors' workforce in the 1990s.

The biggest investment by corporations is overseas, where they keep 57 percent of their cash and fill their factories with low-wage workers. Commerce Department figures show that US companies cut their work forces by 2.9 million from 2000 to 2009 while increasing overseas employment by 2.4 million. They also tap into a "brain drain" of foreign entrepreneurs, scientists, and medical professionals rather than supporting education in America.

One last way corporations see fit to spend their money: executive bonuses. Especially at the banks, where the extra stipends are often paid for with zero interest loans from the Federal Reserve.

The richest individuals and corporations are really good at building up fortunes. They're even better at building up their "job creator" myth.

This article was published by NationofChange at: http://www.nationofchange.org/how-job-creators-really-spend-their-money-1338296463, and is reproduced here by permission of the author.

APPENDIX F:
EIGHT WAYS PRIVATIZATION HAS FAILED AMERICA

Paul Buchheit, PhD

Some of America's leading news analysts are beginning to recognize the fallacy of the "free market." Ted Koppel said, "We are privatizing ourselves into one disaster after another." Fareed Zakaria admitted, "I am a big fan of the free market...But precisely because it is so powerful, in places where it doesn't work well, it can cause huge distortions." They're right. A little analysis reveals that privatization doesn't seem to work in any of the areas vital to the American public.

Health Care

Our private health care system is by far the most expensive system in the developed world. Forty-two percent of sick Americans skipped doctor's visits and/or medication purchases in 2011 because of excessive costs. The price of common surgeries is anywhere from three to ten times higher in the US than in Great Britain, Canada, France, or Germany. Some of the documented tales: a $15,000 charge for lab tests for which a Medicare patient would have paid a few hundred dollars; an $8,000 special stress test for which Medicare would have paid $554; and a $60,000 gall bladder operation, which was covered for $2,000 under a private policy.

As the examples begin to make clear, Medicare is more cost-effective. According to the Council for Affordable Health Insurance, Medicare administrative costs are about one-third that of private health insurance. More importantly, our ageing population has been staying healthy. While as a nation we have a shorter life expectancy than almost all other developed countries, Americans covered by Medicare INCREASED their life expectancy by 3.5 years from the 1960s to the turn of the century.

Free-market health care has been taking care of the CEOs. Ronald DePinho, president of MD Anderson Cancer Center in Texas, made $1,845,000 in 2012. That's over ten times as much as the $170,000 made by the federal Medicare Administrator in 2010. Stephen J. Hemsley, the CEO of United Health Group, made three hundred times as much, with most of his $48 million coming from stock gains.

Water

A Citigroup economist gushed, "Water as an asset class will, in my view, become eventually the single most important physical-commodity based asset class, dwarfing oil, copper, agricultural commodities and precious metals."

A 2009 analysis of water and sewer utilities by Food and Water Watch found that private companies charge up to 80 percent more for water and 100 percent more for sewer services. A more recent study confirms that privatization will generally "increase the long-term costs borne by the public." Privatization is "shortsighted, irresponsible and costly."

Numerous examples of water privatization abuses or failures have been documented in California, Georgia, Illinois, Indiana, New Jersey, Texas, Massachusetts, Rhode Island—just about anywhere it's been tried. Meanwhile, corporations have been making outrageous profits on a commodity that should be almost free. Nestle buys water for about 1/100 of a penny per gallon, and sells it back for ten dollars. Their bottled water is not much different from tap water.

Worse yet, corporations profit from the very water they pollute. Dioxin-dumping Dow Chemicals is investing in water purification. Monsanto has been accused of privatizing its own pollution sites in order to sell filtered water back to the public.

Internet, TV and Phone

It seems the whole world is leaving us behind on the Internet. According to the OECD, South Korea has Internet speeds up to 200 times faster than the average speed in the US, at about half the cost. Customers are charged about $30 a month in Hong Kong or Korea or parts of Europe for much faster service than in the US, while triple-play packages in other countries go for about half of our Comcast or AT&T charges.

Bloomberg notes that deregulators in the 1990s anticipated a market-based decline in phone and cable bills, an "invisible hand" that would steer competing companies to lower prices for all of us. Verizon and AT&T and Comcast and Time-Warner haven't let it happen.

Transportation

As Republicans continue to deride public transportation as 'socialist' and 'Soviet-style,' China surges ahead with a plan to create the world's most advanced high-speed rail transport network. Government-run high-speed rail systems have been successful in numerous other countries, and England and Brazil both lament industry privatization.

As a warning to wannabe Post Office privatizers, Greyhound and Trailways once provided service to remote locations in America, but deregulation intervened. The bus companies eliminated unprofitable routes, and cutbacks and salary decreases, all in the name of optimal profits, resulted in drivers working up to 100 hours a week—a fact to consider any time each of us ride the bus.

With privatization comes automatic rate increases. Chicago surrendered its parking meters for 75 years and almost immediately faced a doubling of parking rates. California's experiments with roadway privatization resulted in cost overruns, public outrage, and a bankruptcy; equally disastrous was the state's foray into electric power privatization. In Pennsylvania, an analysis of school busing by the Keystone Research Center concluded that "Contracting out substantially increases state spending on transportation services."

Banking

The industry is bloated with deceit and depravity. Almost all of the big names have taken part. Goldman Sachs designed mortgage packages to lose money for everyone except Goldman. Countrywide and Wells Fargo targeted Blacks and Hispanics for unaffordable subprime loans. HSBC Bank laundered money for Mexican drug cartels. GE Capital skimmed billions of dollars from its customers. Dozens of hedge fund managers have been guilty of insider trading. Bank of America and JP Morgan Chase hid billions of dollars of bonuses and losses and loans from investors. Banks fixed interest rates in the LIBOR scandal. They illegally foreclosed on millions of homeowners in the robo-signing scandal.

Matt Taibbi explained to us how financial malfeasance led to the bubbles in dot-com stocks and housing and oil prices and commodities that extract trillions of dollars away from society.

This is all the result of free-market deregulated private business. The best-known public bank, on the other hand, is the Bank of North Dakota, which remains profitable while serving small business and the public at low cost relative to the financial industry.

Prisons

One would think it a worthy goal to rehabilitate prisoners and gradually empty the jails. But business is too good. With each prisoner generating up to $40,000 a year in revenue, it has apparently made economic sense to put over two million people behind bars.

The need to fill privatized prisons has contributed to mass jailings for drug offenses, with African Americans, who make up 13% of the population, accounting for 53.5% of all persons who entered prison because of a drug conviction. Yet marijuana usage rates are about the same for Blacks and whites.

Studies show that private prisons perform poorly in numerous ways: prevention of intra-prison violence, jail conditions, rehabilitation efforts. Investigations in Ohio and New Jersey revealed a familiar pattern of money-saving cutbacks and worsening conditions.

Education

The notion that charter schools outperform traditional public schools is not supported by the facts. An updated 2013 Stanford University CREDO study concluded that privatized schools were slightly better in reading and slightly worse in math, with little difference overall. Charter results have shown an improvement since 2009.

An independent study by Bold Approach found that "reforms deliver few benefits, often harm the students they purport to help, and divert attention from...policies with more promise to weaken the link between poverty and low educational attainment."

Just as with prisons and hospitals, cost-saving business strategies apply to the privatization of our children's education. Charter school teachers have fewer years of experience and a higher turnover rate. Non-teacher positions have insufficient retirement plans and health insurance, and much lower pay.

If big money has its way, our children may become high-tech symbols and objects. Bill Gates proposes quality control for the student assembly line, with video footage from the classrooms sent to evaluators to check off teaching skills.

Consumer Protection

Warning signs about unregulated privatization are becoming clearer and more deadly. The Texas fertilizer plant, where 14 people were killed in an explosion and fire, was last inspected by the Occupational Safety and Health Administration (OSHA) over 25 years ago. The US Forest Service, stunned by the Prescott, Arizona fire that killed 19, was forced by the sequester to cut 500 firefighters. The rail disaster in Lac-Megantic, Quebec followed deregulation of Canadian railways.

Regulation is meant to protect all of us, but anti-government activists have worked hard to turn us against our own best interests. Among recommended Republican cuts is the Federal Emergency Management Agency (FEMA), which rescued hundreds of people after Hurricane Sandy while serving millions more with meals and water. In another ominous note for the future, the House passed the Clean Water Cooperative Federalism Act of 2011, which would deny the Environmental Protection Agency the right to enforce the Clean Water Act.

Deregulation not only deprives Americans of protection, but it also endangers us with the persistent threat of corporate misconduct. As late as 2004 Monsanto had insisted that Agent Orange "is not the cause of serious long-term health effects." Dow Chemical, the co-manufacturer of Agent Orange, blamed the government. Halliburton pleaded guilty to destroying evidence after the Gulf of Mexico oil spill in 2010. Cleanups cost much more than the fines imposed on offending companies, as government costs can run into the billions, or even tens of billions, of dollars.

People vs. Profits

As summed up by US News, "Private industry is not going to step in and save people from drowning, or help them rebuild their homes without a solid profit." In order to stay afloat as a nation we need each other, not savvy business people who presume to tell us all how to be rich. We can't all be rich. We just want to keep from drowning.

APPENDIX G:
TIME FOR A NEW ECONOMIC BILL OF RIGHTS

Ellen Hodgson Brown, JD

Henry Ford said, "It is well enough that the people of the nation do not understand our banking and monetary system, for if they did, I believe there would be a revolution before tomorrow morning."

We are beginning to understand, and Occupy Wall Street looks like the beginning of the revolution.

We are beginning to understand that our money is created not by the government but by banks. Many authorities have confirmed this, including the Federal Reserve itself. The only money the government creates today are coins, which compose less than one ten-thousandth of the money supply. Federal Reserve Notes, or dollar bills, are issued by Federal Reserve Banks, all 12 of which are owned by the private banks in their district. Most of our money comes into circulation as bank loans, and it comes with an interest charge attached.

According to Margrit Kennedy, a German researcher who has studied this issue extensively, interest now composes 40% of the cost of everything we buy. We don't see it on the sales slips, but interest is exacted at every stage of production. Suppliers need to take out loans to pay for labor and materials, before they have a product to sell.

For government projects, Kennedy found that the average cost of interest is 50%. If the government owned the banks, it could keep the interest and get these projects at half price. That means governments— state and federal—could double the number of projects they could afford, without costing the taxpayers a single penny more than we are paying now.

This opens up exciting possibilities. Federal and state governments could fund all sorts of things we think we can't afford now, simply by owning their own banks. They could fund something Franklin D. Roosevelt and Martin Luther King dreamt of—an Economic Bill of Rights.

A Vision for Tomorrow

In his first inaugural address in 1933, Roosevelt criticized the sort of near-sighted Wall Street greed that precipitated the Great Depression. He said, "They only know the rules of a generation of self-seekers. They have no vision, and where there is no vision the people perish."

Roosevelt's own vision reached its sharpest focus in 1944, when he called for a Second Bill of Rights. He said:

"This Republic had its beginning, and grew to its present strength, under the protection of certain inalienable political rights.... They were our rights to life and liberty. As our nation has grown in size and stature, however—as our industrial economy expanded—these political rights proved inadequate to assure us equality in the pursuit of happiness."

He then enumerated the economic rights he thought needed to be added to the Bill of Rights. They included:
- The right to a job;
- The right to earn enough to pay for food and clothing;
- The right of businessmen to be free of unfair competition and domination by monopolies;
- The right to a decent home;

- The right to adequate medical care and the opportunity to enjoy good health;
- The right to adequate protection from the economic fears of old age, sickness, accident, and unemployment;
- The right to a good education.

Times have changed since the first Bill of Rights was added to the constitution in 1791. When the country was founded, people could stake out some land, build a house on it, farm it, and be self-sufficient. The Great Depression saw people turned out of their homes and living in the streets—a phenomenon we are seeing again today. Few people now own their own homes. Even if you have signed a mortgage, you will be in debt peonage to the bank for 30 years or so before you can claim the home as your own.

Health needs have changed too. In 1791, foods were natural and nutrient-rich, and outdoor exercise was built into the lifestyle. Degenerative diseases such as cancer and heart disease were rare. Today, health insurance for some people can cost as much as rent.

Then there are college loans, which collectively now exceed a US$1 trillion, more even than credit card debt. Students are coming out of universities not just without jobs but carrying a debt of $20,000 or so on their backs. For medical students and other post-graduate students, it can be $100,000 or more. Again, that's as much as a mortgage, with no house to show for it. The justification for incurring these debts was supposed to be that the students would get better jobs when they graduated, but now jobs are scarce.

After World War II, the GI Bill provided returning servicemen with free college tuition, as well as cheap home loans and business loans. It was called "the GI Bill of Rights". Studies have shown that the GI Bill paid for itself seven times over and is one of the most lucrative investments the government ever made.

An Updated Constitution for a New Millennium

Banks acquired the power to create money by default, when congress declined to claim it at the Constitutional Convention in 1787. The constitution says only that "Congress shall have the power to coin money [and] regulate the power thereof." The Founders left out not just paper money but checkbook money, credit card money, money market funds, and other forms of exchange that make up the money supply today. All of them are created by private financial institutions, and they all come into the economy as loans with interest attached.

Governments—state and federal—could bypass the interest tab by setting up their own publicly owned banks. Banking would become a public utility, a tool for promoting productivity and trade rather than for extracting wealth from the debtor class.

Congress could go further: it could reclaim the power to issue money from the banks and fund its budget directly. It could do this, in fact, without changing any laws. Congress is empowered to "coin money", and the constitution sets no limit on the face amount of the coins. Congress could issue a few one-trillion dollar coins, deposit them in an account, and start writing checks.

The Fed's own figures show that the money supply has shrunk by $3 trillion since 2008. That sum could be spent into the economy without inflating prices. Three trillion dollars could go a long way toward providing the jobs and social services necessary to fulfill an Economic Bill of Rights. Guaranteeing employment to anyone willing and able to work would increase gross domestic product, allowing the money supply to expand even further without inflating prices, since supply and demand would increase together.

Modernizing the Bill of Rights

As Bob Dylan said, "The times they are a'changin'". Revolutionary times call for revolutionary solutions and an updated social contract. Apple and Microsoft update their programs every year. We are trying to fit a highly complex modern monetary scheme into a constitutional framework that is 200 years old.

After president Roosevelt died in 1945, his vision for an Economic Bill of Rights was kept alive by Martin Luther King. "True compassion," King declared, "is more than flinging a coin to a beggar; it comes to see that an edifice which produces beggars needs restructuring."

MLK too has now passed away, but his vision has been carried on by a variety of money reform groups. The government as *employer of last resort*, guaranteeing a living wage to anyone who wants to work, is a basic platform of Modern Monetary Theory (MMT). An MMT website declares that by "[e]nding the enormous unearned profits acquired by the means of the privatization of our sovereign currency...[i]t is possible to have truly full employment without causing inflation."

What was sufficient for a simple agrarian economy does not provide an adequate framework for freedom and democracy today. We need an Economic Bill of Rights, and we need to end the privatization of the national currency. Only when the privilege of creating the national money supply is returned to the people can we have a government that is truly of the people, by the people and for the people.

APPENDIX H:
SAVING THE POST OFFICE:
LETTER CARRIERS CONSIDER
BRINGING BACK BANKING SERVICES

Ellen Hodgson Brown, JD

On July 27, 2012, the National Association of Letter Carriers adopted a resolution at their National Convention in Minneapolis to investigate the establishment of a postal banking system. The resolution noted that expanding postal services and developing new sources of revenue are important components of any effort to save the public Post Office and preserve living-wage jobs; that many countries have a long and successful history of postal banking, including Germany, France, Italy, Japan, and the United States itself; and that postal banks could serve the 9 million people who don't have a bank account and the 21 million who use usurious check cashers, giving low-income people access to a safe banking system. "A USPS bank would offer a 'public option' for banking," concluded the resolution, "providing basic checking and savings—and no complex financial wheeling and dealing."

What is bankrupting the USPS is not that it is inefficient. It has been self-funded throughout its history. But in 2006, Congress required it to prefund postal retiree health benefits for 75 years into the future, an onerous burden no other public or private company is required to carry. The USPS has evidently been targeted by a plutocratic Congress bent on destroying the most powerful unions and privatizing all public services, including education. Britain's 150-year-old postal service is on the privatization chopping block for the same reason, and its postal workers have also vowed to fight. Adding banking services is an internationally tested and proven way to maintain post office solvency and profitability.

Serving an Underserved Market without Going Broke

Many countries operate postal savings systems through their post offices, providing depositors without access to banks a safe, convenient way to save. Great Britain first offered this arrangement in 1861. It was wildly popular, attracting over 600,000 accounts and £8.2 million in deposits in its first five years. By 1927, there were twelve million accounts—one in four Britons—with £283 million on deposit.

Other postal banks followed. They were popular because they serviced a huge untapped market—the unbanked and underbanked. According to a Discussion Paper of the United Nations Department of Economic and Social Affairs:

> The essential characteristic distinguishing postal financial services from the private banking sector is the obligation and capacity of the postal system to serve the entire spectrum of the national population, unlike conventional private banks which allocate their institutional resources to service the sectors of the population they deem most profitable.
>
> Serving the unbanked and underbanked may sound like a losing proposition, but numerous precedents show

that postal savings banks serving low-income and rural populations can be quite profitable. (See below.) In many countries, according to the UN Paper, banking revenues are actually crucial to maintaining the profitability of their postal network. Letter delivery generates losses and often requires cross-subsidies from the post's other activities in order to maintain its network. One effective solution has been to create or expand the role of postal financial services.

One reason public postal banks are profitable is that their costs are low: the infrastructure is already built and available, advertising costs are minimal, and government-owned banks do not award their management extravagant bonuses or commissions that drain profits away. Rather, profits return to the government and the people.

Profits also return to the government in another way: money that comes out from under mattresses and gets deposited in savings accounts can be used to purchase government bonds. In Japan, for example, Japan Post Bank is the holder of fully one-fifth of the national debt. The government has its own captive government lender, servicing the debt at low interest rates without risking the vagaries of the international bond market. Fully 95% of Japan's national debt is held domestically in one way or another. That helps explain how Japan can have the worst debt-to-GDP ratio of any major country and still maintain its standing as the world's largest creditor. If you owe the money to yourself, it's not really a debt.

Some Examples of Successful Public Postal Banks
Kiwibank:
New Zealand's profitable postal bank had a return on equity of 11.7% in the second half of 2011, with net profits almost trebling. It is the only New Zealand bank able to compete with the big four Australian banks that dominate the New Zealand financial sector.

In fact, Kiwibank was set up for that purpose. When the New Zealand postal banks were instituted in 2002, it was not to save the post office but to save New Zealand families and small businesses from big-bank predators. By 2001, Australian mega-banks controlled some 80% of New Zealand's retail banking. Profits went abroad and were maximized by closing less profitable branches, especially in rural areas. The result was to place hardships on many New Zealand families and small businesses.

The New Zealand government decided to launch a state-owned bank that would compete with the Aussie banks. To keep costs low while still providing services in communities throughout New Zealand, the planning team opened bank branches in post offices, establishing Kiwibank as a subsidiary of the government-owned New Zealand Post.

Suddenly, New Zealanders had a choice in banking. In an early version of the "move your money" campaign, 500,000 customers transferred their deposits to public postal banks in Kiwibank's first five years—this in a country of only 4 million people. Kiwibank consistently earns the nation's highest customer satisfaction ratings, forcing the Australia-owned banks to improve their service in order to compete.

China's state-owned Postal Savings Bureau:

With the assistance of the People's Bank of China (the central bank), China's Postal Savings Bureau was re-established in 1986 after a 34-year lapse. As in New Zealand, savings deposits flooded in, showing an extraordinary growth rate of over 50% annually in the first half of the 1990s and over 24% annually in the second half. By 1998, postal savings accounted for 47% of China Post's operating revenues; and 80% of China's post offices provided postal savings services. The Postal Savings Bureau has served as a vital link in mobilizing income and profits from the private sector, providing credit that is available to finance local development. In 2007, the Postal Savings Bank of China was set up from the Postal Savings Bureau and established as a state-owned limited company, which continues to provide postal banking services.

Japan Post Bank:

By 2007, Japan Post was the largest holder of personal savings in the world, boasting combined assets for its savings bank and insurance arms of more than ¥380 trillion ($3.2 trillion). It was also the largest employer in Japan. As in China, Japan Post recaptures and mobilizes income from the private sector, funding the government at low interest rates and protecting the nation's sovereign debt from raids by foreign speculators.

Switzerland's Swiss Post:

Postal financial services are by far the most profitable activity of Swiss Post, which suffers heavy losses from its parcel delivery and only marginal profits from letter delivery operations.

India's Post Office Savings Bank (POSB):

POSB is India's largest banking institution and its oldest, having been established in the latter half of the 19th century following the success of the postal savings bank system in England. Operated by the government of India, it provides small savings banking and financial services. The Department of Posts is now seeking to expand these services by obtaining a license for the creation of a full-fledged bank that would offer full lending and investing services.

Russia's PochtaBank:

Russia, too, is seeking to expand its post office services. The head of the highly successful state-owned Sberbank has stepped down to take on the task of revitalizing the Russian post office and create a post office bank. PochtaBank will operate in the Russian Post's 40,000 local post offices. The post office will function as a banking institution and compete on equal footing not only with private banks but with Sberbank itself.

Brazil's ECT:

Brazil instituted a postal banking system in 2002 on a public/private model, with the national postal service (ECT) forming a partnership with the largest private bank in the country (Bradesco) to provide financial services at post offices. The current partnership is with Bank of Brazil. ECT (also known as Correios) is one of the largest state-owned companies in Latin America, with an international service network reaching more than 220 countries worldwide.

The US Postal Savings System:

The now-defunct US Postal Savings System was also quite successful in its day. It was set up in 1911 to get money out of hiding, attract the savings of immigrants accustomed to saving at post offices in their native countries, provide safe depositories for people who had lost confidence in private banks, and furnish depositories that had longer hours and were more convenient for working people than private banks provided. The minimum deposit was $1 and the maximum was $2,500. The postal system paid two percent interest on deposits annually. It issued US Postal Savings Bonds in various denominations that paid annual interest, as well as Postal Savings Certificates and domestic money orders. Savings in the system spurted to $1.2 billion during the 1930s and jumped again during World War II, peaking in 1947 at almost $3.4 billion.

The US Postal Savings System was discontinued, not because it was inefficient but because it became unnecessary after the profitability of catering to the unbanked and underbanked became apparent to the private financial sector. Private banks then captured the market, raising their interest rates and offering the same governmental guarantees that the postal savings system had.

Time to Revive the US Postal Savings System?

Today, the market of the unbanked and underbanked has grown again, including about one in four US households, according to a 2009 FDIC survey. Without access to conventional financial services, people turn to an alternative banking market of bill pay, prepaid debit cards and check cashing services, as well as payday loans. The unbanked pay excessive fees for basic financial services, are susceptible to high-cost predatory lenders, and have trouble buying a home and other assets because they have little or no credit history. On average, a payday borrower pays back $800 for a $300 loan, with $500 purely going toward interest. Low income adults in the US spend over 5 billion dollars paying off fees and debt associated with predatory loans every year. People with access to banks are better able to resist these services and break the cycle of poverty.

Another underserviced market is the rural population. In May, a move to shutter 3,700 low-revenue post offices was halted only by months of dissent from rural states and their lawmakers, who said the cost-cutting would hurt their communities. Banking services are also more limited for farmers, following the 2008 financial crisis. With shrinking resources for obtaining credit, family farmers and ranchers are finding it increasingly difficult to stay in their homes.

Postal banking could be a win-win in these circumstances, providing jobs and income for the post office along with safe and inexpensive banking services for underserviced populations. Countries such as Russia and India are exploring full-fledged lending services through their post offices; but if lending to the underbanked seems too risky, a US postal bank could follow the lead of Japan Post and use the credit generated from its deposits to buy safe and liquid government bonds. That could still make the bank a win-win-win, providing income for the post office, safe and inexpensive depository and checking services for the underbanked, and a reliable source of public funding for the government.

ADDITIONAL RESOURCES

Chapter 1: Building the New Economy: Ten Steps We Can Take Now

Books and Periodicals

Speth, James Gustave, *America the Possible: Manifesto for a New Economy*. Yale University Press, 2012

_____, *The Bridge at the Edge of the World: Capitalism, the Environment, and Crossing from Crisis to Sustainability*. Yale University Press, 2009.

_____, *Red Sky at Morning: America and the Crisis of the Global Environment*. Yale University Press, 2005.

Alperovitz, Gar, Foreword by Gus Speth, *American Beyond Capitalism: Reclaiming Our Wealth, Our Liberty, and Our Democracy*. Democracy Collaborative, 2011.

YouTube Videos

Manifesto for a New Economy, James Gustave Speth https://www.youtube.com/watch?v=rise0IaqoqM

James Gustave Speth: System Change Not Climate Change: Manifesto for a New Economy https://www.youtube.com/watch?v=gqNi_bxbZ9g

Gus Speth: A New Political Economy https://www.youtube.com/watch?v=wb-BUhzFqdc

Gus Speth: "Liberalism, Environmentalism, and Economic Growth" https://www.youtube.com/watch?v=KSex5t4q9XA

Gus Speth at DEMOS: Capitalism, Environmental Crisis: https://www.youtube.com/watch?v=5Wv2-W0HhcI

Conversations With History: James Gustave Speth https://www.youtube.com/watch?v=uw5VIOSN8p4

Organizations

World Resources Institute: http://www.wri.org/

Chapter 2: The Naked Emperor

Books and Periodicals

Korten, David C., *Agenda for a New Economy: From Phantom Wealth to Real Wealth*. Berrett-Koehler Publishers, 2010

_____, *The Great Turning: From Empire to Earth Community*. Berrett-Koehler Publishers, 2007

_____, *Owning Our Future: The Emerging Ownership Revolution*. Berrett-Koehler Publishers, 2012

_____, *When Corporations Rule the World*. Berrett-Koehler Publishers, 2001

_____, *The Post Corporate World: Life After Capitalism*. Berrett-Koehler Publishers, 2000

_____, *Globalizing Civil Society: Reclaiming Our Right to Power*. Seven Stories Press, 1998

Web Publications

"How to Liberate American from Wall Street Rule" http://neweconomyworkinggroup.org/new-economy-story/how-liberate-america-wall-street-rule

"Religion, Science and Spirit: A Sacred Story for Our Time" http://www.yesmagazine.org/happiness/david-korten-cosmology-landing-page

"The Pursuit of Happiness: A Living Earth Economic Paradigm" http://livingeconomiesforum.org/living-earth-paradigm

Websites

David Korten's Website: http://livingeconomiesforum.org/

David Korten's Blog: http://www.yesmagazine.org/blogs/david-korten

President, Living Economics Forum: http://livingeconomiesforum.org/

Board Chair, *Yes!* magazine: http://www.yesmagazine.org/

Co-Chair, New Economy Working Group: http://neweconomy workinggroup.org/

YouTube Videos

David Korten: Agenda for a New Economy https://www.youtube.com/watch?v =zdsZ_lLz07Q

Radical Abundance: Presenting David Korten https://www.youtube.com/ watch?v=NaqNqw_rm1g

David Korten: Capitalism's Threat to Democracy https://www.youtube.com/ watch?v=rWDn6vQJKE8

David Korten on Occupy Wall Street https://www.youtube.com/watch?v= hhzwgIxqOc0

David Korten and Marjorie Kelly: Building an Economy That Works for All https://www.youtube.com/watch?v=hhzwgIxqOc0

Chapter 3: How We the People Lost the Money Power and How We Can Get It Back

Books and Periodicals

Brown, Ellen, *The Public Banking Solution: From Austerity to Prosperity.* Third Millennium Press, 2013.

_____, *Web of Debt: The Shocking Truth About Our Money System and How We Can Break Free.* Third Millennium Press, 2012.

YouTube Videos

Ellen Brown: Public Banking in America https://www.youtube.com/watch? v=WhKFkKA1qmE

Hartmann: Conversations with Great Minds—Ellen Brown, Web of Debt (Part 1) https://www.youtube.com/watch?v=McVjdNnbEM0

Ellen Brown: The Buck Starts Here https://www.youtube.com/watch?v=aUVQ R945NJc

W.A.N. Radio 3-5-13 hr2 McGrath and Ellen Brown https://www.youtube.com/watch?v=xjuEAcJpQvM

Organizations
Public Banking Institute http://publicbankinginstitute.org/

Chapter 4: Europe's Transition from Social Democracy to Oligarchy

Books and Periodicals

Hudson, Michael, *America's Protectionist Takeoff 1815-1914*. ISLET, 2010.

_____, and De Mieroop, Marc Van, *Debt and Economic Renewal in the Ancient Near East*. Capital Directions Ltd., 2002.

_____, *Finance Capital and Its Discontents*. ISLET, 2012.

_____, *Global Fracture: The New International Economic Order*. Pluto Press, 2005.

_____, *Super Imperialism New Edition: The Origin and Fundamentals of U.S. World Dominance*. Pluto Press, 2003.

_____, *The Bubble and Beyond*. ISLET, 2012

_____, *The Monster: How a Gang of Predatory Lenders and Wall Street Bankers Fleeced America and Spawned a Global Crisis*. St. Martin's Griffin, 2011.

_____, *Trade, Development and Foreign Debt*. ISLET, 2009.

YouTube Videos

Economist Michael Hudson Explains Bank and Bankers Are Parasites and Not Part of the Productive Economy https://www.youtube.com/watch?v=A10bor8FBAk

Michael Hudson: Debt: The Politics and Economics of Restructuring https://www.youtube.com/watch?v=gX5RHhX8E2k

Web Conference with Michael Hudson Michael Hudson: The rich want it all and to hell with the poor: https://www.youtube.com/watch?v=cQkcG68Bdgg

Summit MMT—Michael Hudson: Finances vs Economy, Credit vs Money https://www.youtube.com/watch?v=JZQqrxHGcoQ

Web Conference with Michael Hudson https://www.youtube.com/watch?v =_sbN4bOfLUE

Michael Hudson: Debt & Money https://www.youtube.com/watch?v=cCsx Ky6Lbvg

Michael Hudson: US Black Debt Hole: 'We want you all bankrupt!' https:// www.youtube.com/watch?v=8P1fihT5B7o

Websites
Michael Hudson's website: http://michael-hudson.com/

Chapter 5: Ending the World Financial Crisis
Books and Periodicals

Paul Hellyer, *Agenda: A Plan for Action.* Prentice Hall of Canada; 1st Edition, 1971.

_____, *A Miracle in Waiting: Economics that Makes Sense.* AuthorHouse, 2010.

_____, *Arundel Lodge: A Little Bit of Old Muskoka.* Chimo Media, Limited, 1996.

_____, *Canada at the Crossroads: A Liberal Agenda for the 90's and Beyond.* Chimo Media, Limited, 1990.

_____, *Damn the Torpedoes: My Fight to Unify Canada's Armed Forces.* Toronto: McClellan & Stewart, 1990.

_____, *Evil Empire: Globalization's Dark Side.* Chimo Media, Limited, 1997.

_____, *Exit Inflation.* Thomas Nelson, 1981.

_____, *Funny Money: A Common Sense Alternative to Mainline Economics.* Chimo Media, 1994.

_____, *Goodbye Canada.* Chemo Media, Limited, 2001.

_____, *Jobs for All: Capitalism on Trial.* Carswell Legal Publications, 1984.

_____, *Surviving the Global Financial Crisis: The Economics of Hope for Generation X.* Chimo Media, Limited, 1996.

_____, *Light at the End of the Tunnel: A Survival Plan for the Human Species.*

AuthorHouse, 2010.

_____, *One Big Party: To Keep Canada Independent*. Chemo Media, Limited, 2003.

_____, *Stop: Think*. Chemo Media, Limited, 1999.

Videos

www.youtube.com/watch?v=p8mlwxBpaTU (Public Banking in America 2012)
www.youtube.com/user/PaulHellyer2012 (interview with Steve Paikin)
www.youtube.com/watch?v=RGyFWyNuF3s (Washington, April 2008)

Websites

Paul Hellyer: www.paulhellyerweb.com

Chapter 6: Roadmap to a New Economics: Beyond Capitalism and Socialism

Books and Periodicals

Eisler, Riane, *The Real Wealth of Nations: Creating a Caring Economics*. Barrett-Koehler Publishers, 2008.

_____, and Miller, Ron, *Educating for a Culture of Peace*. Heinemann, 2004.

YouTube videos

Dr. Riane Eisler: We Have to Make the Economic Argument at Congressional Briefings on March 20, 2013 http://www.caringeconomy.org/multimedia/dr-riane-eisler-we-have-make-economic-argument-congressional-briefing-march-20-2013

Websites

TheCaringEconomyLeadershipProgram:http://www.caringeconomy.org/content/caring-economy-leadership-program

Caring Economy Campaign http://www.caringeconomy.org/

Chapter 7: The Role of Bioregional Currencies in Regional Regeneration

Books and Periodicals

Lietaer, Bernard, *The Future of Money: Creating New Wealth, Work and a Wiser World*. London: Random House, 2001; translated in eighteen other languages.

_____, with Hallsmith, Gwendolyn, *Creating Wealth: Growing local economies with local currencies.* New Society Publishers, 2011.

_____, with Belgin, Stephen: *New Money for a New World* (Boulder: Qiterra Publishers, 2011.

_____, with Arnsperger, Christian; Goerner, Sally and Brunnhuber, Stefan, *Money and Sustainability: The Missing Link*. UK: Triarchy Press, 2012.

_____, with Dunne, Jacqui, *Rethinking Money*. San Francisco; Berrett-Koehler, 2013.

Kennedy, Margrit, Lietaer, Bernard and Rogers, John: *People Money: The Promise of Regional Currencies* (UK: Triarchy Prss, 2012)

YouTube videos

Bernard Lietaer: The Potential of Complementary Currencies http://www.ellen-macarthurfoundation.org/education/resources/maths/bernard-lietaer-the-potential-of-complemetary-currencies

TEDxBerlin: Bernard Lietaer https://www.youtube.com/watch?v=nORI8r3JIyw

Bernard Lietaer: Money Diversity @PopTech 2011 https://www.youtube.com/watch?v=T9EI2PrDpmw

Keynotes and Conversations with Bernard Lietaer, Nov. 30, 2011 https://www.youtube.com/watch?v=W6lfWQ2TLlU

New Money for a New World: Interview with Bernard Lietaer https://www.youtube.com/watch?v=OvSrO2c107A

Chapter 8: The Possibility of a Pluralist Commonwealth and a Community-Sustaining Economy

Books and Periodicals

Alperovitz, Gar, *America Beyond Capitalism: Reclaiming Our Wealth, Our Liberty & Our Democracy*, Takoma Park, MD and Boston, MA: Democracy Collaborative Press and Dollars and Sense, 2011.

_____, *What Then Must We Do? Straight Talk about the Next American Revolution*, White River Junction, VT: Chelsea Green, 2013.

Democracy Collaborative, *Building Wealth: The New Asset-Based Approach to Solving Social and Economic Problems*, Washington, DC: The Aspen Institute, 2005.

Hodges, Rita Axelroth and Dubb, Steve, *The Road Half Traveled: University Engagement at a Crossroad.*, East Lansing, MI: MSU Press, 2012.

Williamson, Thad, Imbroscio, David and Alperovitz, Gar, *Making a Place for Community: Local Democracy in a Global Era. New York*, NY: Routledge, 2003.

Web articles

Alperovitz, Gar, and Dubb, Steve and Howard, Ted, "Rebuilding America's Communities: A Comprehensive Community Wealth Building Federal Policy Proposal", College Park, MD: Democracy Collaborative, 2010, available at: http://community-wealth.org/content/rebuilding-america's-communities-comprehensive-community-wealth-building-federal-policy

_____, Williamson, Thad and Dubb, Steve, "Anchoring Wealth to Sustain Cities and Population Growth" Solutions, volume 4, issue 3 (July, 2012), pp. 50-57, available at: http://www.thesolutionsjournal.com/node/1132.

Capital Institute (2011), "Field Study Number 2: The Evergreen Cooperatives," Field Guide to Investing in a Resilient Economy, Greenwich, CT: Capital Institute, available at: http://community-wealth.org/content/evergreen-cooperatives-field-study.

Dubb, Steve and Howard, Ted, "Leveraging Anchor Institutions for Local Job Creation and Wealth Building," Big Ideas for Job Creation, Berkeley,

CA: Institute for Research on Labor and Employment at the University of California, Berkeley, 2012, available at: http://community-wealth.org/ content/jobs-idea-14-anchor-institutions.

_____, and Howard, Ted, "Linking Colleges to Communities", College Park, MD: The Democracy Collaborative at the University of Maryland, 2007, available at: http://community-wealth.org/content/linking-colleges-communities-engaging-university-community-development.

Howard, Ted, "Owning Your Own Job is a Beautiful Thing: Community Wealth Building in Cleveland, Ohio," Investing in What Works for America's Communities: Essays on People, Place, and Purpose, San Francisco, CA: Federal Reserve Bank of San Francisco and Low Income Investment Fund, 2p12, 204-214 available at: http://www.frbsf.org/publications/community/ investing-in-what-works/howard.cfm.

Iuviene, Nicholas, Stitely, Amy and Hoyt, Lorlene (2010), "Sustainable Economic Democracy: Worker Cooperatives in the 21st Century", Cambridge, MA: MIT, 2010. Community Innovations Lab, October, available at: http://community-wealth.org/content/learning-evergreen-and-mon dragon-and-key-differences.

Wang, Elaine and updated by Nathaly Agosto Filión, "Case Study: Cleveland, OH: The Cleveland Evergreen Cooperatives," in Debra Perry, editor, Sustainable Economic Development: A Resource Guide for Local Leaders, Version 2.0, Denver, CO: Institute for Sustainable Communities, Climate Leadership Academy, 2011, 30-36, available at: http://community-wealth. org/content/case-study-clevelands-evergreen-cooperatives

Warren, Deborah and Dubb, Steve, "Growing a Green Economy for All: From Green Jobs to Green Ownership", College Park, MD: Democracy Collaborative, 2010, available at: http://community-wealth.org/content/ growing-green-economy-all-green-jobs-green-ownership.

Film

The Next American Revolution: http://garalperovitz.com/nextamericanrevolution

YouTube
Democracy Collaborative channel http://www.youtube.com/user/Democracy
Collab?feature=watch

Organizations
The Democracy Collaborative at the University of Maryland info@community-
wealth.org
Washington, D.C. office:
6930 Carroll Ave., Suite 501
Takoma Park, MD 20912
Cleveland office
1422 Euclid Ave., Ste. 616
Cleveland, OH 44115

Websites
Community-Wealth.org www.community-wealth.org
Gar Alperovitz.com www.garalperovitz.com
What Then Must We Do book website: www.whatthenmustwedo.org

Chapter 9: The Growing Green Economy

Books and Periodicals
Allee, Verna, *The Future of Knowledge*, Butterworth-Heineman, 2003
Benello, C.G., Swann, R. and Turnbull, S., *Building Sustainable Communities:
Tools and Concepts for Self-reliant Economic Change*, Ed. Ward Morehouse,
A TOES Book, 1997, Revised Second Edition, Bootstrap Press, New
York, available from: http://ssrn.com/abstract=1128862.
Benkler, Yochai, *The Wealth of Networks*, Yale University Press, 2008
Bookstaber, Richard, *A Demon of Our Own Design*, John Wiley, N.Y, 2007
Boyle, D., *The Money Changers: Currency Reform from Aristotle to E-Cash*,
Earthscan, London, 2002.
Davies, G. A, *History of money from ancient times to the present day*. rev. ed.

Cardiff: University of Wales Press, UK. 1996, http://www.ex.ac.uk/~R Davies/arian/llyfr.html.

Douglas, C.H., *Social Credit*, Eyre & Spottiswoode (Publishers) Ltd. London, 1924, available from: http://douglassocialcredit.com/resources/resources/social_credit_by_ch_douglas.pdf.

Dowd, K,. *The Experience of Free Banking*, Routledge, London, 1992.

Ehrlich, E.E., *Review of Economics and Statistics*, 39:4, Nov., pp. 469-471. 1957.

Eisler, Riane, *The Real Wealth of Nations*, Berrett-Koehler, CA. 2007

Ethical Markets Media, International Financial Reform, 5-part TV series moderated by Hazel Henderson, with Kenneth Rogoff, Sakiko Fukuda-Parr and John Perkins on demand at www.EthicalMarkets.tv

Fisher, I., *The Purchasing Power of Money: Its Determination and Relation to Credit, Interest, and Crises*, The MacMillan Co, New York, 1911.

Friedman, M. and Schwartz, A.J. 1971, *A Monetary History of the United States, 1867-1960*, Princeton University Press.

Galbraith, J.K. 1976, *Money: Whence it came, where it went*, Pelican Books, UK.

Gesell, S., *The Natural Economic Order*, 1916, translated by Philip Pye, 2002, available at http://www.appropriate-economics.org/ebooks/neo/neo2.htm.

Griffin, G. Edward, *The Creature from Jekyll Island: A Second Look at the Federal Reserve*, American Media, California, 2002.

Ha-joon Chang, *Bad Samaritans: The Myth of Free Trade and the Secret History of Capitalism*, Bloomsbury Press, New York, 2008

Hayek, F. A., *Choice in Currency: A Way to Stop Inflation*, Occasional Paper 48, 1976a, The Institute of Economic Affairs, London.

_____, *Denationalization of Money: An Analysis of the Theory and Practice of Concurrent Currencies*, Hobart Paper Special 70, 1976b, The Institute of Economic Affairs, London.

Henderson, Hazel, *The Politics of the Solar Age*, Doubleday, 1981. TOES Books, 1998.

_____, *Ethical Markets: Growing The Green Economy*, Chelsea Green, Vermont, 2006 with companion TV series at www.EthicalMarkets.tv

_____, *Beyond Globalization, New Economics Foundation, Focus on the Global South*, Kumarian Press, London, 1999.

_____, *Building A Win-Win World*, Berrett-Koehler, CA , 1996.

Huber, J, and Robertson, J. 2000, *Creating New Money: A monetary reform for the information age*, New Economics Foundation, London available from: http://www.neweconomics.org/gen/uploads/CreatingNewMoney.pdf

Hyde, Lewis, *The Gift*, Vintage, NY, 1979.

Jacobs, Jane, *Cities and Wealth of Nations: Principles of Economic Life*, Vintage Books, New York, 1985.

Kennedy, M., *Interest and Inflation Free Money: How to create an exchange medium that works for everybody*, Permakultur Institut e.v., Steyerberg, West Germany, 1988.

Lessig, Laurence. *Re-Mix*, 2008.

Lietaer, Bernard A., *The Future of Money: Creating New Wealth, Work and a Wiser World*, Century, London, 2001.

Loye, David, *Bankrolling Evolution*, Benjamin Franklin Press, CA, 2007.

Loye, David, *Measuring Evolution*, Benjamin Franklin Press, CA, 2007.

Macleod, Jordan, *New Currency*, Integral Leadership Review, 2009.

Mitchell, Ralph A. and Shafer, Neil, *Standard Catalog of Depression Scrip in the United States in the 1930s*, Krause Publications, Iola, WI, 1984.

Muolo, Paul and Padilla, Matthew, *Chain of Blame: How Wall Street Caused the Mortgage and Credit Crisis*, John Wiley, New York, 2008

Patman, J.W.W., *Congressional Record of the House of Representatives*, September 29, 1941, pps 7582–3, Washington D.C.

Pieterse, Jan Nederveen, *"Is There Hope for Uncle Sam?" Beyond the American Bubble*, Zed Books, London, 2008.

Phillips, Kevin, *Bad Money*, Viking, New York, 2008.

Rawi, Abdelal, *Capital Rules: the Construction of Global Finance*, Harvard University Press, 2008.

Sahtouris, Elisabet, "The Biology of Business," World Business Academy Perspectives, Ojai, CA, Sept-Oct, 2005

Schauf, T.D., *The Federal Reserve is Privately Owned*, 1998, available at http://www.apfn.org/APFN/fed_reserve.htm.

Soros, George. "The New Paradigm for Financial Markets," Public Affairs, New York, 2008.

Speth, James Gustave, *The Bridge to the End of the World*, Yale University Press, 2008.

Stern, N., *The Economics of Climate Change: The Stern Review*, Cabinet Office, HM Treasury, London, 2006, available from: http://www.sternreview.org.uk.

Taleb, Nassim Nicholas, *The Black Swan*, 2007.

White, L.H., "Accounting for Non-Interest-Bearing Currency: A Critique of the Legal Restrictions of Money," Journal of Money, Credit and Banking, 1987, Vol 19. pp. 448-56.

Vaughn, Genevieve, *For Giving*, Plain View Press, Austin, TX 1997.

Yunus, Muhammad, *Creating a World Without Poverty*, Public Affairs, New York, 2008.

Zarlenga, Stephen, *The Lost Science of Money*, American Monetary Institute, 2007.

Videos

Monetary Reform Act, 2008, available from http://www.themoneymasters.com/mra.htm.

Money As Debt, 45 min. video cartoon by Paul Grignon, at www.Ethical Markets.tv

The Money Fix, 9 min. interview of Hazel Henderson, www.EthicalMarkets.tv

Chapter 10: Terra: A Currency to Stabilize the World Economy

Kennedy, Margrit; Lietaer, Bernard and Rogers, John, *People Money: The Promise of Regional Currencies.* UK: Triarchy Press, 2012

Lietaer, Bernard with Dunne, Jacqui, *Rethinking Money.* San Francisco; Berrett-Koehler, February 2013

_____, with Arnsperger, Christian; Goerner, Sally and Brunnhuber, Stefan, *Money and Sustainability: The Missing Link.* UK: Triarchy Press, 2012

_____, with Belgin, Stephen, *New Money for a New World*. Boulder: Qiterra Publishers, 2011

Bernard Lietaer with Gwendolyn Hallsmith, *Creating Wealth: Growing local economies with local currencies*. New Society Publishers, 2011.

Bernard Lietaer: *Future of Money: Creating New Wealth, Work and a Wiser World*. London: Random House, January 2001, also translated in eighteen other languages.

Websites

Takashi Kiuchi, "The Terra TRCTM White Paper" http://www.terratrc.org/PDF/Terra_WhitePaper_2.27.04.pdf

The Terra Mechanism: Stable and Just Global Economic System http://www.slideshare.net/mukhtaralam/terra-islam-nocartoons2

Bernard Lietaer, "Terra: A Win-Win Solution to Monetary Insecurity": http://www.longfinance.net/LongFinance/Bernard%20Lietaer%20-%20Terra_OHW.pdf

Editor's Suggested Resources
Books and Periodicals

Chomsky, Noam, *How the World Works*. Penguin Books, Ltd., London, 2011.

_____, *Making the Future: Occupations, Interventions, Empire and Resistance*. City Lights Publishers, 2012

_____, *Occupy*. Zuccotti Park Press, 2012

_____, *Power Systems: Conversations on Global Democratic Uprisings and the New Challenges to U.S. Empire*. Metropolitan Books, 2013

_____, & McChesney, Robert W., *Profit Over People: Neoliberalism & Global Order*. Seven Stories Press, 2011.

Eversole, Finley, Editor, *Infinite Energy Technologies: Tesla, Cold Fusion, Antigravity and the Future of Sustainability*. Inner Traditions, 2013.

Greider, William, *Secrets of the Temple: How the Federal Reserve Runs the Country*. New York: Simon & Schuster, 1987.

Griffin, G. Edward, *The Creature form Jekyll Island: A Second Look at the*

Federal Reserve. American Media, 5th edition, 2010.

Hawken, Paul, *Blessed Unrest: How the Largest Social Movement in History is Restoring Grace, Justice, and Beauty to the Word*. Penguin, 2008.

_____, Lovins, Amory, & Lovins, L. Hunter, *Natural Capitalism: Creating the Next Industrial Revolution*. Back Bay Books, 2008.

_____, *The Ecology of Commerce Revised Edition: A Declaration of Sustainability*. HarperBusiness, 2010.

Hertz, Emanuel, *Abraham Lincoln: A New Portrait*. Horace Liveright, Inc. New York, 1931.

Lakoff, George, *Moral Politics: How Liberals and Conservatives Think*. University of Chicago Press, 2002.

_____, and Wehling, Elisabeth, *The Little Blue Book: The Essential Guide to Thinking and Talking Democratic*. Free Press, 2012.

_____, *The Political Mind: A Cognitive Scientist's Guide to Your Brain and Its Politics*. Penguin Books; Reprint edition, 2009

_____, *Thinking Politics: Communicating Our American Values and Vision*. Farrar, Straus and Giroux; 1st edition, 2006.

Ludwig, Emil, *Abraham Lincoln*. Tr. from German by Eden and Cedar Paul. Boston: Little, Brown & Co., 1930. Reprinted by Kessinger Publishing, 2004.

McChesney, Robert W., *Digital Disconnect: How Capitalism is Turning the Internet Against Democracy*. The New Press, 2013.

McGeer, Gerald Grattan, *The Conquest of Poverty*. Published 1933. Out of print but available online at: http://www.scribd.com/doc/47883435/Conquest-of-Poverty-1933-Gerald-Grattan-McGeer

Perkins, John, *Confessions of an Economic Hit Man*. Berrett-Koehler Publisher, 2004.

_____, *Hoodwinked: An Economic Hit Man Reveals Why the Global Economy IMPLODED and How to Fix It*. Crown Business; Reprint edition, 2011.

_____. *The Secret History of the American Empire: The Truth About Economic Hit Men, Jackals, and How to Change the World*. Plume; Reprint edition, 2008.

Pollin, Robert, *Back to Full Employment*. MIT Press, 2012.

Quigley, Carroll, *Tragedy & Hope: A History of the World in Our Time*. GSG and
　　Associates, 1975.

Remini, Robert V., *Andrew Jackson and the Bank War*. W.W. Norton & Co., 1967.

Scharmer, Otto & Kaufer, Matrin, *Leading from the Emerging Future: From Ego-
　　System to Eco-System Economics*. Berrett-Koehler Publishers, 2013.

Search, R. E., *Lincoln Money Martyred*. Palmdale, CA: Omni Publications, 1935.
　　Reprint, 1989.

DVDs & YouTube Videos

Noam Chomsky: "When Elites Fail and What We Should Do About It".
　　Keynote Address, Convergence Conference, Portland OR, October 2,
　　2009: https://www.youtube.com/watch?v=5nfNxVW5yi8

Robert Pollin: Globalization of Labor: Is a Race to the Bottom Inevitable?
　　https://www.youtube.com/watch?v=GTZ_jPfseq8

A Dark Truth. DVD, Magnolia Pictures, 2013. Damian Lee, Director

Zeitgeist: Addendum. Peter Joseph, director. DVD, all regions. View online
　　free at: http://www.youtub e.com/watch?v=1gKX9TWRyfs

CONTRIBUTORS

Gar Alperovitz, PhD, is a historian, political economist, activist and author, and is currently the Lionel R. Bauman Professor of Political Economy at the University of Maryland. His articles have appeared in leading American publications including the *New York Times* and *Washington Post*. He has served as legislative director in both houses of Congress and as special assistant in the State Department; is the president of the National Center for Economic and Security Alternatives; and a founding principal of the Democracy Collaborative, a research institution focused on initiatives that promote the democratization of wealth. His latest book, *America Beyond Capitalism,* is described by Noam Chomsky as providing a "concrete and feasible ways to reverse the ominous course of the past several decades and to open the way to a vibrant democracy with a sustainable economy that can satisfy human needs." He is also focused on public banking as a means to achieving a sustainable economy.

Ellen Hodgson Brown, JD, developed her research skills as an attorney practicing civil litigation in Los Angeles. In *Web of Debt*, she turns those skills to an analysis of the Federal Reserve and "the money trust." She shows how this private cartel has usurped the power to create money from the people themselves, and how we the people can get it back. Her eleven books include the bestselling *Nature's Pharmacy*, co-authored with Dr.

Lynne Walker, and *Forbidden Medicine*. Her latest book is *The Public Bank Solution: From Austerity to Prosperity*. In 2012, Ellen organized the first Public Banking in America conference, held in Philadelphia. Proceedings of the first two conferences can be seen at: http://www.publicbankingina-merica.org/speakers.htm.

Her websites are www.webofdebt.com, www.ellenbrown.com and www.public-banking.com.

Paul Buchheit, PhD, teaches Economic Inequality at DePaul University. He is the founder and developer of social justice and educational websites: UsAgainstGreed.org, PayUpNow.org, RappingHistory.org, and is the editor and main author of *American Wars: Illusions and Realities*, Clarity Press. Buchheit's doctorate in computer science from the University of Illinois at Chicago had an emphasis on cognitive processing, with a special-ization in language development. He has contributed numerous articles to scholarly publications. For the past five years he has focused on issues related to economic inequality. His extensive research and writing has been showcased in progressive online sites such as CommonDreams, Truthout, Buzzflash, AlterNet, Nation of Change, CounterPunch, and Brave New World. Paul Buchheit can be reached at: paul@UsAgainstGreed.org.

William A. Collins, MBA, first gained an appreciation for finance and economics while earning a B.S. in accounting at Lehigh University and an MBA from Stanford. After serving in the Finance Corps with the US Army in Germany he interned in a number of congressional offices on Capitol Hill before running for office himself in Connecticut. There he spent two terms in the General Assembly and four terms as mayor of Norwalk, where he led the rebirth of a crumbling sector of that city. Active in state and national mayoral affairs, he served as 1ˢᵗ VP of the CT Conference of Municipalities. He then went on to create his own newspaper opinion syndicate, *Minuteman Media*, which has since been absorbed by the Institute for Policy Studies and is published today as

Other Words. He has been writing public policy columns for over 20 years, focusing often on America's unbalanced economic system. His work has appeared in scores of local papers. In addition Mr. Collins spent 6 years on the National Board of Directors of Veterans for Peace and a lifetime as a peace and justice activist.

Steve Dubb, PhD, is Research Director of The Democracy Collaborative at the University of Maryland, where he has led the development of the Community-Wealth.org web-based information portal and has been lead author or co-author of a number of publications including *Building Wealth: The New Asset-Based Approach to Solving Social and Economic Problems* (Aspen, 2005), *Linking Colleges to Communities: Engaging the University for Community Development* (2007), *Growing a Green Economy for All: From Green Jobs to Green Ownership* (with Deborah Warren, 2010) and co-author (with Rita Axelroth Hodges) of *The Road Half Traveled: University Engagement at a Crossroads* (MSU Press, 2012). Dubb also conducted (with Ted Howard) the initial strategic planning that led to the development of the Evergreen Cooperative initiative in Cleveland, Ohio and currently helps guide efforts to adopt that model to meet the needs of other cities. Dubb received his Masters and PhD in Political Science from the University of California, San Diego and his Bachelor's in Economics (with honors) and Spanish from the University of California, Berkeley.

Riane Eisler, PhD, is internationally known for her bestseller *The Chalice and The Blade*, now in 23 foreign editions and her newest book, *The Real Wealth of Nations*—hailed by Archbishop Desmond Tutu as "a template for the better world we have been so urgently seeking." Her other books include *Sacred Pleasure, The Power of Partnership*, and *Tomorrow's Children*. Dr. Eisler is president of the Center for Partnership Studies, www.partner-shipway.org, She keynotes conferences worldwide, with venues including invitations by Rita Suessmuth, President of the German Parliament, and by Vaclav Havel, President of the Czech Republic. She has received many honors, including honorary PhD degrees, the Alice Paul ERA Education Award, and the Nuclear Age Peace Foundation's 2009 Distinguished Peace Leadership Award, and is in the award-winning book *Great Peacemakers* as one of 20 leaders for world peace, along with Mahatma Gandhi, Mother Teresa, and Martin Luther King. Dr. Eisler is also the only woman listed among the 20 great thinkers discussed in *Macrohistory and Macrohistorians*, along with Hegel, Adam Smith, Arnold Toynbee and Teilhard de Chardin. She can be contacted at: center@partnershipway.com

Finley Eversole, PhD, is a philosopher, educator, activist, and advocate for the role of the arts in the evolution of consciousness. In the 1960s he was active in the Civil Rights and Women's Movements, the anti-Vietnam War movement, and participated in organizing the first Earth Day in New York City in 1970. As Executive Director of the Society for the Arts, Religion and Contemporary Culture, he worked with such cultural leaders as Joseph Campbell, W. H. Auden, Allan Watts, Marianne Moore, and Alfred H. Barr, Jr, founder of New York's Museum of Modern Art. A former university professor, and a small business owner for ten years, he edited and contributed to *Christian Faith and the Contemporary Arts,* is the author of *Art and Spiritual Transformation*, and planned and edited several volumes on solutions to global problems, the first of which is *Infinite Energy Technologies: Tesla, Cold Fusion, Antigravity and the Future of Sustainability.* The second is *Energy Medicine Technologies: Ozone Healing, Microcrystals, Frequency Therapy, and the Future of Health.* In addition to *Creating a Real Wealth Economy,* two volumes, due out later, address environmental problems and solutions and forces shaping global transformation. Eversole is biographed in *Who's Who in the World 2011-2014* and the (30-year) Pearl Anniversary edition.

Paul Hellyer, PC, is one of Canada's best known and most controversial politicians. First elected in 1949, he was the youngest cabinet minister appointed to Louis S. St. Laurent's government eight years later. He subsequently held senior posts in the governments of Lester B. Pearson and Pierre E. Trudeau, who defeated him for the Liberal Party leadership in 1968. The following year, after achieving the rank of senior minister, which was later designated Deputy Prime Minister, Hellyer resigned from the Trudeau cabinet on a question of principle related to housing. Although Hellyer is best known for the unification of the Canadian Armed Forces and for his 1968 chairmanship of the Task Force on Housing and Urban Development, he has maintained a life-long interest in macroeconomics. Through the years, as a journalist and political commentator, he has continued to fight for economic reforms and has written several books on the subject. His many books include *A Miracle in Waiting: Economics That Make Sense* and *Light at the End of the Tunnel: A Survival Plan for the Human Species.*

Hazel Henderson, PhD, has been an active environmentalist since she co-founded Citizens for Clean Air in New York City in 1964 and The Center For Growth Alternatives in 1972. She is president of Ethical Markets Media, LLC (US and Brazil), author of *Ethical Markets: Growing the Green Economy* (2006) and other books and co-creator of the Calvert Henderson Quality of Life Indicators with the Calvert Group, updated regularly at www.Calvert-Henderson.com. She can be reached at hazel. henderson@ethicalmarkets.com

Michael Hudson, PhD, is Distinguished Research Professor of Economics, University of MissouriKansas City; Chairman, Committee of Experts for Renew Task Force Latvia; President, Institute for the Study of Long-Term Economic Trends (ISLET), a research associate of the Levy Institute at Bard College, and Honorary Professor of Economics, Huazhong University of Science and Technology (HUST), Wuhan, China. Prof. Hudson was one of the earliest critics of neoliberal policies alerting his audience to the coming real estate crisis in a cover story for *Harper's* magazine in May 2006. In recent years, Prof. Hudson was a major critic of Alan Greenspan (especially of the Federal Reserve Board's faulty statistical analysis). He has long advised foreign governments, as well as US Government and United Nations agencies. His books include *The Bubble and Beyond* and *Financial Capital and Its Discontents*. His website is: michael-hudson.com.

David Korten, PhD, is co-founder and board chair of the Positive Futures Network, which publishes *YES!* magazine <www.yesmagazine. org>, and a founding board member of the Business Alliance for Local Living Economies www.livingeconomies.org. His most recent book is *Agenda for a New Economy: From Phantom Wealth to Real Wealth*. His other books include *The Great Turning: From Empire to Earth Community*, the international best seller *When Corporations Rule the World*, and *The Post-Corporate World: Life after Capitalism*. Korten has MBA and PhD degrees from the Stanford University Graduate School of Business, served as a Harvard Business School professor, and for thirty years worked as a development professional in Asia, Africa, and Latin America. His website is: www.davidkorten.org.

Bernard Lietaer, MEN, MBA, is an international expert in the design and implementation of currency systems. He has studied and worked in the field of money for more than 30 years in an unusually broad range of capacities including as a Central Banker, a fund manager, a university professor, and a consultant to governments in numerous countries, multi-national corporations, and community organizations. He co-designed and implemented the convergence mechanism to the single European currency system (the Euro) and served as president of the Electronic Payment System at the National Bank of Belgium (the Belgian Central Bank). He co-founded and managed GaiaCorp, a top performing currency fund whose profits funded investments in environmental projects. A former professor of International Finance at the University of Louvain, he has also taught at Sonoma State University and Naropa University. He is currently a Research Fellow at the Center for Sustainable Resources of the University of California at Berkeley. He is also a member of the Club of Rome, a Fellow of the World Academy of Arts and Sciences, the World Business Academy, and the European Academy of Sciences and Arts. Bernard Lietaer has written numerous articles and books about money systems, including *Rethinking Money: How New Currencies Turn Scarcity into Prosperity* and *The Future of Money: Creating New Wealth, Work and Wiser World* (translated into 18 languages). His website is: www.lietaer.com.

John Perkins, BS, is best known for book his *Confessions of an Economic Hit Man* (2004), which remained on *The New York Times* best-seller list for 72 weeks, sold over 1 million copies and was translated into 30 languages. After serving as a Peace Corps Volunteer in Ecuador from 1968–1970, John trained for and later took a position as Chief Economist at a major consulting firm where he worked with the World Bank, UN, IMF, US government, Fortune 500 companies, and heads of state. His work cast him in a role he describes as that of an Economic Hit Man, responsible for persuading countries on three continents to take on heavy debt to fund improvements, which chiefly benefited US corporations and the US government. After an epiphany, in which he realized our entire hemisphere is built on the bones of indigenous people, he resolved never to engage in such work again. Deeply immersed in the spiritual cultures of indigenous people around the world, John writes, travels and teaches with the single-minded goal of bringing people to realize a major global Consciousness Revolution is taking place, out of which can be born a far better world. John has been featured on ABC, NBC, CNN, NPR, A&E, the History Channel, *Time, The New York Times, The Washington Post, Cosmopolitan, Elle, Der Spiegel,* and many other publications, as well as in documentaries including *The End of Poverty?, Zeitgeist Addendum,* and *Apology of an Economic Hit Man*. His many books include *The Secret History of the American Empire, Hoodwinked* and *The World as You Dream It*. His website is: www.johnperkins.org.

James Gustave Speth, JD, joined the faculty of the Vermont Law School as Professor of Law in 2010. In 2009 he completed ten years as Dean of the Yale School of Forestry and Environmental Studies. From 1993 to 1999, Speth was Administrator of the United Nations Development Programme and chair of the UN Development Group. Prior to his service at the UN, he was founder and president of the World Resources Institute; professor of law at Georgetown University; chairman of the US Council on Environmental Quality (Carter Administration); and senior attorney and cofounder, Natural Resources Defense Council. His has long been devoted to combating environmental degradation and promoting sustainable development, serving on the President's Task Force on Global Resources and Environment; the Western Hemisphere Dialogue on Environment and Development; and the National Commission on the Environment. His many awards include National Wildlife Federation's Resources Defense Award, the Natural Resources Council of America's Barbara Swain Award of Honor, a 1997 Special Recognition Award from the Society for International Development, Lifetime Achievement Awards from the Environmental Law Institute and five honorary degrees. He is the author, co-author or editor of six books including the award-winning *The Bridge at the Edge of the World* and *Red Sky at Morning: America and the Crisis of the Global Environment*.

ENDNOTES

Introduction

1   The founding of the Bank of England legalized a scam dating back to 1640—which we now call the fractional reserve system. Prior to that date, wealthy merchants deposited their surplus gold and silver in the Mint of the Tower of London for safekeeping. In 1640 Charles I seized the privately-owned money and destroy the Mint's reputation as a safe haven. Merchants then turn to the goldsmiths of Lombard Street who had fire-proof strong boxes for the storage of their valuables. The goldsmiths accepted the merchants' deposits and issued notes redeemable on-demand. These notes were the precursors of banknotes. The goldsmiths paid 5% interest on their customers' deposits, and then lent the money to needy customers at exorbitant rates, essentially becoming pawnbrokers who advanced money against the valuables in their possession. As these notes became a preferred medium of exchange and only a small percentage of their depositors sought to convert their notes back into gold, the goldsmiths soon realized they could issue notes against the same gold *more than once* and receive interest from multiple borrows. The "money" they were lending did not actually exist. Thus was born the most profitable confidence game in the history of humanity. The founding of the bank of England in 1694 merely *legalized* the fraud. The general public remains unaware that the promised "to redeem in

gold" was nothing more than a sham. Despite bitter opposition by Thomas Jefferson, Alexander Hamilton was able to foist the British banking system on a reluctant America. And so began our modern banking system.

2   See Appendix A for a summary of Lincoln's monetary policies.

3   Anyone wanting a fuller account should consult the works in the editor's Additional Resources section.

4   An interesting side note is that President Lincoln saw a performance by John Wilkes Booth in the play, *The Marble Heart*, at Ford's Theatre on November 9, 1863.

5   Booth's travels to Canada have been confirmed by historians. See Emil Ludwig, *Abraham Lincoln*. Tr. from German by Eden and Cedar Paul. Boston: Little, Brown & Co., 1930, 476. Reissued by Kessinger Publishing, 2004.

6   Quoted by Emanuel Hertz, *Abraham Lincoln: A New Portrait*. New York: Horace Liveright, Inc., 1931, 954. My italics.

7   On the morning of April 14th, the day of Lincoln's assassination, he met with Schyler Colfax to discuss ways of paying off the nation's war debt by employing thousands of disbanded soldiers to mine for gold and silver in the Rocky Mountains and as far west as California, thereby solving the twofold problem of post-war unemployment and addressing the national debt.

8   For that story, see G. Edward Griffin's *The Creature from Jekyll Island*. Western Island Publishers, 1994.

Chapter 5: Ending the World Financial Crisis

1   As reported in the *Globe and Mail*, November 2, 2008.

2   As reported in *The New York Times*, November 17, 2008.

3   Galbraith, John K., *Money, Whence it Came, Where it Went*, (Boston: Houghton Mifflin Company, 1975), 18.

4   Hixson, William F., *Triumph of the Bankers: Money and Banking in the Eighteenth and Nineteenth Centuries*, (Westport: Praeger Publishers, 1993), 46.

5 *Ibid.*, 60.

6 Hellyer, Paul, *Surviving the Global Financial Crisis: The Economics of Hope for Generation X*, (Toronto: Chimo Media, 1996), 1-2.

7 Source: Flow of Funds Accounts, Table L2 through 4, US Federal Reserve Bulletin, from many issues.

8 Data published in the Bank of Canada Banking and Financial Statistics approximately 30 calendar days after each end of reference month.

9 Patricia Adams, *Odious Debts: Loose Lending, Corruption, And the Third World's Environmental Legacy*, (London: Probe International, 1991). *The New York Times*, July 31, 2009.

Chapter 7: The Role of Bioregional Currencies in Regional Regeneration

1 The title of a book by John Kenneth Galbraith.

2 Various sources, including a dozen first hand interviews with local officials during a field trip to Curitiba in 1996-97. Some information about Curitiba's development strategy has also been published in English—see Jonas Rabinovitch "Curitiba: Toward Sustainable Urban Development" in *Environment and Urbanization,* Vol. 4 (no 2), October 1992, 62-73; and Jonas Rabinovitch & Josef Leitman, "Urban Planning in Curitiba" in *Scientific American,* March 1996, 46-53.

3 The 1993–95 data is derived from *Indústria, Comércio e Turismo Gestão Rafael Creca* (December 1996) The respective growth rates are 8.6% per annum for Curitiba, 6% for the State of Parana and 5% for Brazil. The respective *per capita* growth rates between 1980 and 1995 is 277% for Curitiba, 190% for Parana and 192% for Brazil. Statistics from *Informaciones Socioeconomicas,* issued by the *Prefeitura da Cidade Curitiba,(1996)* compared with the Brazilian data bases of SACEN, IPARDES and SICT/ICPI.

4 A research project is now on-going at the Department of Historical Economics of Bocconi University in Milan, Italy. It aims at fully documenting this phenomenon, and providing a theoretical framework to

explain it. See Amato M., Fantacci L., and Doria L. (2003) *Complementary Currency Systems in a Historical Perspective* Milan: Bocconi University.

5   Jackson & McConnell, C. R. (1988). *Economics (3rd ed.)* Sydney: McGraw-Hill.

6   See Amann, Erwin & Marin, Dalia "Risk-sharing in international trade: an analysis of countertrade." *The Journal of Industrial Economics*, Volume XLII (March 1994) pg. 63–77. Williamson, Stev & Wright, Randall "Barter and Monetary Exchange under Private Information" The American Economic Review March 1994, 104–123 . Taurand, Francis "Le troc en Economie Monetaire" L'Actualite Economique, Revue d'analyse economique Vol 52 numero 2, Juin 1986.

7   Fureai Kippu are the brainchild of Tsutomo Hotta and his Sawayaka Welfare Institute. It is a system that is complementary to the national healthcare insurance, given that it covers any services needed by an elderly or handicapped person that is not covered by national healthcare. The unit of account is the hour of service to an elderly and handicapped person. This enables an elderly person to stay much longer in their own house than would otherwise be the case. As of May 2003, there were 372 non-profit organizations issuing Fureai Kippu in Japan.

8   Local Exchange Trading Systems (LETS) is a complementary currency system that uses mutual credit to issue the currency: the currency is created by a simultaneous debit and credit between the users themselves. For instance, if Julia renders a service of 1 hour to James, she gets a credit for one HOUR, and James a debit for one HOUR. The main advantage of mutual credit systems is that they self-regulate to have always currency available in sufficiency. There are over 1000 LETS systems operational in the world. See Lietaer B., *The Future of Money.*

9   See Bernard Lietaer & Stephen Belgin: *New Money for a New World* (Boulder: Qiterra Publishers, 2011); Bernard Lietaer with Margrit Kennedy and John Rogers: *People Money: The Promise of Regional Currencies* (UK: Triarchy Prss, 2012); Bernard Lietaer with Jacqui Dunne: *Rethinking*

Money (San Francisco; Berrett-Koehler, February 2013) Lietaer, Bernard (2001) *The Future of Money* (London: Random House.)

10 Lietaer, Bernard (2000) *Mysterium Geld* (Munich: Riemann Verlag) (also available in Japanese).

11 This concept was developed by Warmoth, Arthur (1995). The metropolitan bioregion as a political and economic unit. *AHP Perspective*, September-October, 20-21. See also Warmoth, Arthur & Lietaer, Bernard (1999) "Designing Bioregional Economies as a Response to Globalization" (http://ceres.ca.gov/tcsf/pathways/chapter2.html)

12 Jacobs, J. (1984). *Cities and the Wealth of Nations*. New York: Random House.

Chapter 8: The Possibility of a Pluralist Commonwealth and a Community-Sustaining Economy

1 Jim Puzzanghera and Don Lee, "Bernanke sharply warns Congress economy is 'close to faltering'," Los Angeles Times, October 4, 2011, http://articles.latimes.com/2011/oct/04/business/la-fi-bernanke-congress-20111005, accessed June 3, 2012.

2 Lindsey Ellerson, "Obama to Bankers: I'm Standing 'Between You and the Pitchforks'," ABC News, April 3, 2009, http://abcnews.go.com/blogs/politics/2009/04/obama-to-banker, accessed June 3, 2012.

3 Franklin Delano Roosevelt, *A Rendezvous with Density*, Philadelphia, PA: Democratic Party National Convention, June 27, 1936, http://www.austincc.edu/lpatrick/his2341/fdr36acceptancespeech.htm, accessed June 3, 2012.

4 David M. Herszenhorn, "Senate Nod to Fed Audit Expected," New York Times, May 7, 2010, http://www.nytimes.com/2010/05/07/business/economy/07regulate.html, accessed June 3, 2012.

5 Victoria McGraine and Michael R. Crittenden, "Senate Passes Amendment for One-Time Audit of Fed," *Wall Street Journal*, May 11, 2010, http://online.wsj.com/article/SB10001424052748704250104575238130707230588.html, accessed June 3, 2012.

6   Laurence J. Kotlikoff, *The Financial FixLimited Purpose Banking*, Boston, MA: Boston University, March 23, 2009.

7   Fred Mosely, "Time for Permanent Nationalization!" *Dollars & Sense*, March-April 2009.

8   Willem Buiter, "The end of American capitalism as we knew it": Financial Times, September 17, 2008.

9   For example, Citibank had a market capitalization fell to $36 billion by December 31, 2008; by contrast, the amount of bailout funds Citi received from the U.S. government totaled $45 billion. See: Citi, Annual Report 2008, New York, NY: Citi, 2009, page 11. On bailout size, see: Jim Puzzanghera, "Citigroup chief thanks taxpayers for $45 billion bailout," *The Network Journal*, March 4, 2010, http://www.tnj.com/news/business/citigroup-chief-thanks-taxpayers-45-billion-bailout, accessed June 3, 2012.

10 Robert Pollin, "Tools for a New Economy," *Boston Review*, volume 34, no. 1, January-February 2009, http://bostonreview.net/BR34.1/pollin.php, accessed June 3, 2012.

11 Roger Runnigen, "Obama Signs Renewal of Export-Import Bank That Boosts Lending," *Bloomberg Business Week*, May 30, 2012, http://www.businessweek.com/news/2012-05-30/obama-signs-renewal-of-export-import-bank-that-boosts-lending, accessed June 3, 2012.

12 Bank of North Dakota, 2009 Annual Report: 90 Years of Evolution, Bismarck, ND: BND, 2010, page 6.

13 Public Banking Institute, State Activity, Resource and Contact Info, Los Angeles, CA: Banking in the Public Interest, 2012, http://publicbankinginstitute.org/state-info, accessed June 3, 2012.

14 Ted Wheeler, "Why creating a 'virtual' state bank is a better idea," OregonLive.com, February 9, 2011, http://www.oregonlive.com/opinion/index.ssf/2011/02/hy_creating_a_virtual_state_ba.html, accessed June 3, 2012.

15 Public Counsel Law Center, Our Stories: Paraplegic Patient "Dumped" Without his Wheelchair, Los Angeles, CA: PCLC, no date, http://www.

publiccounsel.org/stories?id=0003, accessed June 3, 2012.

16 Centers for Medicare and Medicaid Services, Updated NHE Projections 2009-2019, Baltimore, MD: CMMS, September 2010, accessed July 7, 2011, http://www.cms.gov/NationalHealthExpendData/downloads/NHEProjections2009to2019.pdf.

17 Jerry Geisel, "Massachusetts' insured rate hits 98.1%: Analysis," Business Insurance, December 14, 2010, http://www.businessinsurance.com/article/20101214/BENEFITS03/101219966, accessed June 3, 2012. See also State of Massachusetts, Health Insurance Coverage in Massachusetts: Results from the 2008-2010 Massachusetts Health Insurance Surveys, Boston, MA: Division of Health Care Finance and Policy, December 2010.

18 Hawaii Institute for Public Affairs, Prepaid Health Care Act, Honolulu, HI: HIPA, 2004, http://www.healthcoveragehawaii.org/target/prepaid.html, accessed June 3, 2012.

19 Consumer Reports, "Vermont Has a Plan For Single Payer Health Care," Consumer Reports, May 26, 2011, accessed June 23, 2011, http://news.consumerreports.org/health/2011/05/vermont-establishes-road-map-for-single-payer-health-care.html; Linda Bergthold, "Vermont To Go Single Payer—Do I Hear A Second?" Huffington Post, May 6, 2011, accessed June 23, 2011, http://www.huffingtonpost.com/linda-bergthold/vermont-to-go-single-paye_b_858718.html; Doug Trapp, "Vermont Approves Universal Health Program," American Medical News, May 16, 2011, accessed June 23, 2011, http://www.ama-assn.org/amednews/2011/05/16/gvsa0516.htm. David Weigel, "Green Mountain Dreams," Slate, May 11, 2011, accessed June 27, 2011, http://www.slate.com/id/2293634/.

20 Associated Press, "Connecticut Senate Approves Health Care Pooling Bill," Associated Press, June 6, 2011, accessed June 27, 2011, http://www.nhregister.com/articles/2011/06/06/news/doc4ded964cba64b338170157.txt?viewmode=default; Cheryl Harris Forbes, SustiNet: Good Medicine for Connecticut and Small Businesses, Health Justice CT, June 16, 2011, accessed June 27, 2011, http://www.healthjusticect.org/blog/sustinet-good-

medicine-for-connecticut-and-small-businesses.

21 Democracy Collaborative of the University of Maryland, Building Wealth: The New Asset-Based Approach to Solving Social and Economic Problems, Washington, DC: The Aspen Institute, 2005.

22 The Democracy Collaborative, with which both authors are associated, has been a partner in this effort, which began in 2007. The Democracy Collaborative is also involved in the efforts in Atlanta, Pittsburgh, Washington DC, and Amarillo cited below.

23 Rob Witherell, Chris Cooper, and Michael Peck, *Sustainable Jobs, Sustainable Communities and the Union Co-op Model*, Pittsburgh, PA: USW, Mondragón and OEOC, March 26, 2012.

24 Market Creek Plaza, Public-Private Partnerships (Financing): New Markets Tax Credit Loan, San Diego, CA: Market Creek Plaza, http://www. marketcreekplaza.com/mcp_financing_newmarkets.htm, no date, and Market Creek Plaza, Public-Private Partnerships (Financing): Tax Reimbursements, San Diego, CA: Market Creek Plaza, http://www.market-creekplaza.com/mcp_financing_tax.html, no date. PolicyLink, Lifting Up What Works "Community Development IPO" Makes History in San Diego," Equitable Development Update, issue 18, November 16, 2006, http://policylink.info/EDupdates/Issue18.htm. Lou Hirsch, "EPA Grant Will Help Jacobs Center Clean Up Mixed-Use Project Area," *San Diego Business Journal*, October 25, 2010, www.sdbj.com/news/2010/oct/25/epa-grant-will-help-jacobs-center-clean-mixed-use-. Websites accessed March 7, 2011.

25 U.S. Environmental Protection Agency, Building Vibrant Communities: Community Benefits of Land Revitalization, Washington, DC: EPA, 2008, page 4. Lou Hirsch, "EPA Grant Will Help Jacobs Center Clean Up Mixed-Use Project Area," San Diego Business Journal, October 25, 2010, www.sdbj.com/news/2010/oct/25/epa-grant-will-help-jacobs-center-clean-mixed-use, accessed March 7, 2011.

26 Most recent estimate is 576 projects nationwide. See: U.S. Environmental Protection Agency, Landfill Methane Outreach Program: Basic

Information, Washington, DC: EPA, January 2012, http://www.epa.gov/lmop/basic-info/index.html#a01, accessed June 4, 2012.

27 Chris Isidore, "Indiana: An Island of Calm in State Budget Storms," *CNN/Money*, February 14, 2011, http://money.cnn.com/2011/02/14/news/economy/mitch_daniels_indiana_state_budget/index.htm, accessed April 11, 2012.

28 Tom Tresser, "None Dare Call It Privatization," *Commons Magazine*, Minneapolis, MN: On the Commons, July 26, 2011, http://onthecommons.org/none-dare-call-it-privatization, accessed June 4, 2012. Dan Mihalopoulos, "City May Privatize Taste, Recycling," Chicago News Cooperative, August 26, 2010, http://www.chicagonewscoop.org/city-may-privatize-taste-recycling, accessed June 4, 2012.

29 Dan Primack, "Why Obama Can't Save Infrastructure," *CNN/Money*, February 17, 2011, http://finance.fortune.cnn.com/2011/02/17/why-obama-cant-save-infrastructure/, accessed June 4, 2012.

30 Peter Samuel, "NJ Turnpike & unions settle—cuts in toll collector pay but staff jobs kept for now," Tollroads News, April 28, 2011, http://www.tollroadsnews.com/node/5280, accessed June 4, 2012.

31 *Wall Street Journal*, "FAA Grants Chicago Until March 31 to Submit Midway Privatization Plan," *Wall Street Journal*, October 4, 2011, accessed 2/2/12, http://online.wsj.com/article/BT-CO-20111004-711012.html.

32 David Zahniser, "Plan to Lease L.A. Parking Garages Crumbles," *Los Angeles Times*, February 12, 2011, http://articles.latimes.com/2011/feb/12/local/la-me-la-budget-hole-20110212, accessed July 13, 2011.

33 American Sustainable Business Council, White House Briefing: Creating Jobs and Building a Sustainable Economy, Washington, DC: ASBC, June 2, 2011 Jeff Hollender, "Fighting Democracy and Destroying Democracy," Burlington, VT: Jeff Hollender Partners, 2011, http://www.jeffreyhollender.com/?p=1307, accessed June 4, 2012.

34 Ed Wolff, "Table 9. The Percent of Total Assets Held by Wealth Class, 2007," Recent Trends in Household Wealth in the United States: Rising Debt and the Middle-Class Squeeze—An Update to 2007, working

paper 589, Annandale-on-Hudson: Levy Economics Institute on Bard College, March 2010, page 51.

35 Harold Meyerson, "Rush Builds a Revolution," *Washington Post*, April 15, 2009, page A-19. Rasmusesen Reports, 60% Say Capitalism Better Than Socialism, Asbury Park, NJ: Rasmussen, 2010. http://www.rasmussen-reports.com/public_content/business/general_business/april_2010/60_say_capitalism_better_than_socialism. Pew Research Center, Little Change in Public's Response to 'Capitalism,' 'Socialism', Washington, DC: Pew, 2011. Pew Research Center, Distrust, Discontent, Anger and Partisan Rancor The People and Their Government, Washington, DC: Pew, April 18, 201, http://people-press.org/report/606/trust-in-government, accessed September 14, 2010.

36 Gar Alperovitz, *America Beyond Capitalism*, College Park, MD and Boston, MA: Democracy Collaborative Press and Dollars & Sense, 2011, 66. See also Organization for Economic Cooperation and Development, OECD in Figures: Statistics on the Member Countries, Paris, France: OECD, 2002, pp. 6-7.

37 George F. Kennan, *Around the Cragged Hill: A Personal and Political Philosophy.* NewYork, NY: W.W. Norton, 1993, 143, 149.

38 United States Census Bureau, "Projections of the Population and Components of Change for the United States: 2010 to 2050." Table 1. Released August 14, 2008; United States Census Bureau. "Annual Projections of the Total Resident Population as of July 1: Middle, Lowest, Highest, and Zero International Migration Series, 1999 to 2100." Released January 13, 2000, revised February 14, 2000.

39 For further reference, see the discussion in *America Beyond Capitalism*, by Gar Alperovitz, Hoboken, NJ: John Wiley & Sons, October 2004 (2nd Edition, Washington, D.C. and Boston, MA: Democracy Collaborative Press and Dollars & Sense, 2011); and *The Size of Nations*, by Alberto Alesina and Enrique Spolaore, Cambridge, MA: MIT Press, 2003.

40 Paul Pierson, "The New Politics of the Welfare State," *World Politics*, volume 48, no. 2, 1996, 143-179.

41 For further reference, see the discussion in *America Beyond Capitalism*, by ⁿᵇ
    Gar Alperovitz (Hoboken, NJ: John Wiley & Sons, October 2004).2nd
    Edition (Washington, D.C. and Boston, MA: Democracy Collaborative
    Press and Dollars & Sense, 2011).

42 Thad Williamson, Steve Dubb, and Gar Alperovitz, *Climate Change,* ⁿᵇ
    Community Stability, and the Next 150 Million Americans, College Park, MD:
    The Democracy Collaborative at the University of Maryland, September
    2010.

43 Lawrence E. Mitchell, *The Speculation Economy: How Finance Triumphed* ⁿᵇ
    Over Industry, San Francisco, CA: Berrett-Koehler, 2007.

44 U.S. Energy Information Administration, International Energy Statistics
    2010, Washington, DC: EIA, 2011. http://www.eia.gov/cfapps/ipdb-
    project/IEDIndex3.cfm?tid=1&pid=1&aid=2, accessed June 4, 2012.

45 Ralph C. Kirby and Andrew S. Prokoprovitsh, "Technological Insurance
    Against Shortages in Minerals and Metals," *Science,* vol. 191, no. 4227,
    February 20, 1976, 713-719.

46 Juliet Schor, Plenitude: *The New Economics of True Wealth,.* New York,
    NY: Penguin, 2010.

47 James Speth, "Letters to Liberals: Liberalism, Environmentalism and
    Economic Growth," *Vermont Law Review,* vol. 35, 2011, pp. 547-562,
    quote on page 555.

48 George Stigler, "The Theory of Economic Regulation," *Bell Journal of
    Economics and Management Science,* vol. 2, no. 1, 1971, 3-21.

49 Henry Calvert Simons, *Economic Policy for a Free Society,* Chicago, IL: ⁿᵇ
    University of Chicago Press, 1948, page 51.

50 Ian Bremer, *The End of the Free Market.* New York, NY: Portfolio
    (Penguin), 2010.

51 For more on public enterprise, efficiencies, and new developments, see:
    Gar Alperovitz and Thomas Hanna, "Beyond Corporate Capitalism: Not
    So Wild a Dream," *The Nation,* June 11, 2012.

52 Robert Millward, "State Enterprise in Britain in the Twentieth Century,"
    The Rise and Fall of State-Owned Enterprise in the Western World,

edited by Pier Angelo Toninelli, New York, NY: Cambridge University Press, 2000, pp. 157-184.

53 Francisco Flores-Macias and Aldo Musacchio, "The Return of State-Owned Enterprises," *Harvard International Review*, April 4, 2009, accessed 1/9/12, http://hir.harvard.edu/the -return-of-state-owned-enterprises?page=0,0.

Chapter 9: The Growing Green Economy

1 See: Hazel Henderson, *The Politics of the Solar Age*. Doubleday, 1981

2 Cohan, Peter. "Big Risk: $1.2 Quadrillion Derivatives Market Dwarfs World GDP," *Daily Finance*, June 9, 2010.

3 World Development Indicators Database, World Bank, July 1, 2011.

4 See "The Money Fix" TV special distributed to PBS stations in 2009 by Ethical Markets Media.

5 See my "Statisticians of the World Unite," InterPress Service, October, 2003.

NB 6 See my "The Politics of Money," Vermont Commons, January 2006, at www.HazelHenderson.com.

7 See my "And We All Thought that Banks Had Money, September, 2008

*W B*8 See the video cartoon "Money as Debt" at www.ethicalmarkets.tv

Chapter 10: Terra: A Currency to Stabilize the World Economy

1 These statistics are derived from the total daily foreign exchange transactions as reported every three years by the BIS, and compared to Global Annual Trade divided by the number of days.

2 Glynn Davies, *A History of Money from Ancient Times to the Present Day* (Cardiff: University of Wales Press, 1994) 646.

3 John Maynard Keynes, *The General Theory of Employment, Interest and Money* (London: Macmillan, 1936) 159.

4 W. Dolde, "The Use of Foreign Exchange and Interest Rate Risk Management in Large Firms," University of Connecticut School of Business Administration Working Paper 93-042 (Storra, Conn.: 1993) 18-19. There was also consensus that interest rate risks were less important than foreign exchange risks.

5   W. Dolde, "The Use of Foreign Exchange and Interest Rate Risk Management in Large Firms," University of Connecticut School of Business Administration Working Paper 93-042 (Storra, Conn: 1993). The 85 % of the firms that routinely hedge have a capital averaging at $8 billion, compared to $2.5 billion for the 15 %, which have never hedged (See exhibit 1) 23-24.

6   Estimates, as reported by the U.S. Department of Commerce, the World Trade Organization (WTO) and *The Economist* (U.K.).

7   Pepsi-Cola delivers syrup that is paid for with Stolichnaya Vodka. Pepsi has the marketing rights of all Stolichnaya Vodka in the U.S. The deal came about because the president of PepsiCo Wines & Spirits International, Mr. John Swanhaus, had the responsibility to supply the U.S. market of Stolichnaya Russian Vodka. More recently Pepsi has made another innovative step by taking 17 submarines, a cruiser, a frigate, and a destroyer in payment for Pepsi products. In turn, this rag tag fleet of 20 naval vessels will be sold for scrap steel, thereby paying for Pepsi products being moved to Russia. These deals are explained at http://www.barternews.com/approach_marketing.htm

8   Note that the commodity itself that is being sold (in this case, oil) may or may not have to move physically during the process. What matters it that the Terra Alliance becomes now the beneficial owner of the commodity. The legal framework for such transfers is already routinely used today. For instance, the commodity trading departments of an oil company can have a shipment of oil in a tanker change owner several times before it arrives at its destination.

9   A futures market transaction is the purchase or sale today at a given price for delivery at some future date. A spot transaction is the direct purchase or sale of a commodity at the price of today, with delivery today.

10 Note that all exchanges in Terras would occur through high-level secure electronic exchanges, as these transactions would tend to be of high value.

11 The payment conditions would normally have been already determined when the oil rig was put up for bidding.

12 In order to produce the corresponding cash for the Terras that are handed in, the Terra Alliance sells an appropriate volume of commodities of the Terra basket in the commodity markets.

13 Mervyn King, "Challenges for Monetary Policy: New and Old." Paper prepared for the Symposium on "New Challenges for Monetary Policy" (Jackson Hole, Wyoming: 27 August 1999). Sponsored by the Federal Reserve Bank of Kansas City.

14 Benjamin Friedman, "The Future of Monetary Policy," *International Finance*)December, 1999).

15 "Future of Monetary Policy and Banking Conference: A Conference Looking Ahead to the Next Twenty-Five Years" World Bank (Washington, D.C.:, July 11, 2000).

16 "Economics Focus: E-Money Revisited," *Economist Magazine* (July 22, 2000).

17 James Stodder, "Complementary Credit Networks and Macroeconomic Stability: Switzerland's Wirtschaftring", *Journal of Economic Behavior and Organization*, vol. 72 (2009), 79-95.

18 WIR is the first syllable of the word "Wirtschaftsring" (business circle). WIR (German for "we"), unlike "Ich" (German for "I"), means community. This contains the Swiss ideal: to hold together and, together as a community, protect the interests of the individual." (From a speech by Werner Zimmermann, Fall Conference 1954). Source: http://www.ex.ac. uk/~RDavies/arian/wir.html

19 James Stodder, Ibid. 2.

20 James Stodder, Ibid. 3.

21 T. Studer, "Le Système WIR dans l'optique d'un chercheur Américain" WirPlus (October 2000). Online at: http//www.wir.ch.

22 Ames : http://www.geog.le.ac.uk/ijccr/volume2/2js.htm.

23 http://www.barternews.com/archive/06_27_06.htm See for example in chronological order: W.S. Jevons, *Money and the Mechanism of Exchange* (1875); Ian Gondriaan, *How to Stop Deflation* (London, 1932); Benjamin Graham, *Storage and Stability* (New York: McGraw Hill, 1937)

and *World Commodities and World Currency*(1944); Harmon, Elmer, *Commodity Reserve Currency* (New York: Columbia University Press, 1959); Grondona St. Clare *Economic Stability is Attainable* (London: Hutchison Benham Ltd, 1975); Albert Hart of Columbia University, Nicholas Kaldor of Cambridge University and Jan Tinbergen: "The Case for an International Reserve Currency," Document UNCTAD 64-03482 (Geneva: presented on 2/17/1964) (in this last case the purpose wasn't to replace the conventional money, but to stabilize the prices of Third World country commodities)

OTHER BOOKS FROM FINLEY EVERSOLE

Art and Spiritual Transformation:
The Seven Stages of Death and Rebirth

By Finley Eversole, Ph.D.

Published by Inner Traditions

366 pages, oversized paperback,

(16-page color insert)

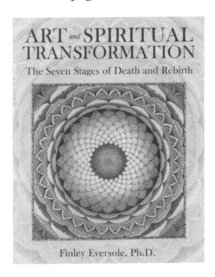

Book Description

Explores the role of the arts in the awakening and evolution of human consciousness.

- Presents a seven-stage journey of transformation moving from the darkened soul to the light of spiritual illumination
- Provides a meditation practice to experience the spiritual energy embedded within art
- Includes artists Jackson Pollock, Mark Rothko, Willem de Kooning, Walter Gaudnek, Alex Grey, and others

Art and Spiritual Transformation presents a seven-stage journey through the dark night of the soul to the light of spiritual illumination as revealed in modern art. Finley Eversole introduces a meditation practice that moves beyond the visual content of an art form in order to connect with its embedded spiritual energy, allowing the viewer to tap in to the deeper consciousness inherent in the artwork and awaken dormant powers in the depths of the viewer's soul.

Examining modern and postmodern artwork from 1945 onward, Eversole reveals the influences of ancient Egypt, India, China, and alchemy on this art. He draws extensively on philosophy, myth and symbolism, literature, and metaphysics to explain the seven stages of spiritual death and rebirth of the soul explored through art: the experience of self-loss, the journey into the underworld, the experience of the dark night of the soul, the conflict with and triumph over evil, the awakening of new life in the depths of being, and the return and reintegration of consciousness on a higher plane of being, resulting finally in ecstasy, transfiguration, illumination, and liberation. To illustrate these stages, Eversole includes works by abstract expressionists Jackson Pollock, Willem de Kooning, Arshile Gorky, Mark Rothko, Adolph Gottlieb and modern visionary artists Alex Grey and Ernst Fuchs, among others, to reveal the powerful and liberating forces art contributes to the transformation and evolution of human consciousness.

Reviews

A very compelling read.

Nexus, *Colorado's Holistic Journal*, Nov/Dec 2009

This visually appealing work will charm artists, students of psychology, and spiritual seekers.

Library Journal, July 2009

Eversole's book begins with an overview of the history of art, and then moves rapidly to well-known 20th century artists such as Jackson Pollack, Willem de Kooning and Mark Rothko, as well as modern visionary artists such as Alex Grey and Ernst Fuchs... As an artist myself, I am indebted to this wonderful, personal, and touching book by Finley Eversole. It made me return to studying my own work from a new perspective.... You do not have to be an artist to enjoy and receive the rich offerings of *Art and Spiritual Transformation.* I believe you will see art and your own creative expressions with different eyes once you have studied it. It is indeed a book to be studied, delved into and intuitively opened to certain pages when the time is right. This book is definitely a 'must have' for any aspiring artist, both of fine arts and prose, as it reveals in very clear terms the link between image, archetype and reality.

Lesley Crossingham, *New Dawn*, No. 120, May-June 2010

In times of anxiety such as these it is heartening to read such a positive book. The author passionately believes, and writes convincingly, that despite the problems facing us we are in fact on the verge of an unprecedented transcendence....

Artists, he maintains, are often prophets, acting intuitively, frequently unconscious of the forces working through them, sensing ahead of anyone else, the shifts taking place around them, making them invaluable barometers of social, psychological and spiritual change.

"'Within our lifetime', he says, 'American art has given us images, like precognition in dreams, of a radical transformation of man and of civilization—a transformation that is just beginning to reach us at conscious levels....art, by its very nature is a transformative process, an act of re-creation. It carries within itself the seeds of cultural change'....

In the final part, 'The Creative Promise of the Coming Age,' Eversole provides not only a brilliant analysis of Existentialism—one of the best I have ever read—but also marshals all his evidence to prove that despite all the negativities of our age there is now an unstoppable process of spiritualization at work leading to immense changes in thought, psychology, politics and spirituality.

The entire work, detailing every step on the journey, is a profound and extensive meditation on the spiritual life. As a guide to that life it is worth reading many times over.

Desmond Scott, Actor, director, and sculptor, Canada

Instead of being simply a well-educated author, who could have easily lost and/or bored many readers by offering highbrow academic-speak, Eversole brings this book to life as he shares his own personal transformations, including his need for therapy at one point, his series of dreams, and his spontaneous mystical experience. Allowing the reader access to his inner life, in a casually intelligent manner, ensures one's rapt attention throughout the reading of this work and shows his inherent bravery in doing so.

G.L. Giles, *MetaCreative Magazine*, March 2010

Art and Spiritual Transformation is a particular treat for anyone with an interest in both spirituality and art.... The book includes a particularly interesting discussion by Mr. Eversole on 'Art and the Evolution of Consciousness'.... This book offers some stimulating, thoughtful, and insightful comments on which to ponder.

***The Beacon*, Vol. LXIII, No. 1, Jan-Mar 2010**

Read an Excerpt
Chapter 6: The Broken Center
Jackson Pollock (1912-1956)

"The human soul must suffer its own disintegration, consciously, if ever it is to survive," wrote D. H. Lawrence. Here we have stated the central problem of our age, evidenced in the art of Jackson Pollock (1912-1956). It is the problem of self-loss, willingly undertaken, in order that the deeper spirit of man may come into manifestation. Nor is it not merely a case of play-acting, of pretending to die to oneself. Dying is a radical experience. It is our destiny as human beings to explore the furthest limits of human existence, to plunge the utmost depths and heights of the human soul and know in fullness its sorrows and joys. How can we know these if we live in a box? We must be free, and we can be free only if we are willing to risk all! As Janice Joplin sang, "Freedom is just another word for nothing left to lose." To be free requires letting go of ourselves, our world, our crutches, our gods. It means plunging into the abyss. The journey of transformation begins then with the experience of the abyss. But how can the abyss be represented in a work of art?

The answer lies in the art of Jackson Pollock—the most dramatic painter of the American Abstract Expressionism movement. Pollock came to be known as an action painter. The "drip technique" of his mature style resulted in works of a highly sensitive arabesque design. Pollock approached his canvases, usually stretched out on the floor or tacked to a wall, with a trowel, sticks, brushes, or hands dripping with paint. Immersing himself bodily into the work at hand, he swirled paint with intense speed and force, forming a veritable network of lines, which, were it not for his near-classical sense of balance, might well have passed off the canvas into infinity. Viewing the athletic Pollock at work, one is reminded of Picasso's statement that every time he began a painting he felt as though he were throwing himself into a void.

The frenzied, Dionysian passion of *Number 1, 1948* provides a prime example of Pollock's particular creative genius. The work employs an all-over style of painting derived from Impressionism and Cubism. Its distribution of lines and color "prevented any climactic emphasis on one point...of his essentially light-dark structured canvases." No one area of the canvas is more important than any other, and the arabesque design is allowed to float freely upon the canvas as though in an empty void, anchored only by the bottom edge of the canvas. The electric speed of Pollock's marvelously sensitive, swirling light and dark lines and the ice-blue terror of the infinite strike a certain terror in the heart. Only the dark, blood-stained handprints reaching outward toward the edges of the canvas reveal the full extent of the agony and tragic suffering that must have overwhelmed the artist while creating this work.

In Pollock's *Number 1, 1948* we are confronted with a modern, abstract form of Gothic expressionism—a kind of "spiritual orgy." The center, the organizing principle in classical art, has all but vanished in this piece. At the horizontal midpoint, two-fifths of the way from the bottom of the painting, a nearly imperceptible "point" appears, giving the work a faint visual center. Its weakness, however, testifies to the difficulty Pollock had in keeping "the center" from vanishing altogether from his work. Oft times it did! Pollock struggled heroically to keep a center, often hand-painting it in at the conclusion of a work. In 1960 I began to refer to Pollock's art as "an art of the broken center." Pollock's *Blue Poles: Number 11, 1952* is another example of "the broken center," in which we find eight "poles" inclining at various angles—all at various stages of disintegration or absorption by the wildly dancing light-dark drips.

The center is the organizing principle in any form or space. But what else, what symbolism gives the center the supreme importance assigned to it in all cultures, both primitive and highly evolved? The symbolism of the center concerns the journey inward, where unity, infinity, transcendence, and the Absolute reside. It is the "abode" of the supreme principle of the universe, the One Reality. Contemplation of the center unites one with the deathless essence of the manifest cosmos. "The most ancient and at the same time the most complete of all symbols given by the Wise Ones for the edification of man is the circle with a dot at its center." Loss of the center means a severance of contact with all that the center symbolizes. An art of "the broken center" is art of alienation, of finitude, of existence in exile—a truly existential art. With the vanishing of the center in Pollock's art we encounter the first stage of transformation—the *dismemberment* motif.

God is a circle whose center is everywhere and whose circumference is nowhere.
   Blaise Pascal

Infinite Energy Technologies
Tesla, Cold Fusion, Antigravity and the Future of Sustainability
Edited by Finley Eversole, PhD
Foreword by John L. Petersen
Published by Inner Traditions, 2013

About *Infinite Energy Technologies*

Clean, sustainable energy solutions from the geniuses of our past and the visionaries of our future

- Explores five great but nearly forgotten minds of the past—John Worrell Keely, Nikola Tesla, Viktor Schauberger, Royal Raymond Rife, and T. Townsend Brown—and their revolutionary discoveries
- Reveals information from leading experts on cold fusion, zero-point energy, power from water, antigravity, and the free-energy potential of the Searl Effect Generator

As the global need for clean, renewable energy grows and the shortage of viable large-scale solutions continues, it is time to look to the geniuses of our past and the visionaries of our future for answers. A society built on limited and environmentally-destructive resources cannot endure. Finley Eversole explains that the key to a pollution- and poverty-free future of infinite energy lies not in pursuing one single method, but in investigating all the possibilities—in uniting as a world in creative pursuit of global transformation.

Exploring five nearly unknown geniuses of our past—John Worrell Keely, Nikola Tesla, Viktor Schauberger, Royal Raymond Rife, and T. Townsend Brown—and their revolutionary discoveries about free energy, electricity, water vortex motion, electric ray and super-microscope technology, and antigravity, this book helps to restore their long-suppressed scientific legacies and bring us one step closer to the destiny they foresaw. Eversole has gathered research from leading experts on cold fusion, zero-point energy, power from water, and the free-energy potential of the Searl Effect Generator to reveal technologies that work *with* Nature's laws and that, if fully implemented, could establish sustainable energy systems in a single generation.

Reviews of This Book

With humanity facing the dismaying prospects of global ecological collapse and geopolitical chaos, there is an urgent need for clear solutions-based guidance that penetrates our dulled consciousness and pulls us back from the precipice. *Infinite Energy Technologies* delivers such guidance. Through a powerfully resonant combination of new energy science, societal analysis, and spiritual insight, Finley Eversole's compilation shakes us awake from our dangerous stupor. The wise voices in this anthology make a compelling case for the immediate embrace of a new wave of energy technologies that is key to launching an era of shared abundance, planetary healing, and unprecedented creativity. I pray that millions will heed this call for action without delay and lead the transformation so desperately needed on our imperiled planet.

Joel Garbon, president of New Energy Movement and co-author of *Breakthrough Power*

Obviously, alternative and free energy systems would save the environment and reestablish a society unlike anything we have ever known. But more than that, they would defuse the fossil fuel economy that is taking us to the brink of WW III by discontinuing the never-ending flow of money into the global banking system that finances the military industrial complex. So the ramifications of what this book is really about go far deeper into manifesting a new social order based on cooperation than one might suspect. If you are wondering about the facts behind alternative energies, this is your book.

Rahasya Poe, *Lotus Guide*

Humanity is on the cusp of an energy revolution, and it's been a long time coming. Ever since Nikola Tesla proposed distributing energy wirelessly via his Wardenclyffe tower in the early 20th century, abundant, non-polluting energy has been nearly within our grasp....

Today, our polluting energy society is the product of a well-orchestrated smear campaign to discredit and/or silence those inventors whose minds stepped beyond the bounds of combustible fuel technology.

Mr. Eversole writes: "Over the past hundred years, according to Thomas E. Bearden—a leading thinker in the free-energy and antigravity fields—there have been at least seventy successfully working free-energy technologies that could have replaced our use of fossil fuels and nuclear energy, met the world's energy needs, and given us a pollution-free environment. Yet every one of these technologies has been suppressed...."

In the past, the powers-that-be could easily suppress public efforts towards free energy technologies and the scientists developing them. Now that we are deep into the Age of Information, such tactics are becoming increasingly more difficult—perhaps impossible at this point. Humanity's consciousness is being affected, and we cannot un-know what we now know. Free and clean energy isn't simply possible— it is abundant. *Infinite Energy Technologies* is the next step towards spreading that message forward into the collective consciousness.

review by Marc Star, *New Dawn Magazine*, Nov-Dec, 2013

Exhilaration, enthusiasm, frustration, depression. These four words describe my reaction to this book.

Exhilaration: Pagan geek alert! "Infinite Energy Technologies" describes several scientists who, over the past 120 years, have developed technologies for cheap, clean energy generation. Part I includes profiles of the early leaders in the field: Tesla, John Worrell Keely, Viktor Schauberger, R. R. Rife, and T. Townsend Brown. All of these scientists realized long ago that reliance on fossil fuels was going to go very badly.

Enthusiasm: A number of viable energy technologies are discussed in Part II, including energy created with water, heavy water, and hydrogen. The Searl Effect Generator, cold fusion, and Zero Point Energy (vacuum) are covered in various essays. Once these methods are mastered and machines perfected, each home (and plug-in cars) could be powered by a small, independent energy generator. Bye-bye grid, so long ugly poles and wires, and *hasta la vista* gas and electric bills and stinky, expensive stops at the gas station!

Frustration: Plenty of obstacles have been placed in the path of development of cheap, clean energy. The book describes how they have been suppressed by "energy cartels, the US Department of Energy, the US Patent Office, the World Trade Organization, and businesses with vested economic interests in maintaining the status quo" (page 1). The science has been rejected, the US Patent office has refused to patent new inventions, or the scientist has been sidelined while his discoveries have been grabbed (stolen) and integrated into super-secret black ops military equipment like the B-2 Stealth Bomber. Energy scientists have been mocked, disenfranchised, omitted from science books, stripped of credit, and their work declared rubbish. In spite of the dire need to stop carbon emissions and reduce pollution and global warming, it's going to be a long time before any of these clean energy technologies are openly available to consumers in the US and abroad. Given the stonewalling and resistance in the US, Japanese and European consumers may benefit from these technologies long before Americans do.

Depression: Is it a fairy tale for paranoid conspiracy theorists, or are multinational oil cartels and onshore power companies actively discouraging these planet-saving energy generators? It may not be as well-organized as a full blown conspiracy, but the results are the same. Industry and government deliberately prevent funding and development, so cheap, clean energy is unavailable to the public. It's an exercise of power over power; the fiscal fist squeezing the planet of every last drop of dinosaur juice and the public of every last shekel. The public 99% in industrialized nations have less and less; the 99% in third world nations are forced into Faustian bargains that forfeit their forests and minerals for rudimentary development. And the third world's 99% is turned into slave labor for first world consumers. All in all, a highly depressing scenario.

This book is a collection of essays with detailed endnotes that supply citations. Several of the writers bemoan the wrongness of the "power over power" hegemony. There are some useful extras at the end of the book. Of the greatest importance is the copy of the "Earth Charter" written at the 1994 Earth Summit with assistance from the Earth Council and Green Cross International. The Earth Charter (Appendix C) is "an international declaration of fundamental values and principles...for building a just, sustainable, and peaceful global society in the twenty-first century." It encompasses environmental protection, human rights, equitable human development, and peace among all peoples. This document needs to circulate on Facebook and on the Web to every aware citizen of the world.

Tom Engelhardt's essay "The Four Occupations of Planet Earth" (Appendix A) gives a scathing summary of the US corporate, financial, and military occupations of the globe in the past two decades. These occupations of greed and force are the reasons why the ethical standards of the Earth Charter haven't gained any traction. The global Occupy movement of 2011 was a "blow-back" occupation reaction to the others, and one that underscored the vast inequities to the populations and the planet. None of the financial or military occupiers have suffered any penalties or imprisonment, either.

This book should be required reading for everyone who gives a damn about the welfare of Mother Earth. It should be mandatory reading for high school science classes. Editor Finley Eversole intends that this book should be the first volume on solutions to global problems with energy, economy, environment, health, food, agriculture, and global change. If he proceeds by gathering work by top-notch, well-informed writers for subsequent books, it will make a difference. This information needs to circulate and be discussed. Loudly. Very, very loudly.

The upshot of all of this is: If we, the people, want clean, cheap (or free) energy, then we must demand it. We must scream it to the sky and pound our little feet until the powers that be bow to massive public demand.

Kudos to Inner Traditions, the editors, and the writers who contributed to this collection of mind expanding essays. In the end, the best word to describe this book is HOPE.

review by Elizabeth Hazel in *Facing North*

Read an Exceprt
Chapter 6: T. Townsend Brown: Suppression of Antigravity Technology
By Jeane Manning

T. Townsend Brown was jubilant when he returned from France in 1956. The soft-spoken scientist had a solid clue which could lead to fuelless space travel. His saucer-shaped discs flew at speeds of up to several hundred miles per hour, with no moving parts. One thing he was certain ofthe phenomena should be investigated by the best scientific institutions. Surely now the science establishment would admit that he really had something. Although the tall, lean physicist—handsome, in a gangly way—was a humble man, even shy, he confidently took his good news to a top-ranking officer he knew in Washington, D.C.

"The experiments in Paris proved that the anomalous motion of my disc airfoils was not all caused by ion wind." The listener would hear Brown's every word, because he took his time in getting words out. "They conclusively proved that the apparatus works even in high vacuum. Here's the documentation ..."

Anomalous means unusual—a discovery which does not fit into the current box of acknowledge science. In this case, the anomaly revealed a connection between electricity and gravity.

That year *Interavia* magazine reported that Brown's discs reached speeds of several hundred miles per hour when charged with several hundred thousand volts of electricity. A wire running along the leading edge of each disc charged that side with high positive voltage, and the trailing edge was wired for an opposite charge. The high voltage ionized air around them, and a cloud of positive ions formed ahead of the craft and a cloud of negative ions behind.

The apparatus was pulled along by its self-generated gravity field, like a surfer riding a wave. *Fate* magazine writer Gaston Burridge in 1958 also described Brown's metal discs, some up to 30 inches in diameter by that time. Because they needed a wire to supply electric charges, the discs were tethered by a wire to a Maypole-like mast. The double-saucer objects circled the pole with a slight humming sound. "In the dark they glow with an eerie lavender light."

Instead of congratulations on the French test results, at the Pentagon he again ran into closed doors. Even his former classmate from officers' candidates school, Admiral Hyman Rickover, discouraged Brown from continuing to explore the dogma-shattering discovery that the force of gravity could be tweaked or even blanked out by the electrical force.

"Townsend, I'm going to do you a favor and tell you: Don't take this work any further. Drop it."

Was this advice given to Brown by a highly-placed friend who knew that the United States military was already exploring electrogravitics? (Sleuthing by American scientist Dr. Paul LaViolette uncovers a paper trail which leads from Brown's early work, toward secret research by the military, and eventually points to "Black Project" aircraft.)

Jeane Manning *has traveled in twelve countries and interviewed dozens of scientists since 1981, researching revolutionary clean energy systems that could replace oil. With Joel Garbon, she coauthored the award-winning book* Breakthrough Power: How Quantum-Leap New Energy Inventions Can Transform Our World. *Her earlier books include* The Coming Energy Revolution *and* Energie, *and several coauthored books, including* Angels Don't

Play This HAARP *with Dr. Nick Begich. Her books have been published in seven languages. Manning now lives near Vancouver, Canada. Her websites are* www.BreakthroughPower.net *and* www.ChangingPower.net

Energy Medicine Technologies
Ozone Healing, Microcrystals, Frequency Therapy, and the Future of Health
Edited by Finley Eversole, PhD
Foreword by Karl Maret, M.D.
Published by Inner Traditions, 2013

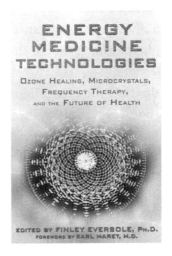

Book Description
New and suppressed breakthroughs in energy medicine, ways to combat toxins and electromagnetic fields, and the importance of non-GMO foods

- Explores the use of microcrystals, ozone and hydrogen peroxide therapy, and how to tap in to healing antioxidant electrons from the Earth
- Reveals the scientifically proven health risks of genetically modified foods
- Examines the suppressed cancer-curing electromedicine of Royal Raymond Rife and Nobel laureate Albert Szent-Györgi

Natural, nontoxic, inexpensive, and effective alternatives to conventional medicine exist, yet they have been suppressed by the profit-driven medical-pharmaceutical complex.

Presenting a compendium of some of the most revolutionary yet still widely unknown discoveries in health and energy medicine, this book edited by Finley Eversole, Ph.D., explores the use of microcrystals to harmonize the energies of body, mind, and environment; the healing effects of ozone and hydrogen peroxide therapy; ways to combat electromagnetic fields and environmental toxins; sources of disruptive energy that cause stress and health problems, including other people's negative emotions; and how to tap in to healing antioxidant electrons from the Earth. The book reveals the scientifically proven health risks of genetically modified foods—the first irreversible technology in human history with still unknown consequences. It looks at the link between industrial farming and the precipitous rise in heart disease, cancer, diabetes, and Alzheimer's over the past 100 years and provides a 10-point Low-Toxin Program to reduce your risk. It explores the cancer-curing electromedicine of Royal Raymond Rife and its suppression by the medical establishment as well as Nobel laureate Albert Szent-Györgi's follow-up discovery of Frequency Therapy.

Offering a window into the holistic future of medicine, the book shows the body not simply as a biological machine to be patched and repaired but as a living organism made up of cells dynamically linked to their inner and outer environments.

Reviews

Energy Medicine Technologies persuasively presents the wisdom of some of the world's foremost authorities on ancient and modern modalities of energy medicine—the only paradigm of healing that can effectively meet our healthcare needs in the 21st century. If you read only one book about this emerging healing model, let it be this one!

Simone Gabbay, author of *Edgar Cayce's Energy Medicine* and *Visionary Medicine: Real Hope for Total Healing*

This meaty volume explores Diseases of Civilization due to electromagnetic pollution, the dangers of genetically modified and pesticide laden foods and other examples of what might be considered "man's inhumanity to man." It also recommends ways to prevent or reduce these in chapters devoted to the benefits of organic foods, light and sound energies, ozone and hydrogen peroxide therapy, as well as intercessory prayer and remote healing.

Paul J. Rosch, MD, FACP, Clinical Professor of Medicine and Psychiatry at New York Medical College, Chairman of the Board for The American Institute of Stress, and Emeritus Member for The Bioelectromagnetics Society

The contributors to this volume are leading experts in their respective fields. There's a media black-out on this information, so it will be a revelation for most readers. There's a balance of information. Some writers discuss new technologies and energy healing methods, while others write about the causes of disease, including the "electrosmog" generated by wireless technology and microwaves, and the damage caused by genetically-modified foods and the man-made toxins dumping into our food, water and environment over the past several decades. The end notes supply citations, and more importantly, contact information and website addresses for additional information and device manufacturers. Contributor bios and an index wrap up the book.

This is an eye-opening volume that sheds light on healing techniques that have been consigned to the shadows for far too long. If you care about health and wellness, get this book.

Elizabeth Hazel, August, 2013

Read an Excerpt
Chapter 5 Rife Therapy: An Innovate Advance in Electromedicine
Nenah Sylver, Ph.D.

One of the most effective and noninvasive healing modalities is frequency therapy, based on the principles discovered by Royal Raymond Rife. Though initially hailed by physicians in the 1930s and 1940s as a major breakthrough for curing cancer and other diseases, Rife's technology was disparaged and censored and has reemerged only in the past twenty years. Did this technology really work? If so, why was it suppressed? And how can we use it today?

Electrotherapy's Place in Complementary Medicine

Rife's technology is best understood in the context of holistic or complementary health. Allopathic medicine regards the body as a machine that is the sum of its parts, but holistic medicine treats the person as a unified organism greater than the sum of its parts, and, because all parts are interconnected, there are no isolated symptoms.

The bioelectrical nature of our bodies is often overshadowed by its more obvious mechanical aspects. But every cell is a transmitter and receiver of electromagnetic (EM) information (which is why electronic equipment is successful in testing). The entire body is a living electrical circuit. Cells and tissues act as conductors, as insulators, as semiconductors, and as capacitors. Human beings, animals, and plants all contain and respond to EM fields, as each cell has its very own frequency with which it oscillates. These various electromagnetic frequencies precede and correspond to biochemical functions. For instance, healthy cells oscillate at higher frequencies than do unhealthy cells, such as in the case of a person with cancer.

Electrotherapy (or electromedicine) is a medical modality that uses electromagnetic, electric, and magnetic energies for therapeutic purposes. Since ancient times humans have used electromagnetic fields from the sun, visible light, electricity, and magnetism for healing. These energies stimulate circulation and normalize the body's cells and tissues. Sometimes they disable and destroy pathogens.

By the early 1900s—a hundred years after the discovery of electrical current—electromedical equipment was considered mainstream. Alternating current, direct current, low frequencies, high frequencies, static electricity, diathermy, infrared rays, and ultraviolet rays were utilized to treat muscular aches and pains, skin conditions, gynecological problems, some heart conditions, respiratory ailments, gastrointestinal disorders, acute and chronic infections, and degenerative diseases.

Today, machines utilizing electromagnetic fields, electricity, and magnetism are used for diagnosis. These include the electrocardiogram and Magnetic Resonance Imaging. Given the widespread historical use of electromedicine and the modern use of machines for diagnosis, it seems remarkable that more practitioners and the general public don't use electromedicine in their daily lives for healing.

A Brief History of Royal Raymond Rife

Born in Nebraska in 1888, Royal Raymond Rife was truly a Renaissance man. Educated in optics, electronics, biology, and chemistry, he studied at Johns Hopkins University before designing and building many medical research instruments. Perhaps his most famous invention, the 200-pound, 5,682-part Universal Microscope, was completed in 1933. The Universal Microscope had extraordinary magnification powers and depth of field, rendering live organisms as small as single viruses visible—something that conventional scopes and even electron microscopes could not accomplish.

Reasoning that once he could *see* how pathogens responded to negative stimuli he could find a way to destroy them, Rife built a ray that devitalized microbes via a specific EM field. This ray disabled pathogens and, once they were disabled, the body's immune cells could eliminate them.

Rife's technology was safe and effective, and he was praised in hundreds of newspapers and journals. His colleagues and supporters were among the most prestigious doctors and scientists of the time. Throughout the United States and Europe, doctors administered Rife Therapy in the treatment of many types of infection, including those caused by E. *coli*, strep, staph, and salmonella. People recovered from cancer, tuberculosis, typhoid, tetanus, gonorrhea, pneumonia, and other ailments. Even most patients given "terminal" diagnoses by their doctors became well when treated with the ray device.

Fourteen highly effective units were made by the Rife's Beam Rays Corporation before a smear campaign was begun in 1939 against Rife, his inventions, and like-minded doctors who practiced Rife Therapy. Virtually everyone who attacked Rife was funded by or connected to the pharmaceutical industry, including the allopathically oriented American Medical Association, the American Cancer Society, and Memorial Sloan-Kettering Cancer Institute. The smear campaign was effective: the abundant funding and resources that Rife had enjoyed in the 1930s evaporated, making mass production of a Rife Ray impossible.

Today in the United States, Rife Therapy is relatively unknown because it is likewise systematically disparaged. The alliance between the pharmaceutical industry, the FDA, and the AMA ensures the prevalence of drugs and surgery rather than nondrug, nonsurgical protocols. Rife Therapy was opposed by allopathic medicine proponents for many reasons. It's much more successful, and thus more cost-effective, than pharmaceutical medicine, because Rifers tend to use far fewer drugs than non-Rifers. Rife machines can be used by more than one person. Moreover, most sessions can be self-administered without a doctor's supervision. Rife Therapy is compatible with all holistic modalities such as acupuncture, chiropractic, and naturopathy. It can even be used with select allopathic procedures.

Today people are seeking alternative treatments—alternative, that is, to the allopathic model most commonly promoted—because they refuse to settle for less than genuine healing. It's time to bring Rife Therapy back into the mainstream by making it freely available to everyone, everywhere.

Nenah Sylver, Ph.D., *is a writer, educator, artist, and agent for social change. Her training as a musician and her interest in healing and the natural sciences led her to study physics before earning a Ph.D. in transformational psychology. For many years she had a private practice in body/mind psychotherapy based on the principles of Wilhelm Reich. Her research in Rife frequency technology and other related fields in holistic health coalesced to form the 768-page volume The* Rife Handbook of Frequency Therapy and Holistic Health. *Her work on the themes of holistic health, psychology, feminism, sexuality, and social change has been published all over the world.*

CPSIA information can be obtained at www.ICGtesting.com
Printed in the USA
LVOW01s0316140814

399091LV00010B/162/P

9 780991 307906